Praise for *Crazy Enough*

"Frank, funny, and caustically un-self-pitying."

—*Publishers Weekly*

"Storm Large has written a bodacious book. Buy it, now!"

—Gus Van Sant

"Storm Large is an irresistibly rambunctious force of nature. *Crazy Enough* is shattering, gorgeous, and uproarious fun."

—Katherine Dunn, author of *Geek Love*

"It's too bad that readers can't have her actually in their lives and feel the true force of Storm, but her book is so true to who she is that it is still a powerful, funny, and outrageous experience. Plus, you won't have to deal with all of those strange sounds and dirty sheets."

—Dan Stern, actor, director, writer

"Storm Large performs with world-class symphonies and hardcore rock bands, and she's written a book worthy of both audiences. If good writing is about taking chances and pushing readers to the edge, then this is a chart buster, as she takes us on a wild and sometimes painful ride into her world of crazy."

—Larry Colton, author of *Goat Brothers, Counting Coup,* and *No Ordinary Joes*

"Like some twisted love child of Mae West and Keith Richards, Storm Large is a force of nature. Her ballsy, heartbreaking, hysterical tour de force of a memoir is not to be missed. *Crazy Enough* is vulgar and fragile, tragic and empowering, and like Storm, it is always entertaining."

—Chelsea Cain, *New York Times* bestselling author of *Heartsick* and *The Night Season*

"We're in complete awe of the blunt, surprising memoir . . . told in honest, poignant prose . . . [Large shows] all of us how to let go—not without fear and doubt, but with it."

—*O, The Oprah Magazine*

"A helluva compelling story."

—*Elle*

"With cleverness and honesty, she transforms a story that in most hands would be maudlin into yet another funny, passionate, and irreverently jarring adventure."

—*Portland Monthly*

"In *Crazy Enough*, Large tells if not all then a whole lot about her loves, her heroin addiction, her eating disorder, and in her voice, it sounds like crazy fun . . . *Crazy Enough* is a good time of a survivor's story, full of funny stories and candid talk from a sex thug who really is, deep inside, a little girl waiting for her mother."

—*The Oregonian*

"A most moving and entertaining memoir . . . The story is edgy, gritty, and fearless, and leaves little to the imagination as Large presents a no-holds-barred journey through her formative years and into adulthood."

—*The Portland Observer*

"Heartbreaking, hilarious and affecting . . . *Crazy Enough* is a starkly honest memoir, a tale of sexual triggering, drug dabbling, and trying to fit in and rebel at the same time."

—*Willamette Week*

"Best recognized as a contender on *Rock Star: Supernova*, Large has the heart of a true exhibitionist . . . This project marks her first literary foray, and her memoir pulls no punches. A no-holds-barred coming-of-age story replete with mental illness, drugs and sex."

—*Kirkus Reviews*

"A memoir that reads like an in-your-face mashup of Augusten Burroughs and Chelsea Handler, combining raw humor and an understandable bitterness with more than a few oversexed anecdotes. Though not for the faint of heart, *Crazy Enough* proves to be a readable account of one woman's descent into madness—and back out again."

—*Shelf Awareness*

CRAZY ♡ ENOUGH

A Memoir

STORM LARGE

Free Press

New York   London   Toronto   Sydney   New Delhi

Free Press
A Division of Simon & Schuster, Inc.
1230 Avenue of the Americas
New York, NY 10020

First Free Press trade paperback edition November 2012

FREE PRESS and colophon are trademarks of Simon & Schuster, Inc.

For information about special discounts for bulk purchases,
please contact Simon & Schuster Special Sales at 1-866-506-1949
or business@simonandschuster.com.

The Simon & Schuster Speakers Bureau can bring authors to your live event.
For more information or to book an event, contact the
Simon & Schuster Speakers Bureau at 1-866-248-3049
or visit our website at www.simonspeakers.com.

Designed by Ruth Lee-Mui

Manufactured in the United States of America

1   3   5   7   9   10   8   6   4   2

The Library of Congress has cataloged the hardcover edition as follows:
Large, Storm.
Crazy enough : a memoir / by Storm Large.—1st Free Press hardcover ed.
p. cm.
1. Large, Storm. 2. Singers—United States—Biography. I. Title.
ML420.L2437A3 2012
782.42166092—dc23
[B]
2011024124

ISBN 978-1-4391-9240-5
ISBN 978-1-4391-9241-2 (pbk)
ISBN 978-1-4391-9242-9 (ebook)

DISCLAIMER

All of these stories are true and as accurate as I could get them, with the help of friends and family who were party or privy to the events described. Several names and identifying characteristics of people and places have been blurred or outright changed to protect the innocent and the dead. Some have been changed to protect myself from the drug addled and psychotic, along with the general douche baggery that is so prevalent in these litigious times. Many of these memories are from more than thirty years ago, so keep in mind there have been a few tankers of alcohol and trash bags full of drugs, not to mention acres of weenie, that have been tossed through my body and brain since then, so I could have gotten a few things twisted around. But I do know for sure that I live at the end.

FOR: Sandra

CONTENTS

CONTENTS

CONTENTS

BIG GIRLS ♡

LOVE YOU,
BYE....

BIG GIRLS WERE NOT BUILT to WALK
The Straight and Narrow

PROLOGUE:

"THE GREATEST GIFT OF ALL!"

People think I'm nuts. They think that I am a killer, a badass, and a dangerous woman. They think that I am a boot-stomping, man-chomping rock 'n' roll sex thug with heavy leather straps on my well-notched bedposts and a line around the block of challengers vying for a ride between my crushing thighs, many of whom won't survive the encounter.

That's what I *like* people to think, anyway. Some actually buy it. My manufactured mythology had begun on stage in San Francisco, and was full-on folklore here in Portland. My band, The Balls, had become a wild success over the past three years, and we packed a downtown club called Dante's once a week, as well as clubs throughout the west coast from Seattle to San Diego. My sex thuggery is reserved for only one man, however. And though we fuck like we

1

just got out of prison, home life is domestic. I help with the care and feeding of my boyfriend's young son, cutting off crusts, giving back tickles. I even own an apron.

Despite my disenchanting normality, however, I get to sing for a living, drink free most places, and I get laid regularly. Life is good.

And now it's Christmas time, so I'm all extra everything with good cheer. December in Portland can be a dreary spectacle. Right around Halloween, a big chilly sog plops its fat ass over the Pacific Northwest and stays parked there until Independence Day. Even in the gray, spitting rain, however, I'm all atwinkle, heading to Hawthorne Boulevard to skip through herds of wet hippies to Christmas shop. And even though I find those pube farmers highly irritating, I am humming "In Excelsis Deo" and in love with the world, so fuck 'em.

Hawthorne is a main thoroughfare in southeast Portland where, on one block, you can buy a latte, Indonesian end tables, pants for your cat, a vinyl corset, or a two-hundred-dollar T-shirt. It's a great place to find perfect gifts for the loved ones in your life, and I am going to buy the greatest Christmas gift ever.

"The Greatest Gift of All": I hear my little fourth-grade voice trilling in my memory bank. It was in a school Christmas play and was the first solo I ever took on stage. It was also one of the few times my mom saw me sing in front of a real audience.

"The greatest giiift of aaall . . . it can come from aaany wheeere!" I sang the heck out of it, if memory serves.

My mom had started beading and was taking it very seriously. She was selling pieces on eBay—seriously—so I'm headed to a store called Beads Forever to get her some killer imported beads, maybe some semiprecious stones. I have a vision of getting her a badass assortment and putting them in a cool, funky box. It's the first Christmas gift I will buy for her in maybe ten years, and it will be perfect.

"Per-fect!" I sing in a fake opera voice.

I see the store ahead through my swishing windshield wipers and, "Fuckyouuu!!" I sing in triumph, to no one, as there is a perfect parking space directly in front of the store. " Rock-star fucking parking!" I pull up, swoosh my wet car into the spot, throw it into park and my phone rings. The little lit-up window reads "BDLarge."

"Dad? Hey, Dad."

"Hi, sweetie." His voice sounds heavy.

"What's wrong?"

He sighed. *Someone must've died. My grandmother. Neeny. God, at Christmas we lose Neeny Cat?*

"Dad?"

"Your mom died last night."

What?

"Who?" *His* mom. Neeny. Ninety-four, lost her mind when her husband of sixty-odd years passed.

"Your ma."

"Who?" More sighing. *Why the fuck is he sighing so much? Should I get out of the car?*

"Your ma. Your mom died last night. They don't know what happened yet sweetie, but . . ."

I'm literally looking into the store where I'm going to get her Christmas gift. Should I still? My hand is on the door, my car is parked . . . rock-star parking and the best gift ever. No. I say no to this. My dad says something about having to call my brothers and will I be okay? He'll call me back right away. Love you. Bye.

Love you. Bye.

It's dark and raining but people can still see into the car, and I must look crazy. I grab the steering wheel with both hands and suddenly I'm sobbing, screaming at the gauges. What the fuck to do?

Where do I go, home? I can't see. I can't drive. I call my boyfriend at work.

"Hi. Can you come get me? My mom is dead and I'm on Hawthorne."

She's gone.

My first thought. She is gone. Not my first thought. No. Fucking no.

I'm thrashing around inside my body. What the fuck do I do?

What am I thinking? No. I peel my mind away like a child turning its face from a tablespoon of cough syrup. No. My first thought. My first?

Thank God. Thank God she's gone.

"Thank God she's gone."

CHAPTER ONE:

CHILD MANIA, Chicken MUSH, Forever AND A Day....

1975.

When I was five years old, I had my first orgasm.

I had played with myself for as long as I could remember, but the gold at the end of that rainbow came courtesy of my first ever boyfriend, Mr. Pool Jet. He was so much fun and such a consistent partner, never asking a thing of me but always eager to give. With my arms folded under my chin at the pool's edge, my body was just the right length to get that warm blast of water right on the money. Tucking my hips up into the stream I remember distinctly hissing under my breath, "Oh my . . . oh my . . . OHMYOHMYOHMY!" Then, kicking away from the wall I sucked in a good lungful of air, dove, and hid at the bottom of the pool to collect myself for a few seconds.

Did anyone see that?

I knew that what I had discovered was huge, but I also knew, instinctively, that it was not for public consumption. More urgently, pressing into my little brains was that once the prickling, throbbing exclamation point between my legs cooled and calmed, I would totally have to do that again.

Like a gateway drug, it started with Mr. Pool Jet, then went on to harder stuff: bathtub faucets and, later, showerhead massagers. Thank you, Waterpik!

I always knew something was wrong with me, and here was the proof. I was a five-year-old secret slut for any stream of water I could get alone. After a couple years of that, I got a real live boy to play with. I was seven and he was five, so, by the third grade, I was not only a water nymphomaniac, I was also a cougar.

We'll call him "ChapStick" as in, "'Zat a ChapStick in your pocket, or . . . ?" We both lived in the same little neighborhood, so he would come over to play. Around adults we would play the usual toddler games: shave Barbie's head, give her a black eye with a magic marker, and feed her to the giant squid that came with my brother's GI Joe undersea adventure series, or we would just space out and watch cartoons. When we could sneak away someplace alone, however, we would play a game called "I Am So Tired!" I would lie on my back in bed or on the floor, cover my head and arms with a blanket or a towel and pretend to fall asleep with my legs open. That was the cue for ChapStick to climb on top of me and ravage my sleeping torso with his fevered humping.

We would be fully clothed during the exchange but still I would tilt my hips toward the onslaught and bite the inside of whatever was covering my face as waves of intense and desperate tickling pleasure would build up in the friction. My face and my breath would get hot and I would pant a little bit, but quietly. Sometimes I felt like my throat was bulging outwards like a water balloon, from hitching and holding my breath and my belly would suck all the way in pulling the tickles in deeper, up higher, then more then yes, and yes, and YES! Then a chickeny flutter and burn and drop, twitch and melt, the weight on my back spread over my bones like hot honey.

He would then get up and go somewhere else in the room and leave me floaty and pink under my covers. A minute or two later, I would get up stretch and make a big deal about how tired I was and how nothing could've woken me, and how was your nap, ChapStick?

Usually we were both very satisfied with this game. Once in a while, though, he would be done before me and I would yell from under my covers, "Ummm, I'm still tired!"

We had no idea what we were doing, yet, we somehow knew not to talk about it. Even to each other. We ignored our little trysts as though they were funny slivers of some wacky kid dream that nobody would understand.

Hypersexuality in children is sometimes evidence of early onset bipolar disorder phenotype, and often is treated with medication, with some success. It's also called *child mania*, I didn't know any of that, but I knew to keep my passion secret, even though I saw nothing wrong with it. I was alone a lot and it was something that made being alone worth it. Suddenly everything turned me on and I would fantasize about, draw pictures of, and obsess over sex.

One of my biggest turn-ons was watching nature shows, like *Mutual of Omaha's Wild Kingdom*. Animals ripping each other apart always made my bathing suit area sparkle. I'd go all hot and twitchy when big predators, like lions or cheetahs, would chase down and kill helpless little antelopes. "Why don't those photographers help that baby deer? Someone has to have a gun out there!" I would lie, deflecting the true cause of my restlessness, counting the minutes until I could get myself alone.

When I was older and in relationships lasting longer than a trip to the bathroom, more than one boyfriend would comment on how much I loved sex, as if it were evidence of something wrong with me. "Were you raped or something?" one even said out loud.

Whatever the psychological hoo-ha was about my early onanistic habits, I called it: "This feels amazing. I'm totally going to do this again and again until I'm dead."

So many guys pray for a girl to *want* to do all the nasty things they think about. Until he gets one. Then there is a realization that she's clearly practiced on a pile of other cocks, and that she can outfuck him.

"You make me feel small" was another constant whine. But, even though my first human scratching post truly *was* much smaller than me, he never once complained.

My burgeoning relationship with ChapStick was around 1976, our nation's bicentennial, but all the fireworks going off in the country didn't hold a candle to the joy I had discovered in myself with masturbation. It was the light and the way out of my loneliest feelings. It was around that time that I started to figure out why my mom wanted to die. If she couldn't feel like that anymore, I could understand why anyone would want to stop living. For the life of me, though, I couldn't figure out why she tried to kill me.

8

I was seven years old. It was more of a mishap on the way to another attempt on her own life, so I can't really say it was deliberately sinister. What made it irritating, however, was that she did it while I had a friend over.

Daphne was my best and, pretty much only, friend. She was a cherubic blonde with cartoon-huge hazel eyes beaming from her porcelain heart-shaped face. We had known each other forever, as her mom and my dad were both teachers in our little town of Southborough. We were born three months apart, were the only members of the Animal Club, and we both loved *Lucan*, the Wolf Boy, the best show ever.

My two big brothers and I were used to Mom being a little off every now and then, but this particular night, she was in a rare state of fucked. She had downed a dozen or so Thorazine washed down with some Tab, before making dinner. She was wobbling around the kitchen, muttering incoherently to herself while puttering at the stove.

Daphne knew my mom was sick. She also knew that my mom had to go away once in awhile, because there would always be some new babysitter living with us, or I would end up sleeping over at her house now and then on school nights.

Daphne's mom and dad never talked about what was happening at my house; they would just set a place for me at the table and treat me like their own kid. Daphne and I would never talk about it, either; we would just do what little girls do. We'd hunt frogs and snakes down at the pond, talk about what we were going to do when we had boobs, steal her brother's *Playboy* and *Penthouse* magazines, stuff like that. Daphne knew there was something funny going on, because she was family, but she'd never actually seen the crazy happen. Until . . .

"Dih-nerrr," Mom creaked in a shaky sigh.

She moved as though through syrup, as she thunked down our bowls of food at our places. We all came to the table. The kitchen was a seventies beige with greasy, flat carpeting. It had probably been nice carpeting once, a million years ago, back when people thought carpets were groovy to have in kitchens. I have no idea what color it had been originally, but now it was sticky and dark, smelling of onion soup and Windex.

Daphne and I sat together, Henry sat across from us, and Daddy sat at the head of the table.

I had been calling my oldest brother, John, "Daddy" since I was four. There was no confusion as to who my real father was, but John, six years older than I, was the man of the house, as Dad stayed at work as long and late as he could. John was thirteen and had the pimples and bad temper to prove it. He sat down, looked at the stuff in his bowl, and shot me a look from under his shaggy mop of brown hair. His dark blue eyes read both angry and embarrassed. Henry, my ten-year-old golden-boy brother, sat down and didn't look at anyone. He just bit his lip and stared at his bowl.

Both of my brothers were already great athletes, but John had recently started to like pot, girls, and Led Zeppelin. Henry had gone the other way completely. Excelling in football and lacrosse during the school year, then off to this or that awesome American camp for sports or just becoming more of an awesome American. He had begun to emulate his namesakes, my father and grandfather, and pursue a military, upstanding, conservative, and painfully normal life. Henry needed normal. He hated this.

I was a weirdo. I was loud and annoying by nature and pretty sure, if I pushed hard enough on the toilet my penis would finally appear. My dearest wish was to be attacked by a werewolf, so I could become a werewolf, too, and live in a secret fort with my werewolf boyfriend, forever. I was also trying every possible way to learn how to fly by flapping magazines in each hand and jumping off cars and furniture. But this . . . even this was too screwy for me.

I got louder and sillier to distract from the thick, weird silence, talking about so-and-so boy at school was a bum-bum head and how when he talked it smells like a bottom burp. I hoped to God that Daphne didn't notice the tension growing in the room. She sat politely with her hands folded in her lap and watched the pretty little blonde lady she also called "Mom" stammering breathy nonsense while scooping food into her bowl. It was clear Daphne knew something was up, as she glanced now and then around the table at us, her eyes questioning.

I gave up my attempt at potty-humor-as-distraction when I saw and smelled what sat in our bowls.

We all stared at Mom who floated into her chair. She made yummy noises as she pulled her bowl towards her and started to eat. She wasn't using a regular spoon, she held on to the long orange plastic one she had used to stir and serve the gloppy food into our bowls.

Her nerves and muscles seemed to jog inside her body, making her head, arms, and torso nod rhythmically as she sat, aiming the huge spoon at her mouth, barely managing to feed herself. She looked like a toddler pretending to eat imaginary food with toy utensils and a severe lack of coordination, without a whiff of embarrassment. The table was quiet except for Mom humming and gurgling and a rhythmic thudding of her leg hammering lightly on its heel.

I mouthed the words "don't eat it" to Daphne.

"Mom," John said finally.

"Ye-hessh, shweetie?" she said to something about four feet over John's head.

"What is this?"

"It's shicken mush! Who-ooo wants mo-ooore?" Then half asleep on her feet, she drifted in a zigzag path back to the stove to refill her bowl.

Daphne and Henry stared quietly at their food. John got up from the table and trotted upstairs. "Why is it *blue?*" I asked, trying to sound tough and accusing, but it came out as an embarrassed whine.

I didn't see any chicken anywhere in the frothy, teal colored gruel that sat in my bowl like a wet, poisonous frog. It was lumpy and foamy and had a bleachy smell. Mom had slurped a whole bowl of it into herself, and was scraping out the saucepan for the rest. John came back to the table, gave Henry some money, and told us all to go get a pizza. Then he took off out the door to get our dad, who was at school a football field away. Henry, Daphne, and I didn't talk about what we had seen as we walked downtown, but I wondered what Daphne was going to tell her family when they asked, "How was dinner?"

Later, back at home, I saw my mom being walked into an ambulance with Dad behind her carrying her little blue suitcase.

Shicken mush. It turns out, after they had pumped her stomach, there really was chicken in it after all. There was chicken soup, oatmeal, and Calgonite dishwashing powder.

I loved my mom more than anything. She was a cross between Grace Kelly and Sandy Duncan, but with two good eyes. When I was little I knew she was the most beautiful woman in the whole world. To me she looked like a Disney princess, a magical lady that birds and baby deer would follow around, eating out of her hand. Not an elegant lady about town, more a pretty, pixielike girlie girl. I had no idea that a lot of people in our sleepy little town thought she was . . . odd.

As I got older, I started to notice eyes rolling her way. My mom was bright and chatty—a chime-in-loudly-on-any-conversation type person—but it turned out that was a social no-no for the prep-school set. Plus, she was a mere twenty-two when she and my dad took up residence at St. Mark's School.

My dad always comments on his lucky break in landing a job at St. Mark's. When he was done with his tour of duty in the Marine Corps in 1965, he went to his alma mater, Princeton University, to meet with the woman in charge of placing graduates into their ideal employment situations. She asked him where he wanted to live, what did he want to teach, and would he also like to coach football? Then, she handed him a piece of paper with a name, phone number, and an address. In July of that same year, Dad, Mom, and three-year-old John moved from my grandparents' farm in Pennsylvania, to St. Mark's School, in Southborough, Massachusetts, where Dad would teach, coach, and mentor, nonstop, for forty-five years.

Friends referred to them as "the golden couple." My dad, an Ivy League, ex-Marine lieutenant, was manly handsome. He stood a healthy six foot one, one blue eye, one green eye, with jet-black Superman hair. My mom looked like a giggling tow-headed fairy that could pirouette across a field of buttercups and not bruise a single one.

I think some of the older, dumpier ladies around school took my mom's youthful sparkle as the antics of someone who thought a bit too much of herself. Most of the faculty wives at St. Mark's were bookish and preppy, embracing a more matronly aesthetic. Think lots of brown wool skirts with pale ankles dumping into squeaky duck boots. My mom stood out. Stood out like a slice of summer sun beaming into a punishing cold January. She twinkled in complete contrast to those dour prep-school hens, and they did not care for it at all. Within the stiff, Tudor walls of St. Mark's, if you stood out, or thought you were special in any way, you were on your own . . . a lesson I learned for myself years later.

I remember witnessing affectionate moments between my parents, even though things would soon get to the point when it became hard to imagine them even in the same room together without getting a stomachache. But they loved each other long enough to get pregnant three more times after John.

Mom always had trouble with her girl parts, she'd say. Her pregnancies and her periods were rough going, but her miscarriage nearly did us both in. She was four months or so along when she lost the baby, and it knocked her out for awhile. Mom was twenty-six, John was five, Henry was two, and the doctors recommended a hysterectomy. They told my parents that Mom's endometriosis wasn't going to get any better, and since they already had two healthy boys . . . But Mom wouldn't hear of it. She wanted a baby girl. She promised to have the surgery, as soon as she had a girl.

Mom loved telling me, and anyone in earshot, how I nearly killed her, but June 25, 1969, twenty-four hours of labor and one blood transfusion later, she got her little girl and all the terrible tales of woe that would come with me. Yay! You're welcome, Ma!

When I was around six months old, the doctors finally got to melon ball her reproductive system. And, supposedly, that was just the ticket, until she started trying to kill herself.

Before Mom had any official diagnosis that I knew of, it was just, "Mom's tired." It would go like this: We all came flying in from school in a blur of noise and book bags. My brothers were usually caked with mud from sports or brawling, while I would be covered in paint with some huge piece of construction paper with leaves or some other crap glued all over it. We would barrel into the house and stop short at the sight of Dad by himself or one of our rotation of babysitters. "Where's Mom?" one of us would ask.

"She's resting."

"Resting where?"

"At the hospital." And that would be the end of the conversation.

The whole "tired" explanation made sense for awhile, because right before she would disappear she would usually seem . . . well . . . tired. She'd either be in bed for days and days, or she would move sleepily, and appear brittle and frail. She would stare at her food, out a window, or at one of us. She would get all weepy, and then, she'd just be gone.

I *loved* hospitals in the beginning. Mom was my favorite human being on the planet, so when she was in the hospital, well, that was the place to be! Plus, visiting Mom was like a big family outing. My dad, brothers, and I would pile into "Sunshine," the yellow Volvo, and off we would go. We'd usually stop at a drugstore to buy her some smokes or some candy or her favorite perfume: "Muguet," a soapy, lily-of-the-valley scent my mom absolutely soaked herself in.

Sometimes, my dad would give us a couple of bucks each to buy her a present, if it was a special occasion like her birthday, or Mother's Day. I'm pretty sure every single Mother's Day of my childhood was spent in some smoke- and psycho-filled hospital common room. Now that I think of it, pretty much the same goes for any holiday, *our* birthdays, Easter, Arbor Day, but if it was Mother's Day, we were definitely headed for this or that hospital with sparkly drugstore presents.

We would all crowd around her, in her room or the common room. I would tell her about something stupid the cat did, sing her songs, and make friends with all the doctors and hospital people. Mom was in so many different hospitals for the first ten years of my life that some of the details blur together. For example, in the seventies, there was a common theme among all hospital common rooms. They stunk, for one. No amount of weapons-grade disinfectant could combat the stench of terrible coffee, pharmaceutical BO, despair, and about nine gajillion cigarettes. Those people *smoked*. In pretty much every hospital common room I ever saw, the walls, windows, and ceilings were slathered with tobacco sludge.

There would also be, without fail, a ping-pong table. I played more fucking ping-pong as a kid in more hospital common rooms, that when I so much as *hear* the *ker-plip-ker-plop* of the game, my stomach drops.

In general, something about seventies aesthetics were creepy even *in* the seventies. Even when grownups were growing their Chewbacca pubes and rapist mustaches, yanking up their camel-toe spandex to go roller skating around to key parties, I think even while the times swung, the people in it were creeped out by their own sepia-toned pre-Reagan-era, Polaroid existence.

Regardless of bad taste and smelliness, if Mom was *resting* in any hospital, when it was time to see her, I was into it. When she would finally come home from the hospital? That was just emotional mayhem and the best! thing! ever!

The second she got home with her little blue suitcase and plastic name bracelet, I would squeal, do a little dance, and be a tiny fireworks display of embarrassing little girlness. I would have a ream of pictures, fists full of whatever flowers were around, and have planned exactly what song I would sing for her, all the sentimental little things I wanted to share with her all planned in my head. She was gonna laugh, cry, and be so glad to be home that I wouldn't have to worry about her leaving anymore.

That was my movie. As the uplifting music would swell, the scene would fade to black, as the little girl and her mother would be holding hands, walking away from the camera, and toward the house as the sun went down, thus signifying completion of a trial or difficult period.

It wasn't until I was five when I realized that Mom and I were watching very different movies.

I remember one time when Mom had just gotten home from a substantial absence, about two months. But home again, home again, jiggety jig. There she was, sitting on her bed with the green bedspread, her powder-blue suitcase at her tiny feet.

She looked exhausted.

I remember I hugged her where she sat with my arms around her tiny waist, my head in her lap, and I looked up at her.

"Are you home forever?"

"Forever and a day," she said, stroking my hair.

Panic. What does *that* mean?

"Just a day?"

"Forever *and* a day." She was tired, but I could hear a tiny shred of amusement in her voice. Still confused, she's using *day* and *forever* in the same sentence. If she's home forever, days don't matter, right?

"Just a day?" I said quietly into her boobs. I didn't get it. I wanted her to just say *yes, sweetie, I'm not going to the hospital anymore, I will be here for breakfast and when you get home from school, we can watch television, and we can get married.* It wasn't hard to promise forever; I did it all the time. All she had to do was stay home.

She didn't say anything but I could tell she was looking at my dad while she stroked my head.

Turns out, forever and a day equaled about a week and some change before she was gone again.

I came flying in from school screeching for Mom to show her the marvelous ashtray I had made *and* glazed, myself, just for her, because my love for her was so amazing. I found, instead, the broad back of my father, as he hunched over the sink washing dishes.

"Where's Mom?"

"She's resting."

"Resting where?"

"At the hospital."

"Why can't she rest here?" I yelled at his back.

I couldn't help it. I had been promised forever and a series of days after that. We were going to be together every day for the rest of our lives. She was going to smoke and use this unbelievable ashtray and love me so much more than God knows what, forever.

My dad said nothing, but his body visibly cringed and tightened against my tiny air raid siren. He sighed into the sink.

Everything with me as a child—and later on—was either the mostexcitingwonderfulamazingyougottacomeseethis*now* thing ever or else the sun would be going black, it was raining frogs, and the hooves of plague were thundering around me. Sometimes, I wondered if I was too sensitive to even be alive. I still feel that way now and then, like a turtle yanked raw and naked from its shell and tossed, torn open and shrieking, into a sandstorm.

To cover my sensitivity, I would be loud and annoying. Well, to my mind, at the time, I thought I was hilarious and entertaining. I could sing anything I heard on the radio, television, or eight-track; I could recite my favorite lines from Monty Python and Mel Brooks movies. I had no brains for books or math but, after the first time I heard *Abbey Road*, I could sing along to it the next time it was spun. I secretly thought I was a genius. But, in truth, to everyone else, I was just loud and annoying.

So, standing in the beige, sticky kitchen, staring at the silence of my father's huge back, the air still ringing with what my family referred to as my "burglar scream," it dawned on me.

Mom can't rest at home because of me. Because I'm so loud and I talk too much, this whole thing was my fault. I have to shut up, I have to be quiet . . . mute . . . Marcel Marceau. Then she can come home.

So, I practiced being quiet. No fighting with my brothers. No singing any *Godspell* . . . quiet. When I heard she was on her way home I knew I couldn't get too excited. I damn near chewed the inside of my mouth bloody, but there would be no "Yay you're home!" or "Are you home forever?" or tackling hugs or stories about poop or snakes or endless streams of "I love you."

When she finally *did* get home, I was ready. I was hiding in the stairway around the corner from the kitchen, where she sat with the babysitter, Michelle. I had a big bunch of flowers, black-eyed Susans and Queen Anne's lace, and I had drawn her a picture of a horse with a flower in its mouth.

I had it all planned. I would walk up to her, quietly, I would give her the presents, and then I would bow, without saying a word. Yes. Then I would walk away having shown her sufficient love and yet not budged a single decibel.

I would wait for a break in the conversation. I would not interrupt. I listened, ready to quietly pounce, or just appear.

Suddenly I heard my mom crying. Then I heard my name.

"Stormy hates me because I'm sick," she whimpered between little, hitching breaths. "She *hates* me."

At the bottom of the stairs, there was a mirror painted to look like the cover of a magazine. It was red and blue and read *TIME* at the top, then "Man of the Year" at the bottom. From where I stood on the stairs, I could see my face in the mirror. My mouth hung open like a little o. I had never seen myself cry before, but I watched my own face crumple, listening to the accusation. I bit my lower lip. Don't cry. Don't cry. Be quiet.

No! How can you say that? I was already in front of her, my kid brains scolding my mouth to stay shut. I crushed the picture and the flowers in my little fists. I wanted to scream at her that I knew this whole thing was my fault and the fact that she thought I hated her was proof right there. I wanted her to know that I knew I was too loud and too much, but when I'm loud I'm just saying I love you over and over again, now being quiet you think I hate you? What am I supposed to do, Mom, don't you know how this is killing me? But I'm five.

All I can manage is, "I love you, Mommy." And dissolve into snotty little-girl tears.

Roll camera. Mom started crying, Michelle the babysitter started crying, everybody cried.

Aaand scene.

That was Mom's movie. Her movies ended with all the children around the bed of the dying mother who, with her last breath and iota of strength, says the inspirational catch phrase. The children all cry because they realize, finally, what a miracle mother they had all along. Then, she tries the catch phrase again, only gets half of it out, dies, and then starts glowing.

She *lived* for moments like that. Tearful goodbyes, bedside vigils, and when her kids cried over her, ka-boom. Oscar time. That was love. The only love she understood, anyway.

It took a few years of this back and forth for me to figure it out. Shortly after that, I started to be a little glad when she was gone. And, not much later, I started to hate her guts.

CHAPTER TWO:

MANIC DEPRESSION, SADVILLE, HELGA The WHORE, C-R-A-Z....

Manic depression: A mental disease that causes mood swings that range from the lows of depression to the highs of mania. More commonly known, in modern terminology, as *bipolar disorder*.

The first official-sounding disease I heard in relation to my mom was manic depression. When it looked like she had an actual disease, it made it hard for me to hate her. It was frustrating, but, if she were *sick*, that meant she could possibly get better. The doctors knew what she had, so they had to know how to fix it, or even make it a teeny bit better at least. Right?

Just keep her from killing herself and all of us, maybe?

By the time I was around ten years old, though, Mom had been through a dozen hospitals, scores of doctors, specialists, and drugs by the truckload. And she was not better at all. *Au contraire.*

"Your wife is chemically imbalanced," said the doctor whose

expertise was chemical imbalances. "Your wife is classically depressed," said the depression expert. Schizophrenia, multiple personality disorder, mental epilepsy, which still doesn't even exist. She needs this drug, that drug, this or that treatment, and it will only cost another few thousand dollars . . . *more*.

Meanwhile, my father had to pay for all of this with some help from his parents, as insurance didn't automatically pay for mental-health issues during that time. When mental health was finally covered by the insurance my father had through St. Mark's, it was highly restricted, and ran out shortly after it kicked in. My dad could barely keep up financially, and was quickly shutting down inside himself. He would lock his jaws and get through each episode, each drama, each time in relatively stoic silence until something would snap. His frustration was always felt, but only seen in flares of temper. Those were rare, but as huge and scary as a grenade going off in a Dumpster.

"If you don't come down here and pay what you owe us, we will have no choice but to put your wife out on the street!" shrieked a doctor on the phone one night. It was after dinner, and Dad had just cracked a beer when the call came.

"Excuse me? You must be mistaken; I gave a check to the business office this morning after I got my wife checked in."

The doctor called my father a liar and continued with his threatening. Dad hit the roof. Not only had he paid, he had taken out a loan out against his life insurance policy to do it. "You better get us that money by tonight or she's out!"

"You put my wife out on the street and I swear to fucking God, by morning you will be crawling with lawyers!" roared my dad into the receiver before slamming it down. Not surprisingly, they did not kick her out of the hospital. They kept Mom, kept the money, and never offered an apology or an explanation for the doctor's threatening phone call.

That was Dad's reality for most of my growing up, so we never blamed him for losing it now and then.

Years later, I asked him why he didn't share with us what was going on, why did he shoulder the whole thing and rage at the world alone. He said simply, "How do you tell a four-year-old that her mommy wants to die?"

The hospitals weren't all that bad. One, McLean, was downright opulent. I remember marveling at the nicely appointed rooms, decent food, and celebrity guests. When I was a teenager, visiting Mom at McLean, we went into the dining area, where she introduced me to her new best friend, Ricky. "He's a singer, too!" she crowed at us both, one hand on my shoulder and the other on his. He was shiny and sad, with trembling hands and a thick macramé head of beaded braids. I wondered if Rick James told my Mom to call him *Ricky*. I somehow doubted it.

Mom often had a new favorite person in the whole wide world that she would meet in these hospitals. When we would visit her it would go like this: "Stormy, this is my new bestest *bestest* friend Sheena. Her husband is a shit and so she tried to jump off of a building, but she's not going to do *that* again, are you, *Sheeny?*" Then they would have a knowing laugh and Sheena would look at her bandaged arms and chuckle as if to say, "Yeah, I'm such a silly pants!"

Most of my mother's bestest bestest friends, I could tell, were lifers, either hopeless addicts or so horribly damaged that they could only find connection or community in a medical or chemical environment, and destined be locked up, somewhere, forever. Some of these new friends would want very much to sit near me or hug me in a wrong, hungry way. When those people were Mom's new friends, I knew never to go to the restroom without my brother walking me there and waiting for me.

Mom would collect these new favorite people because she was the princess of the ward. She was never *ever* as fucked up as the poor souls she was bunking with, so she was like a powerful beacon to the rejected and disenfranchised. Build them up and try to love the sick and sad out of them. Mother Teresa for maniacs. A batshit bug light. It always seemed as though she was everybody's favorite little person in the hospital. I guess that's why she loved it there so much.

As glorious as McLean Hospital was, on the other end was a pit of hellish proportions. One hospital was so bad that my father wouldn't let us go there at all. I was much older when he told me about it, and it shocked me because I was sure there couldn't possibly be a place more ghastly than Sadville.

It was a doctor from Sadville who had threatened to throw my suicidal mother out in the middle of the night if my dad didn't pay up. It came as no surprise to anyone in my family that this pit of an institution was closed. I would even hazard a guess that some of the people who were in charge back then are either behind bars or mopping up their own shit in a soggy cardboard box under a bridge somewhere in hell. For purposes of describing this particular institution without incurring any potential legal ramifications, or conjuring any demons from its ashes, we'll call the place "Satan's Anal Deluge-Ville," Sadville for short.

Sadville was a mental institution that looked exactly like you would expect a loony bin to look like had you only seen them depicted in horror films: a monolithic, gulag-type building with walls the color of yellowing chicken bone. The kind of place where, as a kid, you'd stare up at its horribleness from your tiny spot of sunshine, and you'd swear you saw thunder clouds gathering and a flock of screeching black crows or bats flapping around it.

There was no ping-pong at Sadville.

I remember one particular visit from when I was nine or ten, and still into visiting Mom wherever she was because I missed her so much. Dad was having a meeting with one of Mom's doctors, or, for all we knew, having another fight over whether he had paid the bill. Either way, I'm pretty sure he was happy to miss the mess his wife was in at the moment. We were closing in on 1980, the beginning of a terrible time for Mom. There was no better evidence of how hopeless the situation was with her than when she was at Sadville. When Mom was in that hole, things were not good. The place had hardcore security (read: lockdown), as it was home for the dangerous lunatics who were generally called *criminally insane*. There were thick, scary doors and gigantic nurses with big arms that looked like big legs. Their even bigger legs were stuck into itchy white tights and stomped around under their square asses, barely shifting under the white uniforms. Like blocky, scowling ships, they swept through the wards, checking straps and giving Thorazine enemas.

The supercrazies were either holed up in the never-get-out ward, or doped up within an inch of their lives in the drooling-medicated-coma ward. Mom was in another section of the hospital, where patients were free to bump into things, rage maniacally at shadows, or stare blankly at the blaring television. Let's call it the seriously-deranged-but-not-terribly-dangerous ward or, simply, the Unwanted Relative Area.

We had to sign in at the front desk and wait to be escorted to Mom's floor. One of the linebacker-shaped nurses would appear like Lurch from *The Addams Family,* and we would follow her into the elevator and up to the proper floor. The nurse never spoke. She looked like she could flip over a car and eat the passengers, so we never spoke to her either. Once on Mom's floor, Nursezilla would haul open three massive, medieval iron locks, then pull open the thick metal door with a *ka-chunk*! Out would waft the scents of stale cigarette smoke and old coffee stink. The industrial fluorescent lighting gave a constant bug-light buzzing, the television was blaring, and there was someone screaming from a locked room.

The door opened to a long, straight hallway with patient rooms all along it. Immediately on the left was the small TV room. In the hallway were slumped a few catatonic bodies, someone in a broken wheelchair, someone leaning on the wall drawing with her finger, someone else stood swaying in the center of the hallway. I noticed her staring hard at us as we came in.

She was very thin, but looked like she had been pretty once, with high cheekbones and wide-set eyes. Her hair was a teased blonde-gray mass that would have pouffed around her head like a wiry cloud had she not woven it into two rough braids on either side of her head with childish bows at the end. "Helga the whore" said my brain. She stood in the hallway, staring slack-jawed until she saw my brother John, when she sprang to life hopping like a toddler into a room with a squeak.

"She has sex prawblums," spat a fat, wall-eyed woman in front of the television.

"Hi, Mom!" I said, and went into the common room to give her a hug. Mom was wasted.

"Hi-, sh-shhweetie," Mom groggily cooed back.

The TV room was small and stuffy. There were about five patients already in there watching *Donahue,* taking up all the seats, so we could only visit one at a time, while the rest stayed near the door or out in the hallway. I went first, while my brother Henry leaned on the wall just inside the door awaiting his turn. Mom was rocking and wobbling in her chair so I held her hands and stood in front of her. "How are you?"

"Shooo-ooo mush better, babe." She swayed my hands in hers as if in a dance. "Mu-uuush better. H-hooome soon," she sang.

I wanted to leave so badly, run out of there. I loved my mom, but it was all so much. I knew she wasn't as crazy as all this. She didn't need to be here. She looked like a tiny, fucked-up, baby bunny, huddled in her chair, flanked by genuinely psychotic humans straight out of central casting. The wall-eyed schizo lady chimed in, chuckling in a slurred south Boston accent, "She's good naow, but you shoulda seent 'er when theyz brung 'er in heeyuh."

With that my mom shook to her feet, swung her arm in slow motion to point at the lady. I saw bruises spreading out from under a wide bandage on her forearm.

"Don'tchoo talk to my children!!!" She was shaking and crying as the woman cackled and snorted, all satisfied with herself on the couch. It seemed like everyone started to wake up at that point, and make some kind of crazy noise in response to the weird confrontation unfolding during *Donahue*.

"Don'tchoo dare!!!" Mom wailed.

I looked back to the doorway at my brothers. Henry started toward me. I looked at John, I wanted him to come in and intervene, too, but he wasn't looking at me, or even aware of the medicated mayhem unfolding in the room. He was staring hard at something down the hall. He had both his hands on either side of the door, as if bracing himself. Henry and I do-si-do-ed in front of our weeping mom, so that I could get to the door and he could calm her down. He took her hands.

"Mom," he started.

"She's soo *mean!*" she said.

"Sit down, Ma," he said calmly as he got her to sit back down. Even at thirteen, Henry had a solid presence, normal and unflappable. He quieted Mom into her chair and everyone seemed to settle back into their haze-and-stare mode. Mom finally noticed my brother was holding her hands and lit up a little as he squatted in front of her, "How are you, Mom?"

"So-ooo mush better . . . home soon . . ."

John was still blocking the doorway, looking down the hall, his jaw set and his body stiff. I got to the door and tried to get on the other side of him but he wouldn't budge. Before he put his hand on my shoulder to turn me to face inside the TV room again, I got a good look at what he was watching.

Helga the whore had come back into the hallway with a slash of red lipstick on and was in a semisquat plié, knees cranked open to my brother, rubbing herself desperately with the bristles of a paddle hairbrush. John pushed me back in the room by my shoulder, and stood firm. I heard a nurse thump up the hallway to get Helga to stop. I heard little of the exchange other than Helga saying, "But he's so beautiful!" Then she sang like a child, "Gimme ten more minutes! Gimme ten more minutes!"

When the nurse got Helga handled, John finally let go of the door and came in. He gave Mom a quick, awkward hug and we were done.

We were silent all the way home.

CHAPTER THREE:

JUST LIKE YOUR MOM DR. LOVEY, THE HEAD BOX....

The Seventies

I looked just like my mom, everyone said so, but, in no time, I grew taller than her. Way taller, in fact. She was five foot two, and by my ninth birthday, I had at least three inches on her. My height, plus my big, smart-ass mouth, made people think I was much older. They also assumed I was tough. Mouthy and fisty, I had started a bit of a fighting habit that was giving me trouble in and out of school. I could shoot my mouth off and back it up with a swift kick in the nuts or a wildly swung roundhouse to the head. I told teachers to go to hell and meant it. I was starting to notice things sucking, and it was ticking me off.

The whole hospital thing was getting old. My mom had become the weakest girl that ever lived, in my opinion, and she seemed to relish the title. The world echoed with a chorus of "your poor mother," and Mom would sing backup. She would cry and cry and stare at us all, sucking all the hope and joy out of anything in a desperate, begging need to be the most hopeless of cases, and, "Isn't it so awful!"

I learned how to bite holes inside my mouth, say "I don't care," and make no big deal about it when she would go lame. By all outward appearances, or as far as I would let any grown-up know, I was doing fine with everything, blissfully ignorant to what was going on with my mother, or stiff-upper-lipping it. I was neither. I was just big, loud, and broken. I had started to hear myself say things I didn't mean, but couldn't stop it. I would lie in bed and say, "Fuck you, God." Slap my hands over my mouth only to hear it ringing in my head on a dirty loop.

God can hear your thoughts.

I didn't mean it, but it played over and over, hissing like a dusty hi-fi in my head. *It's not me, but what if God can't tell it isn't me? I don't really mean it!*

He hates you, too.

God was going to see to it that I would live a miserable, lonely life for my terrible words to him. I was sure of it. It was like people spreading shitty gossip about you to a teacher or parent that wasn't true, but nobody believed the truth, because, well . . . it *is* you, and you are a bad person. Bad people think bad thoughts and bad things happen to those people.

Terrible voices were tiptoeing through my two lobes all the time. Many nights I would bite my lip and punch myself in the head to try to shut the voices up, but they would just laugh. I would also suffer paralyzing anxiety, knotted stomach cramps, and outbursts. I walked around, constantly feeling like an exposed tooth nerve, but I did everything I could to make the world at large think I was doing just fine. I was a big strong girl.

It wasn't just the punching myself to sleep and all the rest that let me know something was wrong with me. I was a weirdo, a total outcast. Every day at school was the worst day of my life. I didn't have a lot of friends, but I had invisible pets that I talked to in public. I was just as quick to be completely destroyed by an unkind word as I was to smash someone in the face for hurting someone else. Everything mattered more to me than everyone else. And no matter how hard I tried, I was always in trouble, because I could never be quiet or disappear. And the one person, in the whole world, who I knew loved me completely, the only one who told me I was beautiful and could do or be anything, kept running away to die.

My grandmother on my father's side, Neeny, told me that she never liked the way Mom looked at me. "She was obsessed with you. It just wasn't right." I loved it, though, Mom really could light up a room or a rainy day like no one else. Besides, Neeny used to drive her Chrysler LeBaron around, wearing huge black postcataract surgery glasses, and scream at those GODDAMNED WOMEN DRIVERS!

My mom loved me so much it made me feel famous. But that had been a long time ago, and at around nine or ten, it stopped being so great. Her loving me that much was just a trick. Around that time, I also stopped wanting to be just like her. She was weak and needy, so I acted tough. Everyone was still compelled to say how alike we were, but I figured if I acted strong and practiced not giving a fuck, they would eventually stop saying, "You are just like your mother!" Boy, was I wrong.

The doctor wasn't even looking at me when he said it; he was writing something down for a nurse. It was so casual that he didn't seem to think that he was really dropping some bomb on my skull. He acted more as if he were reminding me of something I had always known, like my middle name or where my grandparents lived.

This happened during a bad visit. Generally speaking, a *bad* visit was anything from being turned away because Mom was too fucked up to see anyone or the hospital staff would let us up to see her, only to find out when we got there that she was too fucked up to see anyone, and *then* we'd have to leave.

On this day, it was the latter.

Mom was wasted and had thrown herself on the floor in front of us in the hallway begging for forgiveness, "Please don't hate me!" She cried and keened, her breath so pitifully short that she could barely talk. She collapsed on the floor in a dead heap, but was so tiny that my father and a nurse could scoop her up like a wet hand towel to help her walk down the hall back to her room. She was never really loud or scary, no wailing or screaming. She would bend under some inescapable sad weight, and slowly break in front of us.

As she slumped against them padding limply back down the hall, she begged my dad to forgive her and "Please don't stop loving me Henny, please . . ." She wept helplessly.

My brothers and I knew to stay put. John and Henry went around the corner to the common room. I hung back with Dr. Lovey.

Mom called everyone Lovey. If she knew you for five minutes, you were Lovey.

Her psychiatrists were no exception. They were all familiar characters as Mom got locked up more and more frequently, and I was used to being around them. It was nothing for me to chat with Dr. Lovey and practice being the tough little girl who was totally unfazed by the madness or sadness she'd just seen.

"Oh, well," I shrugged, my sneakered heel bouncing on the floor.

"Your mom's been having a hard week, but she'll be okay, Stormy," he said.

"Yeah, I know; it's no big deal."

He was still writing with his head down. I hated the quiet.

"At least I'm not gonna be crazy like her. Right?"

You know when you ask a question you already know the answer to, and you're just trying to make conversation? You're being friendly, engaging, filling up any uncomfortable, quiet gaps? Like, "Dontcha just love chocolate?" or "What the heck is the deal about cats and Christmas tinsel anyway? You know it ends up in their poop, right? Stupid cats."

I expected that he would guffaw and say, "Oh, silly girl, of course not!" Then he would ruffle the hair on my silly head as he passed by me on his way to do some doctoring elsewhere.

But, barely giving me a glance, Dr. Lovey nodded and said, "Oh. Well, yes. It's hereditary. You will absolutely end up like your mother."

My heel stopped bouncing.

As he tore off the piece of paper he'd been scribbling on and got up to leave he said, I imagine to comfort me, "Probably not until your twenties, or when you have children, whichever comes first."

All I remember after that was getting very hot in my face and standing very still in the doorway. I bit my cheeks, heard the ker-plip-ker-plop of ping-pong around the corner. I wanted to walk away, take back the question, go back in time, ask him about something else, change the subject, or shut up. But, instead, I was frozen. Dr. Lovey, on his way out, said something about how lucky I was that we knew so much about my mother's illness, now, so that when the time came for me to get treatment, not to worry, we'll know how to take care of it, then left.

Just like your mother.

My dad never mentioned it to me. At some point, I know, my mom and one of her Dr. Loveys had suggested examining us, but my father would have none of it. I remember hearing him say, when he was recalling the let's-have-the-children-looked-at conversation with a friend of his, "You already got my wife, I'll be damned if you think I'm gonna give you my fucking kids." Dad didn't call any of the doctors *Lovey;* he called them all a bunch of screaming assholes.

No, Dad wasn't going to send me into treatment. Hell, it pissed him off enough when I had to go to the hospital just to get stitches. In that regard, I knew I was safe.

But asshole or not, Lovey was a doctor. He wore the white coat and name tag and had that chilly white voice we were so used to hearing. All swoop-y with pretend caring. He was clearly a medical authority, a grown-up, so I believed him.

I was going to be just like her. And everyone said so.

The next time that Mom got sent to Sadville was the summer my brother John and I seriously considered killing her. I was eleven and all summer the universe conspired to take my childhood and give it to that little blonde. She was so greedy, mewling for our love and attention, taking it, then turning around and telling anyone in earshot that we hated her. Dad had pretty much washed his hands of the whole thing, and nobody blamed him. He worked so hard only to give every penny to this or that institution or pharmacy, each promising to bring his wife, life, and sunshine back. All it seemed to do, though, was embolden all the stupid doctors to make more and more ridiculous diagnoses and write dopier prescriptions, some that would make my mom weave and wobble in her body like a cartoon chicken on a unicycle. Each doctor acted as though they had all the answers, and every single one was wrong. It was as if they were all horny to find more stuff wrong with her, and keep her sick and medicated.

After many sad and frustrating years of that, Dad checked out. He worked all school year, teaching history and coaching, then in 1980, took a summer job as a lifeguard at a water park near Little Boar's Head, or Boarsie, a town near Rye, New Hampshire. He and his dog Tilly could live all summer at the beach and have a nice, ninety-odd miles between himself and reality. Henry was off at awesome American camp. John and I stayed home, smoked pot, and grew thick calluses all over our hearts. John had his license now, and that meant we had Mom duty.

Mom duty basically involved us going to the hospital, bringing her a carton of Kool Milds, chocolate-covered cherries, and clean underpants.

"Something's gotta give," we would say every time we left. "She's gotta go." We weren't complete bastards, but Mom clearly wanted out, so why not give her a hand? We were mostly kidding when we joked about putting a hit on her or going through the phone book to find Mafia-sounding names. Callous humor was the only thing that made the crazy tolerable. Whenever we'd hear an ambulance siren blaring by we'd say, "There goes Mom." when someone asked what our parents did for a living we'd say, "Our dad works but our mom is broken."

It was a long, hot summer with varying degrees of horrible after each hospital visit. There was always some new drama with one of her new pyromaniac rapist friends, or Dr. Lovey would be changing her medication and she would be a complete mess. She would rattle her pink plastic pill dispenser, like a doll's ice cube tray, embossed with M T W T F S S for the days of the week, and say, "Lovey is taking me off all my meds. I'm better now that we know what's wrong! See? No more pills! I'm only taking this one for voices, this one for shaking, this one for sleepy-sleepy-nye-nye and this one . . ."

One of the last times I saw my mom in that hospital was a blazing late-August afternoon. John and I pulled up to Sadville, armed to the teeth with her smokes, clean underpants, and loads of sarcasm. The air was smudged with humidity, wavering a couple feet above the ground, blurring the edges of everything. A great day to be slathered in Bain De Soleil and flirt with the tattooed carnies at my dad's water park, or just run into some cold water, like kids were doing everywhere else that day.

Instead, we walked up the cement steps into the main office to sign in and wait for Nursezilla to come grunt us up to our mom's floor. When we said Large to the sign-in nurse she looked on a clipboard and quickly sat up very straight, smiled phonily and awfully, and said, "Um . . . yes. Could you please wait over there for a moment? Someone will be here soon, to talk with you."

To *talk* with us?

John went stone quiet. His face was stiff under his long rock 'n' roll hair.

We sat on the sofa across from the front desk, the sign-in nurse smiling nervously if she caught us looking her way. She busied herself with some papers and kept her head down.

John and I stared blankly forward.

"She's dead. She fucking did it. She's dead," I said out loud, not looking at him. I knew full well my big brother had already come to that conclusion. What I wondered was, did we make this happen? Does *John* think we made it happen?

I was immediately ashamed of myself. All the joking . . . I felt like a bully who had terrorized a little dog and then watched it sprint into oncoming traffic. A tiny living being, so twisted and miserable from God knows what, but all she wanted in the whole world was to be loved. And one by one, all the loved ones in her life gave up on her and pulled away. Including her children. My faced burned. I wanted her to die, and now . . .

"Hi there," someone was singing at us. "You must be Stor-meee!"

I looked up to see a middle-aged woman in a pink pantsuit standing in an office doorway. John and I were pulled from our reverie and beckoned into a bright office, blasted with air conditioning. I instantly had gooseflesh all over my arms and legs. We sat on one side of a massive desk, she on the other. A plaque on the desk read Dr. Candy Something-ski.

"So, how are you kids doing?"

Next to her name plaque was a menagerie of ceramic Siamese kittens, frozen and shiny. They were posed to look like they were suspended in midplay. All around the room were the trappings of someone who had to bullshit families as their primary source of income. On the walls were framed posters of soft-focus vistas, those typical shots of seascapes and rainbows with birds stretching across them. Some had motivational phrases about footsteps and paths and shit. There were other glass critters here and there, all peeking their heads around, giving the impression that they were all paying attention. Like they cared.

I wanted to smash everything I saw.

Dr. Candy opened her mouth to sing again, this time to my brother who just stared at his thumbs.

"Is she dead?" My voice did not sound as tough as I'd hoped.

An expression twitched over her before the cough-syrup smile of gigantic fake empathy returned. The look that lit for a nanosecond on her face was a cold, sharky indifference with a barb of "I've heard about you, you mouthy little fucker, don't interrupt me again or you'll be frozen in glass faster that you can read the motivational messages on my wall."

I could feel the bitch, and she hated me. Fuck her.

"Is. She. Dead?" I refused to look at her, staring at the tiny ball of yarn in the grip of the tiny ceramic cat whose tiny butt pointed up. Someone thought it a good idea to paint a tiny butthole under its upturned tail.

"Suzi's had a bad day." She turned her lollipop charm back on me, talking at me as if I weren't real. I looked at John, then at his thumbs as he didn't lift his eyes, then back to the ceramic kitty butthole. "And it seems she's been trying to hurt herself, and, and . . ."

"We know she wants to fucking die already, that's why she's here. Do we need to identify her body or sign something, because I have to get the fuck out of here, okay?"'"

I jumped to my feet, swatting the little animals off the desk and onto the floor.

"Not dead," said the candy-coated Disney bitch without singing.

She tried to regain her cough-syrup tone, saying that Mom was okay but we could not see her. She offered us no condolences or details. As we got up to leave, she told us someone from the hospital would let us know when it was okay to come back and visit. My brother thanked her, I think. But his voice was so low that he could've said "Fuck you, lady." And made it sound like thanks. John was so cool. I was not. I made sure my feet crunched over the bits of porcelain kitty heads and snapped little paws on my way out.

We found out, later, that Mom had smashed her lily-of-the-valley perfume bottle in the sink and carved herself up pretty good with a shard. She probably had no idea we had even come that day, as she lay somewhere wearing gauze opera gloves, barely able to form a sentence from all the drugs they pumped her with.

I tried so hard to *be* hard. To not care, make no big deal, and be tough. My brothers could do it, but me? I sucked at not caring.

My dad was the best at looking tough. He told me his secret, once. We were in the car heading back to Southborough from Boarsie. It had been a glorious day of sun and ocean. As the afternoon crept into a warm, orange evening, we all enjoyed an impromptu clambake, with my brothers and I, Dad's parents and family, all my cousins, extended summer friends, dogs, and Frisbees. We all stuffed ourselves with clams, lobster, and buttered heaps of corn on the cob. The grownups smoked and drank beer and the kids ran amok in the cooling sand.

My brothers had stayed behind, and Dad brought me with him as he went back for some Mom-related crisis. I sat in the front seat with my sand-sticky feet on the dash, staring hard out the passenger side window. I didn't want Dad to see my face, crumpling around my stupid, indulgent tear ducts. We were rolling under passing streetlights on our way to I-95, and I didn't want him to know I was crying. Crying was weak.

My throat was tight and big fat tears welled behind my lids. I tried to do the tough thing, the correct thing, and quickly wipe anything that fell from my lashes. I guess only a dumb kid would think holding one's breath and wiping each eye every three seconds while staring ferociously out the window wouldn't betray the truth.

"What is it?" my dad asked sweetly. Of course, it made me cry harder. I strained every facial muscle I had, trying to stop the tears. I folded my arms tighter and higher and shook my head quickly.

"In a minute," I tried to say, but my voice was that gapping, breathy, crying girl voice. Mom's voice. I was so embarrassed. I was scared that Dad might get angry if he knew what I was thinking. As soon as we were on the dark highway, headed south, my breathing smoothed out and I could talk without sounding like Mom. "I loved today. I love our family," I started.

"Me, too," he said, waiting.

"It's just that . . . Mom doesn't have this. She never did, and it's all she has ever wanted. It just doesn't seem fair, you know?" I felt tears coming again, but my dad spoke up immediately.

"You know what I do, when it all gets to be too much?" He wasn't angry at all. He sounded like his teacher self, wise and calm, not the hurt man ready to flip out if someone burnt a pot of hot cocoa. "I take all of those feelings, all the sad and scary feelings, and I lock them in a box inside my head. You don't have to feel them at all, just put them away. You can deal with them later."

Oh, how I tried to find that manly box in my head, to stuff it with all my crazy thoughts and feelings, but I just couldn't do it. All my emotions whipped and jumped through me like a pack of cracked-out monkeys. I was convinced that I *felt* more than anybody else. Not only my own, but I could also feel other people's feelings, too. Though I tried on the mantra "He who cares the least wins," trying not to feel, for me, was crazy making.

$\sim$

Back at Sadville, John and I sat in the car, hot as a fevered ear from baking in the parking lot. I broke down, hot tears spitting through my stinging eyes. "Something's got to give, and it was almost *her*. She did it again; I can't believe she did it again."

John must've thought I meant the attempt itself. I didn't. I meant that I had just started to get my footing that summer, where I could laugh and be okay with the way things were. Giving the world the finger from a nice, sarcastic place to hide. Mom got her sad, little girl fingers into my guts, to fuck me up again. "I fucking wish she'd done it, man, *fuck* her." She got me to care. Again.

Gotcha.

CHAPTER FOUR:

YAY PORN! ♡ PUTTING IT IN

Since I knew I was going to lose my mind, I figured the best thing to do was lose my virginity. Fast. I wasn't super attached to it anyway.

In the provincial enclave of Southborough, Massachusetts, there was a lot of chatter one year about *the white van*. Ask anyone who was around St. Mark's School in the seventies and say, "Remember *the white van?*" Chances are someone will, and say, "'Oh yes, the rapist." By all accounts, nobody was ever raped by anyone in any white van, but it was a hot topic for awhile, and Mom loved it. Rape was a big thing with my mom. It's how she told me about sex.

"I'm going to catch snakes."

"Oh, no, you're not. You'll get raped."

"God, Mom. There is no guy in a white van at the pond."

"The answer is no."

"Mom!"

"He will hold you down and stick his penis right in your vagina," Mom said, as if there would be a dramatic swell of music and we would go to an Ovaltine commercial. I was eight, and I knew it was horseshit.

"And what if I like it?" I said in a snotty voice to Bowser in bed that night, pretending I was smarting off to my mom. Bowser was my huge teddy bear I practiced making out with.

Fast forward to twelve years old. My childish ideas of sex were not at all on par with my advanced ability to please myself. I was a genius masturbatrix. But though I knew what everything was and where everything went, I had no tangible idea of how it was all supposed to happen.

Thank god for porn.

Watching grownups have sex with no subtlety or innuendo, just straight up doing it, was a huge leap in my awareness. The film was *Candy Goes to Hollywood*. Not a terribly clever story, or superattractive people, but in the twenty odd minutes I sat glued to it, I learned everything I needed to know about sex before I actually did it. The only bummer was, I was getting this deep education while wedged, shoulder to shoulder, between my mom and my aunt Bitsy.

My father's family lived in rural Pennsylvania, about five hours from Southborough. We spent some summers and many Christmases there. My grandparents and aunt and uncle lived in these huge old farmhouses, filled with generations of antique furniture, silver, and gleaming lemon-oiled wood floors. There were wide fields and golf courses, tennis clubs where we could have watercress tea sandwiches with the crusts neatly trimmed. It was a blue-blooded WASP-y land, but my dad's family were farmers and railroad workers and some of the best people I had ever known. My aunt Bitsy, Dad's sister, was a tall, gorgeous blonde with a filthy sense of humor and a heart too big for this world. She had the porn tape hidden in the study, behind the red- leather encyclopedias.

The details of how I ended up watching the porn with my mother and my dad's sister I cannot recall. However, I remember absolutely everything about Candy and all the misadventures she and her giant droopy boobs got into.

She was a big dumb blonde from nowhere, stepping off a bus on Hollywood and Vine. Her fake Marilyn Monroe-isms were not lost on me. "Hollywood! I can't believe it! Here I am in Hollywood!" heaving her chest with every H. In no time, a talent scout sees her and gets her on the casting couch. He hypnotizes her to get her over her stage fright. "By the way, what's your favorite flavor ice cream?"

"Va-NILLA!" Heave-heave-heave.

Later, as the talent scout crams his joint into her mouth, telling her it's a vanilla ice cream cone, my mom whispers into my ear, *"That's* not making love."

I nodded slightly, making a mental note that, yes, yes, it was. I was all tingly and hot and couldn't wait to scoot my butt under a bathtub faucet.

I kept my tingles and prickles well to myself throughout the stretch of film we watched. My aunt finally clicked it off and put the VHS tape back behind the encyclopedias on the bookshelf. Both women feigned disgust and I quietly agreed, mumbling something like, "Yeah, she was so stupid." I couldn't wait to try it all out on somebody.

Valuable lesson number one: I learned that when the guy is done, *everybody's* done. Lesson number two: When he's shot his stuff in or all over you and is kneeling or standing over you panting, you need to stare at him or just his dick, with a mixture of fear and total amazement. Lesson three: No matter what is happening to you sexually, you must respond in all excited affirmatives, *Yes!* and *Yeah!* or

Oh, yeah!!! were all you needed to say to stoke the action further, and keep things positive.

My only concern was the whole penetration thing. Besides my fingers, nothing had actually been *in* me, and that was worrisome.

What if it hurt? What if I said *ouch* or, worse, cried? I had heard that you bleed when you lose your virginity and that was way too embarrassing to even remain in the realm of possibility.

I'd have to break myself in.

I found a plastic, tapered cylinder in an old junk drawer in our guest room in Southborough. It was cream-colored and hollow with a screw-off bottom. When I opened it, I saw a place for two C batteries. "Personal Massager" was embossed around the bottom along with "Johnson and Johnson."

I never put batteries in it, but I washed it really well and took it to bed with me every night for a long time. Every day I would wash, dry, and return it to the junk drawer. Just in case. After a few weeks, I was confident that I was ready for my first time.

Sex was already important to me. It was my thing. And I believed once I got past the physical initiation, once I was *cocked and loaded,* as I liked to call it, the old me would dissolve, leaving a pink and fresh new me. A me that might not go crazy, but wherever I went, I would definitely not go alone.

He was twenty, I think. I met him in a cloud of college kids outside of a concert. He got a six-pack and we walked into the huge park called the Boston Common. He seemed cute enough, not too big, dark, spiked hair, his collar pointed upwards on his jacket. I noticed he had acne under his jaw and down his neck a bit, but he had beer, and that made him perfect. I told him my name was Nina and I was nineteen years old and would he like to go hijack a swan boat?

Nineteen was my go-to lying age *until* I was nineteen, then I told everyone I was twenty-two. This night, however, I was a few months into thirteen.

We couldn't find the swan boats in the dark, so we ended up in a nice dewy patch of grass near some Hare Krishna twirl-off. They chanted and sang and hopped around in their saffron sheets about twenty yards from us. I could smell the incense as we sipped beer and talked about music we liked. I told him how it was so cool to meet him, but, "Gosh, it is such a shame I have to leave day after tomorrow, back to London."

Because of course, during this entire exchange, I was faking an English accent.

Besides my lie "I'm nineteen," the accent was something else I did constantly when I was on my own in the city, or when Daphne and I met new people. We watched a lot of Monty Python; I can still recite huge chunks of *Holy Grail* and *Life of Brian.* John Cleese was my dialect coach for snowing guys and sounding as cool as possible.

And though I only suspected it at the time, there is nothing quite so hot as a girl who's going to be leaving soon, and going far, far away.

We made out. We lay down and he got on top of me. My heart sank when his hands went up my shirt. I was wearing a padded bra with basically bee-sting boobs underneath. At this point, though my body was long (I was as tall as he was), in his fumbling hands I probably felt like a squashy ribbed ironing board . . . an ironing board with a hole in it. He looked for that next.

"Yes," I tried to say, but the weight of him on top of me was a thing I hadn't yet encountered. I had made out before, but only sitting up, or leaning against something. In this position, everything I would try to say sounded strained. So I was quiet.

My tightest and sluttiest corduroys were probably not the best choice for this adventure, but they got pulled down past my bum eventually, and far enough to get my legs open, just enough.

I steeled myself.

Hare Kriiishnaaa! Hare Kriiishnaaa! Thrumming in the background.

My bare butt in the cool wet grass.

Hare raammaaaHare raaammaaaarammaraaammaaa. . . .

Desperate breathing in my ear, and Storm, the virgin, was gone.

It didn't hurt.

I did get to say *yes,* and *oh yeah* a couple of times (in my fake accent) when he would do a push-up over me and I could breathe. I bit his chin at one point, he seemed to like that, so I decided later it would become my signature move.

The moments leading up to his finish line, I felt this weird burst of feverish heat push out of him and onto me. He made a sharp, surprised sound, shook, then collapsed. His breathing became long and happy-sounding, like he'd just run to catch up with someone he loved and truly missed. It felt amazing to me to be buried under a big hot body that felt so grateful.

It took me awhile, after getting cocked and loaded, to figure out how to get more of that transient, love-you-for-a-split-second action. I was determined to become *good* in bed. I hadn't the foggiest idea what that even meant, but knew the power was in that. And like anything else, I knew with practice, I could become a pro, a passionista, and, in time, a dick whisperer. I would be in demand, like the cool kid who gets chosen first for dodgeball.

On television, girls always got mad at boys for kissing and telling. Me, I wanted a full-on word-of-mouth campaign. I wanted guys to call each other and marvel at my skills. "Dude. Isn't she fucking amazing? Did she bite your chin?"

I lived for that moment when the guy was about to get off. Simultaneously melting and exploding, he became simple. The world would disappear, but I wouldn't. And whoever he was, for a brief bit of time, he was so glad I was there.

Those sweet, pounding seconds, to me, were like little drops of love. The only love I understood. I know it wasn't really love per se, it was more carnal gratitude than anything, but it was all I had, so it was enough.

Just like with Mr. Pool Jet and ChapStick, I knew not to tell anyone in the beginning. I told anybody and everybody I was a virgin, unless, of course, they were about to fuck me. I kept everything hidden, especially from Mom. It wasn't hard, since she was home less and less. And I didn't even want to acknowledge her existence, let alone talk to her about anything. But when she got released one day, without anybody knowing, she sneaked home while everyone was out, and found condoms and pot in my dresser drawer. She insisted we go immediately to the gynecologist. I thought the jig was up.

I was fourteen and, at this point, hated everyone, especially my mom. Whenever she came home from the hospital, she would try to mom the shit out of me, I guess to make up for lost time, but she would give absurd advice about boys, my weight, or try to ground me for talking back. It was too little, too late. Every blessed thing she did reeked of an obvious need to draw attention to herself. Every overly mom shtick she pulled on me had to be in front of an audience.

In a clothing store, I'd try to run away from her and look for boys, "I'm going to the restroom." Then she'd wait until I was within shouting range,

"Stormy! Tell them you just got your period!!" Then, every human in the store, boys included, would suddenly burn holes in my crimson cheeks with their embarrassed-for-me stares, then, one by one, picture me bleeding and struggling with a tampon.

Friendly's is a fast food chain that has family-friendly, greasy-spoon food and ice cream. They call milkshakes "Fribbles." It was also my mom's favorite theater of hideous and public discussion of my fertility and other cringe-worthy topics.

We would get all the way there in silence, me just staring through my running black eyeliner and cigarette smoke, stinking boots on the dash, she singing gaily along to the radio and not talking to me about anything until we got inside. The ambush would spring as soon as we were surrounded by strangers in line, waiting to be seated, or in front of the waitresses.

"Welcome to Friendly's! Can I get you girls something to drink to get started?"

"Oh, boy! Can I please have a big ginger ale with a cherry in it? Stormy, when you DO get your period, did you know you can bleed up to a tablespoon's worth a day?" She would say this out of nowhere.

"Um, thanks, Mom. Yeah, I'll have a chocolate Fribble and a hand grenade. No pin, thanks. Awesome."

I would eventually run away or make her cry, so she would hide in her room. But every time she would come home, she'd try to mother me or ground me, and find absolutely any opportunity to talk loudly and publicly about my menstrual cycle.

She also had a strange habit of grabbing her boobs in public.

Like an actress in an old black-and-white film who would clutch at her chest to emphasize her passionate sincerity, Mom would go for that effect. Only she would straight up grab one tit and hold it. Arching her back and sighing, dramatically, "Oh, my stars above!"

She loved doing the boob clutch thing in front of any boy in her presence. I had a guy come over while she was home exactly once. She pulled him into a room, closed the door, and held him hostage for about twenty minutes. I could imagine her grabbing her tits and telling him how completely insecure I was about my weight and how this whole punky thing was such a cry for help. She went on about how I had a big, wounded heart, which she understood because, "You know, I was raped when I was ten and now I hear voices I have named 'the Judges.' They tell me to hurt myself, but oh, my stars (grab-squeeze-hold), I am doing so much better since they found out that I am the only person in the world who has this rare illness. It is SO new and unresearched it doesn't even have a name yet! Right now they are calling it 'mental epilepsy.' They say I'm going to be written about in a medical journal, and I said 'A medical journal? Oh, my goodness gracious!' (grab-clutch-hold)."

Then she hugged him for an awkwardly long time, thanked him, and let him leave.

Never saw him again.

Suffice it to say, I would just run away to get laid. However, I did keep condoms in my dresser drawer with my pot. Unluckily for me, Mom got a ride home from the loony bin while no one was home and went through my stuff. Lucky for her, she found just the things to inspire some phony-baloney mother-daughter moment.

I came home to find her on the couch next to our neighbor, Suzi2, from across the street. They were both sitting straight up, knees together, hands folded—a serious talking-to posture. She was trying to not crack a smile as the camera in her head started rolling on this pivotal moment in her life as a mother. The Intervention.

"I found these in your room."

Three little square condom envelopes sat on the coffee table in front of them.

"You're home," I responded flatly, fighting the urge to pick up a nearby lamp and smash it over my own head.

"Stormy. Are you still virginal?" Both women were fighting off a full-on giggle fit. I guess they had found my stash as well.

"Yes," I lied. "Mom, did you smoke my pot?"

"We flushed your drugs straight down the po-po," she lied, fully snickering now.

"Great. Thanks." I walked into the kitchen to get something to eat. Her performance continued as she shouted from the couch about how WE were bringing ME to the gynecologist to get me on the PILL.

Fast forward to where my heels were dug into the cold metal stirrups and my stomach was in my throat. We girls often find ourselves on our backs, legs cranked open, hoping for the best. During sex: "Please don't be another douche bag." In childbirth: "Please be healthy . . . and look like your father." Our gynecological visits are no exception. Most of the time, in these episodes of legs akimbo, one simple hope is, whoever is dealing with us down there, is at least cool . . . and not looking like someone's creepy old uncle, like my last gynecologist did.

No problem. Act cool. Count ceiling tiles.

The creepy doctor was actually humming as he thumbed through my girl parts like a damp paperback. I was pretty sure I wanted to die. This guy will see I'm not a virgin and tell my mother.

I could just picture her making a spectacle to the horror of women and girls waiting for their own round of personal, and some humiliating, tests, discussing her bold confrontation with her wild teenage daughter who's been using food and now sex to cover up her feelings of insecurity. "It's so hard for Stormy, but I understand. My nanny was a Satanist and she used me in some terrible rituals when I was just a baby. Oh, my heavens, it was awful. Just. Awful." Grab-squeeze-hold.

I was up to twenty-odd ceiling tiles when I realized Dr. Creepy wasn't really talking. Does he see something weird? He's gotta know. He will totally be able to tell. Will he tell my mom? Isn't it a law or something? Shit, I'm going to have to have yet another hideous talk with my mom, and it will probably take place at Friendly's. God damn it. Every time she comes home from being locked up . . . ow! Is his whole fucking hand in me??

"So, what d'you use normally?" he finally said from between my shaking knees.

"Huh?"

"G-K-S?" He actually smirked at my open and brightly lit sexbits.

"What . . . um . . . what is . . . I don't know what . . ."

"Greasy kid stuff," he said to my insides.

Great. My very first gynecologist is clearly a pervert, and thinks he's down with what the kids are sayin' these days. Fucking *great*.

"Oh . . . um . . . ha-ha . . . no . . . um I'm still a . . . um . . . a virgin. Yeah," I said to the ceiling tiles.

"Uh-huh. Little pressure now." Was he chuckling? He moved the speculum, then I heard a click and something pinched deep behind my belly button, like a ragged toenail getting caught on a wet sock.

Later in the car, headed to the drugstore with a prescription for birth control pills in my hand, and a dull aching in me, Mom and I, again, smoked in silence. Thankfully, we did not go to Friendly's. She had already put on a great performance for her girlfriend and the cringing girls and women at the doctor's waiting room, so I guess she was satisfied.

We got to the drugstore and I got my pills. Mom got some pills, too. By the time I started taking mine, she had already taken one too many of her own, and was gone again.

CHAPTER FIVE:

HARVARD SQUARE AND SHIT.

I didn't really get to notching up too many bedposts until starting around fifteen. It was a slow turn of the crank until I went full throttle slut bag. Probably because I wouldn't fuck anybody weird, or anyone I knew and certainly no one I liked. That seriously limited my pool.

Most of my trysts were with my many punk-rock acquaintances in Cambridge and Boston. If I liked someone, though, I was a disaster. There was a boy in a neighboring town I loved desperately, forever.

Bill.

Saying his name now, I can still recall the ache and how I would sigh. My first blowjob recipient, he also taught me about handjob etiquette, put hickies on my boobs, smelled *really* good, and was a fantastic kisser. But we never ever had sex.

I couldn't figure out how to get the two together, the liking and the fucking. If I had feelings for someone, for me it was a sad guarantee that they would never like me back, no matter what I did. It was instant agony. If my heart leapt at the sight of them or the sound of their name, I knew it was hopeless. I was that chick who would call the guy maniacally until he (or better yet, his *parents*) would pick up and yell "Stop calling!" I was the girl who'd show up uninvited to parties and stare miserably at whomever it was I was obsessed with. I couldn't see it then, but when I felt anything like love for another person, I would really be just like my mom, who confounded and terrified the people she loved the most until we all scattered away from her as if she were a bad smell. I spent most of my tweens feeling like a turd in a punch bowl, but having feelings for someone turned me into an insta-leper. That, coupled with the fact that I actually *wanted* someone to love me, filled me with hot-faced shame.

I had no shame about sex though, nor anything around it; it all seemed normal and natural. My biggest problem was that I made too big a deal about it, secretly wanted it to mean more. A desperate flutter in my chest, hoping that what's-his-name or whoever was bending me over in a bathroom stall, would see something in me and think I was special. That they would see I was more than that, and try to fuck some sense into me. Then one day the flutter gave a cool thud, my heart balled into a fist and gave the world the finger.

The guy was, I think, thirtyish. He was some muckity-muck business professional with a law degree, and we were both guests at a wedding. It was a sweltering day in a deep green part of New England, and we were all partying around a pool. Everyone had bathing suits on under their formalwear, and as soon as the word came down from the mother of the bride that the classy part of the wedding was over, people peeled off their clothes quickly. Through the wavy blur of humidity, the huge lawn was littered with discarded poufy dresses. The grass looked like it had sprung a bunch of prehistoric flowers, all pinks, blues, and multicolored, wilting in the oppressive temperature.

I was sixteen years old and in a bit of a Goth phase, short spiky blonde hair, black cat eyeliner and black everything. I wanted to be too cool for the pool, but it was superhot and the party was quickly turning into a drunken free-for-all, and getting fun, so I peeled out of my witchy-poo dress, tossed it behind me with a flourish, and walked off the diving board.

I could feel the guy staring, and once I confirmed that he was, swam under water and hid among groups of people to see if he would look for me. Once *that* was confirmed, I commenced fucking with him. Swimming around his legs, kicking water in his face, then taking off to the opposite end to glare at him. He asked a bridesmaid about me; I could tell what the topic of conversation was, because he was grinning, she was not. She shook her head at him and I could read her lips. "No. No . . . she is *not* eighteen. No." He mouthed okay at her but kept glancing over to me to see me smile and give him the finger before I submerged among a pile of partygoers.

"Sure I am," I lied to him a bit later, a bit drunker, and still sixteen. "I'm actually nineteen. How 'bout you come back here when everyone's asleep . . . midnight."

As the party wound down, I chatted up one of the hired bartenders as he was packing up the booze and getting ready to split. He had a homemade-looking tattoo that I could see the tip of, sticking through his shirt sleeve. He asked me if I might want a drink before it all got put away. I told him I could find forty bucks for something else.

Later, I helped him carry a box of glasses to his catering truck where he sold me a decent amount of blow, neatly packed in a rectangular fold, a torn piece of a page out of a porno magazine.

At the height of summer, it seems to take forever for the dark to take hold and steep the world in one of its rare and fine velvety nights. It was near nine when the sun finally gave up the day and that plummy, hot black soaked in. Most of the people had left, or gone off to bed and the big old house grew quiet and settled as it ticked towards midnight.

I did a fat line in the bathroom, then walked around the wide dewy yard in the dark, away from the house lights, waiting. My bathing suit was still damp but the summer night was a warm breath, silk around my skin. The grass and earth were cool and wet under my feet and the dark jangled with cricket songs. Delicious nerves were ringing throughout my young wires, waiting, nearly invisible in the inky black.

I felt like a kid on an adventure. The frosty numbness in my nose and lips and the tickling excitement of the night and the blow, my belly feeling suspended by a strumming rubber thread. In the dark I pretended I was a dancer, swaying my hips around and grinding in wide exaggerated circles. I was an animal, a creature. I could hide in the bushes and scare the shit out of this guy as he walked up the lawn, or I could run away and howl at the moon, pouncing through the cool grass, naked and hidden in the deep backyard. I could blow this clown off and skip the whole to-do. Then I saw someone ambling up the street, and held my breath for a split second.

Here he comes.

This was the first time I had experienced somebody exerting any effort to get to me. He had to sneak out of his house and walk about a mile in the pitch dark up a country road, all based on the hope I would be where I said I'd be, and that he would get some when he got there.

The distance from the street to the pool was about seventy-five yards, so I had a minute or so to set the scene. I wanted to have it arranged so, when he saw me, it was like the movies. I trotted through the dark and slipped into the pool, dunked under and dragged the backs of my fingers under my eyes to right my eyeliner that had started to run. I stretched my arms out along the edge and gently kicked my legs in a slow, rhythmic, cancan. Hair wet and slicked back, I smiled at him as he walked out of the dark, towards the eerie blue glow of the pool.

Been waiting for you, sailor.

He smiled back, stopping at the edge. He undressed and walked into the blood-warm water and swam towards me.

No talking. Nice. I dove deep through the water under him to a ladder at the deep end and spun around to face him as he followed. We made out at the ladder a little, kissing deeply, groping, wet and clumsy, still a little drunk. His mouth was pool water and scotch. I slid down into the water to take him in my mouth a few times as I held my breath, blowing bubbles around his cock and between his legs. After more splashing around we found an empty room where we could go at it for hours.

It was one of those stinging, sweat-soaked marathons where parts of your body ache and cramp where other bits lose all sensation from the desperate pounding. I don't know if it was the coke or the booze, but the guy stayed marble hard and could not come.

I refused to stop or even wince, for fear of betraying the hurting parts. I was all pornographic moaning and a squealing good time.

My stubbornness in keeping the good times rolling wasn't so much for Mr. Marathon Esquire; he was good looking enough and not too bad a guy from what I could tell. No, my hell-bent determination to fuck through the pain was to bruise this into his memory banks. All of his future encounters would be compared to this one, to me.

This was my power. This was my only grip on being something, anything. I would replay in his head while he throbbed in his hand or some other sucking mouth.

Raw and sore himself, he finally called a temporary ceasefire. I tucked him into my mouth cooling off his dick by swirling ice cubes around it with my tongue. He was holding my head up by my hair. Suddenly, looking down at my face, with my makeup having been all fucked off, he must've seen the kid I actually was.

"How old are you?" he asked, a bit out of breath.

"Mmmummph?" I hummed around him and the ice.

"How. Old. Are. You. Really?" The word *really* trailed off with the unmistakable ring of already knowing the answer and that the answer was all kinds of bad. I never really considered the legal ramifications of these scenarios. Pretty much every man I screwed around with was older than me except one guy in high school who was my age. Mr. Marathon actually sounded scared. Jesus, friends and some family were all over this house sleeping off the hot day and the buckets of free wedding liquor.

He could be seriously fucked if anyone even saw him here. Poor guy.

He pulled my head up quick by my hair and looked at me harder through the dim light.

His cock popped out of my mouth so I tapped it lightly on my chin, smiled and cooed sweetly and reassuringly up his sweaty torso. "Okay, okay, I'm thirteen." I went back to licking him. "Why?" I asked, tapping him against my lips, smiling.

Gotcha.

To this day I don't know why I lied to the guy, but the look on his face was priceless. The surge of panic, wrestling with desire, wrestling with eons of law school, reputation, more panic, and more lust stoked by the very, very, wrong thing going on, so dirty, so bad.

"Hurry up and finish," was all he could manage.

Power.

⟊

Right around that time, my dad showed me how to break a guy's thumb by pinning it back against his wrist, a trick he picked up in the Marine Corps. It's a move so painful, he explained, I could drop a guy much bigger than myself. I assumed that he taught me that trick because he thought I was strong enough to be on my own, and didn't mind that I was always gone. I asked him recently why he didn't freak out or punish me: make me stay home, send me to military school, break my legs, and so on. He said he was terrified that if he tried to control me, it would push me even farther, that I would have run away for good, gotten arrested, or worse.

I had plenty of run-ins with cops, but thankfully didn't get arrested until I was eighteen (for possession of a class B substance, cocaine, and contributing to the delinquency of minors; the second charge was ironic because the sixteen-year-old, whose delinquency I was supposedly contributing to, was my dealer). Being eighteen, though, meant my dad wasn't called. I spent one chilly night in a cell by myself, was fined four hundred dollars, and was told, if I paid on time, since it was my first offense, the charges would be taken off my record.

We'll see, if I ever run for office or try to marry a prince or something.

Besides that tiny footnote from my late teens, there were, of course, stupid injuries, car accidents, wicked fights, and oodles of drugs. I was part of a small crew of kids that the dealers loved. They would say things like, "Hey, Storm, I think these are Quaaludes, will you take one and tell me how you feel in twenty minutes? Oh, and don't drink."

My punk-rock beggar friends and I all hung out at the Harvard Square T stop. There is a brick, circular, patio-type structure there where we could sit around and complain about society, talk about how punk was dead and harass passers-by for spare change. The boys would do skateboard tricks, and the girls would smoke and put on black, black eyeliner, using little circular mirrors on their superpale pressed powder compacts. It was where we heard about parties, fights, who was fucking who; the T stop was a great hangout.

On one particular day, to our collected rage and disgust, the city of Cambridge had festooned our hangout with blue plastic port-o-potties. Five of them, in a row, along a low wall, which happened to be my favorite sit and bitch place.

It was Harvard's 350th anniversary and the whole area around the campus had become a fucking glut of blue-blooded, overly entitled douche bags snobbing around in their maroon blazers talking like Thurston Howell III from *Gilligan's Island*, and they were all peeing out their gin and tonics in our hangout.

We were appalled.

The cops kept trying to roust us from the area, but like bees to a barbecue, we all buzzed back and continued our very important loitering. Since the public crappers were stationed where we normally all sat, a couple of us climbed to the top of the T stop itself. One of the guys was my buddy Starchild.

Imagine a featherless and emaciated turkey with a crooked, baby curl Mohawk and put a motorcycle jacket on it. Now, set its head on a swivel, so the head constantly swims on its neck as if trying to break free of it, and you might get a picture of poor Starchild.

He had done more drugs than Hunter S. Thompson. He was so completely brain-damaged; it sometimes seemed like he had been trepanned (when a hole gets drilled into your skull so you're high forever). Mental stability aside, he was a complete and total sweetheart.

The day of the reunion, he was very quiet. He sat up straight, eerily staring at everyone below our little rooftop perch.

My friend Keith and I were snickering at the preppy bastards tiptoeing around, trespassing on our land. We started to play a little game we'll call "Audacity Tag."

As in, if you have the audacity to come into our house, then tag! You're it.

As soon as some poor sucker would get all situated in a port-o-potty, we would jump off the roof and knock on the thing, shake it and yell into the vents, literally scaring the piss out of them. Then, we'd clamber back onto the roof and duck down, so the sad sack wouldn't know from where the attack had come. When a corpulent man in a craptastic red-and-white Hawaiian shirt stepped into one, we launched our attack, trying to outdo the fear factor of the last.

We pounded, yelled, and pushed, and suddenly it rocked at such a treacherous angle, Keith and I backed away nervously.

"Whoa," Keith giggled, as we heard a muffled expletive from inside the thing.

Just as it was wobbling back to right itself, with Hawaiian Punch still cussing inside, we heard a scream. We looked up just in time to see a low-flying, peeled swivel turkey sailing quite beautifully through the air.

Starchild had suddenly launched himself from the station roof onto the roof of the Johnnie on the spot, screeching, "Kaaa-yeee-haaa!" sending himself, Hawaiian Punch, and the port-o-potty crashing over onto the bricks, the latter landing on its door, trapping its ill-fated occupant.

Starchild sprinted down Dunster Street cackling. Keith's and my mouths hung open and time froze for a second. We were about to start laughing when the bottom of the Johnnie splooshed out its entire day's contents onto the bricks.

There was a hideous, muffled screaming and pounding coming from inside the shit sarcophagus. Hawaiian Punch's wife came running towards the fallen thing with her hand on her face, but stopped short when the stink choked her away. The cops held their breath, righted the thing, and H.P. came stumbling out, looking for someone to kill. Starchild was long gone. Half the people in the immediate area were laughing, the rest too horrified by the scene to move to or fro. I was in full paroxysm and looked guilty as hell, so Keith and I bolted to the Cambridge Common.

In the middle of the Common, a park across from Harvard campus, stands a monument with Abe Lincoln standing inside. All around this monument, several thousand well-heeled WASPs milled about with their pet names and trust funds as the sun went down.

Keith and I laughed hysterically over the horrendous spectacle we had just been privy to, as we clambered up into the monument. I don't know how no one saw us do it; the park was packed with alumni-ratti, but we crawled under the old president's bronzed legs, and fucked like kids without a future.

CHAPTER SIX:

MEET the BANKS. A Silk Upholstered Heck.

By the time I turned sixteen, my brothers and I hardly went to see Mom in the hospital anymore. We wouldn't even go to bring her home. She would get rides back to our house from friends or just take a cab.

We barely spoke to her parents anymore, either. There was no official conversation between them and my father about Mom's staggering health-care costs, but after the separation was official and divorce was imminent, they were finally helping with her bills. Which was nice, since my father, a teacher, was struggling and mom's parents were multimillionaires.

My brothers and I always felt that our maternal grandparents—we'll call them the Banks—blamed us for Mom's troubles. God knows what Mom told them about us when she was with them. She probably sang her favorite, *my children hate me* song, but what she told us of her life with them, she made it sound like she was raised in an evil yacht club full of stiff-jawed, overprivileged rapists who made her young life a silk-upholstered hell.

〜

Mom was adopted a little before her fourth birthday, from an orphanage near Yale University. Mr. and Mrs. Banks were a wealthy couple from Snob-Ascot, Connecticut, and had one natural son, Dicky. It might have been because of Mrs. Banks' delicate health they adopted a little girl instead of having another baby. Mom was about seven or eight when Mrs. Banks number one died of brain cancer.

Enter Mrs. Banks part *deux*. The second Mrs. Banks was a gourmand and a highly paid interior decorator. She did a room in the White House and bought tchotchkes for the Shah of Iran. She was a friend of the family, and recently widowed, so she and *her* natural son, Claude, moved in. Daddy Banks has his son, Mommy Banks, hers, and then there's little Suzi. The girl the dead lady wanted.

Now, everything Mom told us about her life, growing up a Banks, was clearly mommified. It's not so much that it was *all* total delusional bullshit, but so much of what came out her mouth about *anything* was baloney, that one had to take it with a grain of salt. Or maybe, a ton of salt, like, as much sodium as one might find *in* baloney. So I can't really say much about her childhood other than the obvious: She was raised with loads of money, was a debutante, sent away to schools, given horses and French tutors, and then sent to Paris to study dance, where she met my dad. I can't really speak to the alleged abuse, rapes, neglect, and satanic nannies who drugged her, or any of the other colorfully horrific things that supposedly happened to her at the Banks house. However, I can tell you about my personal experiences with the Banks.

Mr. Banks was a hoity-toity CEO or some such thing for a fancy hospital in New York City. I have no idea if my uncle Dicky ever actually had a job, but I'm certain he suffered a rope burn or two while docking his yacht in various ports of call. The other uncle, Claude, seemed nice enough, but we barely ever got to know him.

For a while, we would spend every Thanksgiving at their house in Connecticut, where we were sequestered in the downstairs apartment. Not a bad place to hang while the grownups got crocked upstairs. There was a wall of closets to go through, full of old pictures, board games, plastic horses, and croquet mallets. We would play Chinese checkers, usually, or ding around on the old sixties-style organ that had a built-in rhythm machine. Pop, waltz, and calypso were a few of the selections. Push a button and a cheesy booping pattern would play to accompany whatever number you planned to rock on the keys.

The kids would eventually be called to walk, not run, up the stairs, thickly carpeted with a lush, leopard pattern, into the wide, airy living and dining room. The house would be jammed with family and friends of the Banks, people whom we would only see at Thanksgiving, then never see or hear from for the rest of the year.

I think we stopped going there by the time I was nine. I remember wanting to like them but, even as a little one, I got the impression my brothers and I weren't liked very much by most of the people there. Grandfather Banks, throughout dinner, would get redder in the freckles and gruffer in his voice. I suppose he was very funny because many of the grownups would laugh at things he said. In a room full of drunken partygoers, he would snarl jovially at me, "Hey, Stormy! C'mere. Hop up in my lap! Atta girl! Hey, you wanna see smoke come outta my ears?"

Being in his lap was always weird because I was fairly sure the man hated me, but, when a grownup pays attention to you, and is holding your little four-year-old person in their lap, that's a sign of affection, right? And, of course, I wanted to see smoke come out of his ears!

"All right, now, I'm going to take a drag off my cigarette and you're going to push on my chest with both hands, okay? Ready? Watch my ears now!"

He had big, red, sticking-out ears. I wondered if the smoke would puff out or maybe, hopefully, he could somehow make smoke rings. He took a drag, and I pushed and watched, and I didn't see. . . .

"OWWW!"

While I stared at his ears, he'd puff his cigarette to a glowing cherry, then quickly poke the lit end into the back of my hand. I yanked my hands away as he laughed two lungs full of smoke at me. Everyone would laugh, I guess, because, it was a grownup joke. I must admit it was a neat trick, because I fell for it more than once.

Regardless of whatever the truth was about the Banks and my mom's childhood, it was clear that a lot of her loneliness, and her unfixable broken heart, had taken hold partly on their watch.

The longer I lived, the more I understood why she needed to be sick. And why a new diagnosis was like a new crush, and she would fall all over it like a swooning teenager.

"I've finally figured it out! They know what it is!" Mom announced, catching me in the living room one afternoon. "I have *alters*." The timing on her diagnoses blend together a bit, but I know I was at least at an age where I did not give a flying fuck anymore, and John had his own place, so I must have been around fifteen.

Multiple personality disorder was a big one for Mom. She was positively giddy with it. It was as intoxicating to her as her other go-to malady, bone cancer. More on that later.

She could barely contain her enthusiasm as she explained how, like in the movie *Sybil*, there were these different personalities, or *alters,* that would come out and make her do and say crazy things. According to Mom, the most extreme case of MPD her doctor had ever heard about involved a woman with nearly two hundred personalities. While I burned holes in the television with my eyes, trying to tune her out, Mom went on to marvel at herself because she, Suzi Large, somehow, had amazed her medical team by having more alters than that other woman, thus beating that record. "By forty-three percent," she said.

The doctors were so confused at the intensity of her disorder, yet her ability to still function, somewhat, that one of them was going to cite her condition at his next lecture and her case would end up in yet another medical journal.

Wow, so I guess you win and congratulations are in order.

"It explains everything! The voices, the wobblies, how I suddenly can start speaking fluent German."

The *wobblies* we knew about. They were dramatized dizzy spells that, we believed, were used as an excuse for her to fall down on purpose, in public. Weddings, graduations, or funerals, pretty much anywhere people were gathered or participating in an event geared toward loving and celebrating somebody who wasn't my mother. The *fluent German* thing was a new one. When she tried to show us, she seemed to be parroting all of the German one could learn by watching *Hogan's Heroes*. "Nein! Dummkopf! Schnell! Macht schnell!"

Mom's award-winning multiple personality phase lasted quite some time, as it was creepy, and people had heard of it. She got a load of mileage out of the disorder.

My brother John was the best of all of us at forgiving Mom and her curiously revolving ailments. As much as she pissed him off and broke his heart, he would visit her in the hospital long after the rest of us had given up.

During Mom's "schnell dumkopf" period, John brought his new girlfriend over to visit Mom in her temporary digs at some halfway house. Mom met the girl, made tea, and some small talk. The young lady was studying to be a nurse and, though her focus was on pediatrics, she had taken some psychology classes and oh, yes, she had heard about multiple personality disorder.

Green light.

Not long after tea, Mom excused herself for a minute and came back with crayons and paper, plopped on the floor, and cooed like a toddler, "Sumbuddypwaywiffme!" John must have wished he could blow away like a palm full of talcum powder. John's girlfriend, however, was new to all the many splendors of Mom, so she snapped into nurse mode. She crouched in front of Mom and said firmly, "If Suzi is in there, I'd like to talk to her. May I please talk to Suzi?"

My brother burned against the wall he was leaning on, grinding his teeth into stony little nubs, as he watched Mom dip her head as if nodding out, then looking up and around, feigning confusion, saying, "Oh, oh my. How long have I been on the floor?" Then to John, "Are you all right, darling? Did Mommy scare you?"

As loyal and diligent a son as John was, I think it was about a year before he ever saw or spoke to her again. I, on the other hand, was more than ready to cut her off forever.

∞

Even though Mom allegedly had a cast of thousands within her, not a single one was very motherly. So naturally I sought the affections of other mother types and, thankfully, struck gold with a few.

The first and longest-running momstitute was Daphne's mom, Annie Leavitt. In the early days of Mom's illness, Annie and the Leavitt family made me feel totally at home whenever I had to stay over.

Annie was a biology teacher and easily one of the most knowledgeable people on the topic of all things in existence. Any bug, bird, rock, cloud, bone, leaf, she would know its name, origin, purpose, and, in most cases, an historical anecdote about it. A true Anglophile, she was also a badass gardener, and kept a girly mass of flowers growing in all directions in her sunny backyard all spring and summer.

Annie taught at Fay, the grade school down the way from St. Mark's. Fay was a fancy boarding school that went up to ninth grade. My brothers and I went there for awhile but, for some reason, we never finished there. I went there from third to fifth grade. I heard we couldn't afford the tuition because of the terrible hospital bills that decimated my dad's savings. I also heard rumblings that my brothers and I started displaying behavior problems and were asked to leave.

I hated it there. Every day was the worst day ever. Fay was where I learned that if you were rich, or pretty, you had quite an advantage over other humans. If you were both, well, then, you could be as big a cunt as you could be and it would be just ducky with the whole world. I wasn't rich or pretty. I had behavior problems. Fay was where my werewolf phase started.

However, Annie was a ray of sunshine that would peek through the black, preppy clouds at that school. I only had her as a teacher once in three years, but I would see her now and then in the hall or in the dining room and I would literally gasp like a kid lost in a huge foreign mall finally seeing her family. I would hug her, trying to soak in as much of her big cinnamon and nutmeg scented, roundy round momness as I could. That would carry me through the day.

One day, as spring seemed to be on its way, it was warm enough, in my estimation, to wear a dress. I pulled on my dress, slipped into my brother's rain boots, had a bowl of Cheerios and hoofed it off to Fay. My dad was already long into his first class or meeting or checking light bulbs in his office, (any old thing to keep him away from the house) by my first bite of sugar heaped oat-y goodness. Otherwise, he might have not let me leave.

The beautiful, rich Izod princes and princesses laughed at me openly for my big mouth, crazy dreams, and fashion limitations, but on this day the amusement was apparent before I even put my book bag down. Word must have gotten to Annie, or maybe it was dumb luck, but she swooped in, gave a look that silenced the cackling bastards and took me to her house down the road.

"A little cold for a summer dress, Stormy. Put these on." As she laid out some of Daphne's clothes for me, hot tears started pouring down my face. I thought the dress had maybe been too short, but I wanted it to be spring, so I wore it. Standing in my best friend's Laura Ashley bedroom as I put on some of her corduroys, I realized my faux pas. The dress, which had been fine last summer, was a little seasonally inappropriate. More important, I had grown so dramatically since the summer, that it was now, technically, a seasonally inappropriate shirt that barely covered my ass.

Annie passed no judgment, nor scolded me, and, most important, did not tell my father. He heard it years later as an amusing, and now harmless, look-back-and-laugh story. I went back to school with her and nobody said a word to me about it afterward. She was magnificent.

Daphne loved *my* mother and called her Mom as well. Besides the shicken mush episode, when we were seven, she had been privy to some other kinds of crazy from my mom. But Daphne felt sorry for her, and would reprimand me, now and then, for being hard about it.

When we were twelve, Daphne came over to see if I was home, and found Mom all alone in the kitchen, crying, smoking cigarette after cigarette. "What's wrong, Mom?" Daphne asked as she gave her a hug, waiting for her to compose herself.

Mom blew her nose, wiped her face, lit another Kool Mild, and, as if she were an actress in a TV movie about her own life, looked at my little friend and said, "I have bone cancer." She then proceeded to tell Daphne that she didn't know how to tell us because, she explained, we all hated her. She was afraid nobody would care, "They're already so mad at me; please don't tell anyone!"

What Daphne didn't know was that Mom had not been diagnosed with anything of the sort; it was just wishful thinking on her part. Mom simply longed to get bone cancer. If she could've caught it somehow, or contracted it by sheer will, she would have been all over it.

Mom loved the idea of having cancer. Her mental-health issues were looking more and more like attention-seeking, made-up BS, but cancer? The big C was a capital T tragedy. Cancer tore families apart, took down babies, athletes, and movie stars. Weeping crowds would fill the streets to walk, wheel their stricken loved ones to raise awareness and money to fight this monster. Everybody loved somebody with cancer, and for my mom, that was reason enough. Why *bone* cancer? Possibly because it sounded horrible enough, painful and scary enough, and as sure a death sentence as anything else in the cancer menagerie. A perfect thing to tell a child to get her completely freaked out.

Daphne didn't know any of that. She just saw the sad little lady she called Mom crying and smoking and supposedly sharing a heavy secret with her. For weeks following this news, Daphne later told me, she would stare at me in school, wondering if I had been told yet. And if I had, how could I just be my big, loud, silly self, and not totally crack knowing my mom was dying of a hideous bone disease? She thought that maybe I hadn't heard, or, maybe my mom was right, that I didn't care. For awhile she thought I was the coldest kid on the block, or just crazy.

CHAPTER SEVEN:

BORN TO LOSE.
BONE CANCER BLUES.

At the beginning of my junior year of high school, I made a declaration to myself to be more positive. I was determined to get more involved in school, and make the best of it. I knew I was a huge disappointment to my father for much of my growing up. I went from little shit to complete asshole with very little variety between the two. But I knew, somehow, that it was a temporary thing. I had a feeling that one day, I would make him proud of me. The man had done his darndest with the hand he'd been dealt, and so far had gotten hosed. I wanted to give the poor guy a little happiness in his bleak, locked-box-up-in-his-head life. I had been so miserable; I figured it was up to me to turn it around. So I gave it a go and was victorious! Well, for a minute, anyway. It was a nice minute, too.

I started to give little concerts after dinner, quickie concerts with my vocal coach, Ruth Cooper. She was a tough old broad who had no patience for the preppy brats at St. Mark's, but she loved me to pieces. "You get a lot of crap here, I can tell," she'd growl at me. "You know why, dontcha? It's 'cause you're good. They don't like you, 'cause you're good. You're talented. They don't like that." I didn't get it, but I loved that she was into me and hated everyone else.

I also tried to get into sports. Not only playing, but cheering on the teams and having some spirit, some spunk, some school pride! Yay, everything!

The only thing that seemed to bring my father any joy at all was sports. He was a football captain when he was in school and had grown up to be a celebrated football and baseball coach at St. Mark's. Both my brothers were captains of football and lacrosse. They both kicked all kinds of athletic ass to the tune of multiple injuries for both of them. I was fat and liked Bauhaus. But that was the old me, the new me gave a hoot, gosh darn it.

Sports ruled our house. I guess because it made sense. There were rules, goals, a motivation to win, obstacles to overcome, and methods to overcome them. My dad and brothers would have lively and impassioned talks around sporting events. Football, especially. Upcoming games, games of the recent and distant past, pro and college games, stats, players . . . when our house and family would shatter, sports acted as glue for the boys.

When there was a game on the television my dad would be hermetically sealed to it, and to his cigarettes and a bottomless glass of Heineken, until the final whistle. I would try to get in on it, chiming in at commercial breaks, "Hey, Dad, if a player had a glass eye and got tackled and it popped out, would they stop the game to find it? There's a kid at my school with one and it falls out all the time. Oooh! I love this commercial 'The UN-Cola-ah-ah . . .' Do the players go to the bathroom during the commercials, Dad? Is that why they even have commercials, Dad? Hey, Dad?" Try as I might, however, he and his smoke and drink of choice were in a soundproof and daughterless vacuum. I could never get in on any of it. Around the Super Bowl one year, I asked my dad to teach me about the game so I could join in the festivities. He tried to, but to me, it sounded like a lot of math and confusing dance moves performed by big, unattractive men. So, I just gave up.

So, imagine my surprise when I suddenly found myself being called a star athlete.

At fifteen, I weighed in around 190 pounds and was a thick chunk of girl muscle. Still plushly upholstered with baby fat, but I was as strong as a bear with a similar temper.

I fucking hated sports and the rapey testosteroids who loved them. But the new me, the me who was trying to be all right and fit in, grit my teeth and went for it. And in very little time, I found myself growing in athletic reputation. First, I was asked, nay somewhat begged, to be the varsity goalie for the girls' soccer team. The coach so wanted my big blocky, rageaholic self in the net, he pretty much let me do whatever I wanted there.

I relished my position. I didn't have to run with the other ponies at practice. I could just hang around in my sweats and be a menace. Another girl from the team and I would go to my house right around practice, get stoned, then go to the field. It was my first feeling of being a spoiled rock star. Very little was asked of me, but I was awesome at my job. It was the perfect outlet for my frustration to vent on other people. The coach and my teammates encouraged me to be as brutal and scary as I wanted. At games I would smoosh mud all over my face, and straight up tackle chicks. It was great.

I had also become a bit of a superstar in varsity crew as well.

My giant body and black little heart made me a monster with an oar, and I was ranked in the top rungs of New England and the Eastern seaboard for my age group. The ergometer is a rowing simulator, and a measuring tool for your strength and stamina. And, though I loved my Marlboros, and cocaine was becoming a more frequent treat for me, I constantly made the ergometer my bitch.

Suddenly, my dad thought I was great. He positively glowed when the St. Mark's athletic director announced my name at assembly, telling the crowd how I would be spending the summer, training and kicking ass for St. Mark's at the Junior Nationals in upstate New York. There was finally something about me he understood and could be proud of. At least, for a minute.

He would come to my meets, chat with my coach, and I was suddenly awesome. His little girl, who had saddened and confounded him for so long, had grown into a giant meat triangle of broad back and shoulders, huge, shoebox thighs, and no boobs or booty to speak of. So, not only was I now an athletic asset to the school's rep, I was so fucking unattractive that, in my dad's mind, no boy would ever want a piece of me. I was the perfect daughter.

For those of you who don't know about crew, allow me to inform you that, while it is the preppiest sport this side of croquet, it is one of the least attractive. Brutal, grunting, yanking, there was very little room for hotness. Field hockey girls were plucky and quick, usually superhot with wide, swinging ponytails and delicate limbs plunging out of flippy skirts and grass-stained jerseys. Soccer girls were a tad more boyish, tougher, more contact and aggression. Crew ladies are moose. Big, butch moose.

Crew, by all appearances, attracted young lesbians. Everyone's sexuality is pretty malleable during the agony that is being teenager. However, I can say with confidence, while I was doing the sport, there were many vagitarians in those sleek and skinny boats. I, too, like girls from time to time; I consider my sexuality as opportunistically omnivorous. If it tastes good, I'll eat it. However, I tend to go for field hockey player types.

I rowed for weeks in early summer in upstate New York, training for the Junior Nationals. Every day, there were speed trials and long, heavy workouts. Every night, I would smoke out my dorm window and wonder what the fuck I was doing there.

I was in a two-man boat with a superhuman girl, a solid chunk of muscle with a mop of bright blonde curls named Kara. Kara was a star athlete in just about anything she put her body behind. She had a healthy competitive sense, she wanted to win, but she primarily wanted to outdo herself and be better every time. She was the most outstanding teammate anyone could have hoped for.

God must have been mad at her for something, though, since he threw her in that little boat with me.

Kara was a tough little nugget, but built out of pure sunshine. She had a gruff and easy laugh, and her fine sportsmanship also made her a fount of encouraging talking-tos, bitten with her old New England vernacular. On the water, she was a teacup Clydesdale, grunting and huffing, her body and breath in perfect synch. I, on the other hand, was always hocking up gray tobacco loogies into the lake and complaining about the weather, or the breakfast, or the air, my huge feet, and so on. Kara would bolster cheer and accentuate the positive! Eliminate the negative! She would try, anyway.

Kara should have drowned me. I totally deserved it.

On our last day in New York, there was a regatta for placement in the Nationals. We were a shoo-in, as our times had been stellar all week. I even noticed other teams checking us out with a sliver of intimidation, nodding our way: "That's *them*." Apparently, we were the ones to beat.

The boats you row in for crew are long, slippy blades, built for speed. They are also super lightweight and eggshell delicate. Just before the finish line, there were warning buoys to let you know you were headed into the final stretch. The buoys were a signal to pull your strongest, but to keep a good eye open because, just past the finish line, were some old dock posts. Should you overshoot the line, you might hit one and utterly demolish your shell. It had never happened before, we were assured, but they had to warn us just the same.

Ten two-man boats lined up at the starting line. Kara was in the zone, muttering some ass-kicking mantra about winning to herself. I wanted a cigarette and suddenly had to take a shit.

"Oars at the ready!" The ref's voice echoed over water.

"I gotta poop!" I laughingly whispered.

Kara's back cringed, "Ugh."

I pinched the urge back up into me.

We were in position for a racing start. You never start a race with a full stroke. You do a racing start, which are quick, explosive half-strokes; the head oar barks them out. Then you go to three-quarters stroke, then full. The whole start takes maybe seven seconds to get to your top speed. Kara and I were in position, ready, set, 3 . . . 2 . . . 1.

"Bang!" The starting gun cracked through the morning air and our boat launched out of the line. Muscles bulged all over Kara's back all the way up to her bright-blonde ponytail. I pulled in synch with her, my guts up into my chest, and my breathing ragged.

"One half! One half! One half! Three quarters! Three quarters! Pull! Fucking pull! Pull!" Kara called out the strokes. My job, since I was in the rear, was to keep an eye over my shoulder every few seconds to make sure we were going straight.

I'm not sure if we were winning, but we were damn close. We were easily going to place and then be on our way to the next heat that would send us to the Nationals. After that, the Olympics. That's where Kara's head was. Unfortunately for her, my head wasn't fixed on winning anything that day. I'm pretty sure my head was quite a distance up my own ass.

We whooshed past the warning buoys and were in the final stretch, I glanced over my shoulder and saw the finish line, but the view from inside my rectum was, of course, obscured.

"Wane off! We're gonna hit a post!" I said, Kara pushed her oar up and we coasted until she looked back.

"That's the finish line, not the posts! We haven't even finished! Racing start!" Kara screamed a new start but it was too late. Four boats swept past our coasting shell and we didn't even place.

I threw the race. Not sure if it was a conscious decision, but I disappointed my coach and teammate to the point of sickness. I ended up driving back to Boston with a different team because I couldn't face my own. Kara and our coach drove separately.

Looking back, the whole trying-to-fit-in thing just wasn't me. I was good at some stuff, even great at some of the things most kids would have loved to have been able to do at all. But the competitive angle, the trying to win, the be your very best, felt like an iron maiden–type torture device. Kara and my coach were lovely, and I only encountered terrific people on this quick and clean detour, but my dark, twitching insides still felt like all I could be was a loser. So I lost.

Though I would have loved to have skulked off into a dark comfy hole to be null and void, my crew adventure had one more stroke. I was driven to and dropped off at Harvard University for Crew Camp. I imagine it was just like one of those awesome camps my brother Henry often got to attend. I stayed at the university, woke up at six in the morning, ate breakfast, then trudged to the fancy boathouse to haul the big shells into the water. I miserably rowed every day on the Charles River with the rest of the Izod-clad moose.

They were all really nice, and very excited for this great opportunity. I was a loser and a bad one at that. My head and mouth rang with so many *who cares, I can'ts, fuck its,* and *why bothers,* that no one wanted to even talk to me there. Coaches bristled when I was around and the other rowers barely tolerated my presence.

So, I'd run off at night to bum change off strangers, get high, and fuck whomever, come back wasted and stinking of weed, beer, and boys.

It didn't take me long to get kicked out. I stayed out all one night doing coke and taking Xanax. Then, my fuck buddy, Keith, and I broke into someone's basement to have sex and pass out. I showed up just in time for practice, only to be confronted by the head coach telling me I had to leave. The good news was the cops weren't called.

Bad news, my dad was.

He swore and shook and asked me what my fucking problem was as I packed up my room. He moaned and kept saying over and over how he had fucked up as a father. We walked across the yard and out through the university gates into Harvard Square. Me with my bags slung over my back and him with a lit Viceroy pointing at me while he yelled. I tossed my bags into his car as he continued to rail on me. Some street kids I knew were looking on, one of whom I had slept with. He smirked wickedly as my dad noticed them watching us.

"What the fuck are you looking at, you fucking freak?" He

pointed at the kid. The kid's smirk spread into an evil grin, with many terrible things to say behind it.

"Don't," I said to both of them. "Dad, just go home. I'll see you later."

"Fucking freak," he said again, to everyone in earshot, as he slammed into his car with my bags in the back and took off, leaving me on the sidewalk.

Looking back now, I guess it was odd that my father would just *leave* me there, with no place to stay that he knew of. Southborough was forty-five minutes away by car, and I had no car. He was well aware that I had been kicked out of camp, so I couldn't stay at Harvard anymore. Dad was inconsolable with rage and, clearly, didn't want to see me for awhile.

At least that was *something* I could do right, I could stay away from home like a pro. As I watched him drive away, my heart broke for him. And, though I was relieved I wasn't in the car with him right then, I knew I would make him proud of me one day. I remember clearly thinking, *I'm fucked up right now, Dad, but one day, you will be proud to tell people that I'm your daughter.*

CHAPTER EIGHT:

"CLOTHES ARE A LIE!" MY OFFICIAL INSANE DAY.

One of those fucking freaks my father hated so much was one of my dearest friends. Her name was Stitch, and she saved my life.

I was sixteen and I still had a mind to lose. My sanity was careening on a mad rolling bike with no handlebars, and I was blindly flailing into an inevitable belly flop into the abyss. But not until my twenties. I could still go crazy my way and collect all the exclamation points life could swing at me. So I decided to go crazy, officially, a week or so after my sweet sixteen. Fuck Dr. Lovey.

There were loads of girls in the punk-rock scene who wanted to kick my ass for one reason or another, mostly because I was so loud and uncool, but I had one or two aces on my side.

Stitch was a super badass, had never lost a fight, and, for whatever reason, she was my friend. She looked six foot nine with her Marlboro-box-red Mohawk and greyhound lean body. She was a few years older than me, but had a job at a nightclub and her own apartment on Mission Hill. I would often crash with her in exchange for cooking spaghetti and canned white clam sauce (my specialty at the time). We would eat, drink beer, smoke tons of pot, and talk about music, fights, and whatever we dreamed for ourselves in the future.

Stitch knew that I was going crazy, and she thought it was cool. She wanted to see it happen.

And it did, on the Fourth of July, 1985.

It was an established fact, or rather, someone read somewhere, that if you take acid seven times you are thereby clinically insane, so, for a pile of fucked-up kids, it was a celebration when one of us would hit lucky number seven.

My birthday had been just a few days earlier. My sweet sixteen. Everyone had forgotten about it. Dad was up at Boarsie, Henry was at awesome camp, and John was anywhere he wanted to be. Eventually, I got a call from Henry, a hug and a joint from John, and my dad left me a present on the sofa on one of his microvisits, before he split again. It was a poster of a kitten sitting in a wine glass. He was still pissed at me for the whole crew thing.

So on June 25, 1985, I made myself a key lime pie that I ate, by myself, while drinking a stolen bottle of dry vermouth. That night I ended up in the backyard, with my arm around my dog Rosie, hacking up bitter green foam and crying like a girl.

A week or so later, I get a few hits of acid and decide to share it with Stitch. She told me about the whole clinically-insane-after-seven-trips factoid, and we were both into it. My brain was going to go bye-bye anyway, so why not help it along?

It was the Fourth of July, and it was bloody hot. Hot like deep in a panting dog's mouth hot. Everything in Boston looked smudged with a piss-yellow halo of hanging, soggy air. The plan was for me, Stitch, and a couple other kids to hang in Faneuil Hall to trip, scare children, beg for change, then hit Harvard Square at sunset to drink bagged 40s and watch fireworks over the Charles River. Then we could all pass out in the park. A perfect teenage day.

⌖

Once in Faneuil Hall, the acid churning in our empty bellies, we made our way to the Christian Science Center. The CSC was a great place to have a picnic and enjoy a summer's day if you were normal. It was also an ideal location to get all twisted on drugs, if you were a jackass punk with a middle finger for a moral compass. There was an impeccable little grassy park stretching away from a massive reflecting pool and a fountain. The park was dotted with small ornamental trees and an adorably manicured path. We parked ourselves under some rare maple tree, and went on to stare at normal people.

We were surrounded by Ronald Reagan's America. The clean people trying to stay all clean and look normal. Our very presence was a ringing *fuck you*. We were a handful of angry little turds floating in their Perrier, and we loved it.

The drugs started to tingle and shake me loose from my mid-spine, into my chest and up my throat. I felt a gag rise but a swig of cold Coke knocked it back down. When that wild juice starts kicking open your spackled brain holes, there isn't a lot of nuance to your thinking. There are those fleeting sweet and terrible moments where you think that you may not come back from this trip.

The visuals swim and expand. The first thing you notice is how utterly repulsive some humans look. Facial features get blown way out of proportion, babies look like mewling larvae, and any woman with makeup on was a greasy horrible clown whore that eats raw bacon with her huge clawed hands.

Whoa, come back, okay.

The giggles kick in. Giddy, nervous snickering that gives way to hysterical, total, pee-leaking, laughter. Like a crazy bag of tickle bugs bust open in my chest. I would laugh at anything and everything. Cancer? Child prostitution? A five-year-old with no arms or legs turning tricks to pay for chemo? Hilarious!

Reality vaulted from under my feet, and the world became a swimming, sweaty cartoon. Trying to suppress the maniacal giggling, I started going off on my friends. "It is so fucking hot, you guys. Why the fuck are we wearing so many damn clothes?"

We all had on studded leather motorcycle jackets and army boots. I had on a torn-up black thermal shirt and army pants. It was very important you wore the required punk-rock attire, the grubbier and more torn up, the better. But, on such a muggy hot day, it was, as they say in Boston, re-tahded. We were walking around under heaps of unnecessary fabric, growing heavier by the minute in the heat. It was completely ridiculous. I suddenly felt a bolt of truth, logic, clear and unarguable, blast to the surface. I leveled my wide-pupiled gaze to my fellow revelers and spoke my truth: "Clothes are a lie."

It occurred to me that our outfits, everyone's outfits, were just costumes declaring wordlessly to the world who and what we were; who and what we would and wouldn't do, what we listened to. It was like waving our own little flag for our own little fucked up country, but underneath it all we were the same! Smooth and simple, scared and yearning little meat tubes full of poop, hopes, and fears and now, most important, we were all, collectively as one, fucking unbearably hot. Sweating like hot dogs in our stupid, societally appointed declarations of identity! I say, fuck that! Say it with me!

"Clothes are a lie!" My friends laughed, repeating my battle cry. I tore off my jacket, flopped onto my butt in the grass to yank off my boots. I looked at my partners to join me. No? No one? Really? I went to unclip my studded belt, smiling, "C'mon you guys. Let's do this!"

"Clothes are a lie!" They were now crowing and laughing but staying totally dressed. I yanked open my belt with a ta-da! And they cheered. I knew I was going to be on my own in this, but I was high, on fire, and diamond-hard committed.

There's always that one standout moment, good or bad, in every acid trip, that one recalls forever, and right now it was mine.

And it was time for my pants to come off.

I was so high everything made sense. I was Susan B. fucking Anthony, Iggy Pop, and Patti Smith. I was Bill Murray when he gives that awesome speech in *Stripes,* and later, he gives a similar speech in *Meatballs,* when he gets everyone to chant, "It just doesn't matter! It just doesn't matter!" I was a liberator. I was taking off my clothes *consciously.* I was stripping for freedom, throwing off the shackles of society, and peeling away my own teenaged ego. It was my insane-dependence day!!!

"Nice underpants," Stitch guffawed.

Uh-oh.

Because of my mother's literal and figurative absence, nobody ever took me shopping for clothes, certainly not for underwear, so I had on threadbare, butter-yellow little kid underwear with light blue baby turtles all over the butt. I'd had them since I was eleven. Not terribly punk rock.

I soldiered on; I was on a mission. Self-consciousness was for those nine-to-five slaves with clean fingernails and love lives. I was free and there was no going back. Besides, I'm already mostly naked and I don't wanna look like an asshole. I was officially crazy and committed.

I start to notice other people in the park, the clean normal people, I notice them noticing me. It's scary and wonderful. As soon as I peel off my sticky shirt, I hear the unmistakable shrill mom voices calling to their kids. Someone yelled, "Oh, my Gawd, what is she *doing?*"

I yell, once more, triumphantly, "Clothes are a lie!" My friends cheered, sounding like a throng, a stadium of adoring fans, and I am winning. Arms pumping skyward, I go bounding straight into the reflecting pool, singing "Flight of the Valkyries."

In case you didn't know, running naked in public can really heighten a trip.

I could actually *feel* the attention, shocked eyes, glued all over my every pore and crevice. The fatty air felt like a thing that slid past me. I was very aware of my bones jostling in my wet body meat. The water ahead of me shimmered with spirits. Was I there yet? Am I doing this? Images were all stop-motion photography of shuffling medicine men in huge skull masks in a conga line, the concrete lip of the reflecting pool looked like the rim of a massive sandpaper toilet.

Sailing over the lip of the pool I plunged into the water and splooshed about six big strides into it. The water was knee deep, scummy, and spit hot.

Suddenly, I snapped back, momentarily sober. My bare feet slipped and squashed, and I felt warm old pennies in the slime.

I stood still for a moment in the foul, bleach-scented tea and thought, What if the Christians put sulfuric, flesh-eating acid in this fountain to keep people out? Oh, my God. My legs. Am I gonna clack out of here on bleached and exposed femurs?

I kept looking down to check if my skin was bubbling and foaming. No. I check again. I start to giggle. Shit.

Acid? Acid? I reach down to touch check. Whoa, is that guy gonna drive into the fountain?

I focused my eyes best I could. About fifty feet in front of me on the other side of the pool, two big, loud men jump out of their dark car pointing and shouting at me to come outta they-ah.

Oh, my God. Cops. Be cool.

I tried to act sober and casual, like I'm not naked. I pretend I don't see them. I start looking into the water as if I may have lost an earring or something through some silly accident. I'm just looking for something in the fountain and, whoa, hey! Where are my clothes? Whoops!

Still playing deaf and dumb to their shouts, I turn to exit the scene, quickly. I'm going to have to make a run for it with my friends. As I high step through the water like a wasted baby giraffe toward freedom, however, I see my friends pointing and laughing, as they run away.

With my clothes

Shit. Be cool.

The cops meet me at the edge of the fountain, one is holding out a dark shirt to cover me. I feign confusion at the cops' approach, and casually cross my arms to hide my small boobs and say, "I'm really sorry, officers, it's just so damn hot, you know?" They are both sweaty. One looks like a cat, but starts to turn into an owl skull. The other is so pink I can't look at him because I see his impending stroke, heart failure, or choking death and I have an urge to comfort him. The poor man had no love in his life and would die alone.

The peeled owl takes my arm and we start toward the police car.

"You see, my friends dared me to jump in the fountain and it just seemed like a really good idea, I mean, all those little kids are in their underwear, sir, and . . ." High as I was, I couldn't help catching glimpses of pinky and owly smirking at each other. They were amused, they might even think I'm funny and *like me*. I continue as normally as I can manage, "Seriously, if you didn't have to work today, wouldn't you want to jump into some water? I mean, Gawd, it's broiling. Look at you poor boys in your heavy uniforms. Right? Don't you agree that on a day like today?" The caged backseat of the police car yawned open like a dark medical chamber. *Nonono.*

Just then, like an action figure come to life, Stitch appears, her Mohawk cutting through the crowd like a bloody shark fin. She was as bright as the sun and, I thought for a second, she had on liquid reflective black armor. She had my clothes bundled up in my leather jacket under her skinny arm.

"Hey, officers, I'm sorry, it's our fault. It's her birthday and we took her clothes to play a prank on her. I promise I'll get her out of here right now." My birthday? God, Stitch was a deep genius.

The cops were still trying to look serious and hard, but clearly had no interest in processing the stoned and chatty naked kid. They tell us to get out of the area and to not come back. Stitch and I promise they will have no trouble from us, sir, thank you sir, happy Fourth of July, sir, clothes are a lie, sir.

We damn near pissed ourselves on the T back to Cambridge. I couldn't help but think how close I came to spending the hottest day of the year in a beige, concrete holding cell packed with screaming bipolar whores, drunken hags, and bag ladies with missing eyes and inexplicable, open wounds, while I tripped my teenage brains out of my mind for lucky number seven.

Stitch had saved the day all right, and probably my life as well.

That wasn't the first, nor last time that Stitch saved my stupid ass from my own stupid assness. She was a powerful creature, one I tried to emulate often. She was so cool that I couldn't believe she was my friend.

Later, in my twenties, I was living in San Francisco. I got a drunken message from her about some huge party in Manhattan, Tompkins Square Park. The Drunk Punk-Olympics, where, according to her message, a bunch of folks from the old crew would shotgun beers and attempt made-up sporting events. She promised a great time and absolutely guaranteed vomiting and heinous injuries, as part of the entertainment factor.

It was great to hear from her, but I was not doing too well when I got the call. I couldn't make it to New York, anyway, but I promised we'd see each other soon. She lived in my heart and mind as a keeper.

Nearly ten years after our last exchange of messages, I was in New York at a bar just off Tompkins Square Park, ironically, and even more weird was the fact that the bartender was one of those girls from back in the Harvard Square days who had wanted to kick my ass, but she was happy to see me and we chatted about the good, bad, and ugly old days. "You ever hear from Stitch? Where is that woman these days?" I asked.

My heart sank at her expression.

"Stitch got killed."

Got killed?

The bartender went on to say that there was an investigation, but she died six months ago. Supposedly, Stitch was living in London with a *bad* guy. He was a drug dealer and she had been apparently using heroin pretty regularly. One night, the cops were called to their flat and found her hanging by her neck in the shower. It was believed that the boyfriend had beaten her to death and hung her up to make it look like a suicide. But, nobody seemed to know the truth, and hey, junkies die all the time over nothing.

Stitch got killed. Even writing it down now seems crazy.

CHAPTER NINE:

43 IS A MAGIC NUMBER, MOOSE AND MULTIPLE MOM.

"I've finally figured it out!" Mom said, again, coming into the living room with a stack of books and her best friend behind her. She wanted to play me her new single, and I was lucky enough to be home to hear it. I wanted to walk out of the room, the house, the town, but I had a fresh pack of smokes and I was practicing how to not give a fuck.

"Lovey is so amazing, I swear," she said, putting the books on the coffee table. They were all magic books, witchcraft, Wiccan, whatnots.

"Do tell," I said, French inhaling.

Mom took a breath and made her serious, I'm about to blow your mind with this information face. "Okay, you know how I always say the number 43?"

"In German?" I muttered under my breath to my cigarette.

". . . I called you *forty-three* times; I ate *forty-three* thousand blueberries? I always say it and I never knew why." Dramatic pause, looking around. "Until today." Here's where, in the movie, everyone perks up, listens expectantly, and the music gets all hopeful, signaling a change in everyone's fortune. In reality, I light another smoke with the end of my last one and wonder if she has any idea how little I care. I am so far from giving a fuck about what she has to say that I don't even see her as my mother at all. I am completely separate, staring back at what should be a grown woman, and see instead a child of four, showing me a frog that she is convinced will become a prince once her lips touch it.

I care nothing for the woman, but start to pity the little girl.

I was a miserable, angry teenager, sure, but I loved what little scraps I could muscle out of life. Laughing and breathing and music and sex, feeling and fighting and fucking up, I loved it all. The movie in my head was the hero's journey, where the ugly underdog achieves the impossible, gets the girl, and punches out the bad guy everyone had thought was the *good* guy, and so on. Mom could only scrape a speck of happiness out of being the sickest person in the room. Like those kids who, when in a race or some kind of game, when they realize they can't win, instead of trying anyway, they fall down on purpose and act like they hurt themselves so everyone has to stop playing and focus on them.

I wanted so much to not care, to humiliate and belittle her. To make her see how pathetic her whole reaching for something to be so terribly wrong with her that everyone would, finally, care. I did care though. My heart broke for this tiny little blonde. She had a cold, whistling hole in her, so bottomless that no amount of drugs, hugs, or promises would ever fix her.

"So, what did he say?" I played along.

"Four plus three, *seven*. Stormy, I'm a witch." Her friend exhaled and stared at my mom, amazed and relieved.

"A witch." I said.

"Yes, sweetie, but I'm a *white* witch, I'll only do good spells and love potions."

"Mom, the *doctor* told you this?"

"Yes! He said it was my subconscious telling me that I am a magic person, and that's why I have such a hard time fitting in!" She was so pleased with her new thing, I didn't even have the heart to laugh out loud at her. She and her friend started right into her magic books to look for love spells as I walked out of the house.

Christ.

I'm sure Mom thought she could cast a love spell on my dad to win him back. When *that* didn't work, Mom thought it a good idea to start dating, while still living with my dad.

That'll show him.

However, Mom's dating pool was pretty shallow, occupied, mostly, by guys from halfway houses, and friends of friends from halfway houses. She met a nice idiot named Moose. I don't mean to say folks in the halfway house / rehab / psychiatric outpatient world are idiots, but Moose sure was. I don't know what his illness or chemical situation was, but he was appropriately massive, hence, I suppose, the name. He also had one of those annoying habits of chuckling after saying absolutely everything.

"Oh hey there, ha-ha, you must be Stormy, huh huh huh, is your mom home?" Moose said as he stood, taking up the whole entire doorway. It seemed he was oblivious to the fact he was picking Mom up at my dad's house. Mom trotted down the stairs and stepped in front of me as I stood slack-jawed. She was overly made-up and positively reeked of lily of the valley.

"Moose, *darling*! Come in, sweetie. Come in," she said, extra loudly. Mom wasn't quite ready for their date, even though she'd been crowing about it all week, so she grabbed one of my dad's beers, stuck it in Moose's huge paw, and sent him shuffling into the living room to "hang a tick."

In the living room, a Patriots game was on the television, watching said game were my dad and brothers. Moose smiled around the room as he thunked his heft onto the sofa next to my brothers. "Henry, this is Moose," she said to Dad, with soap-opera iciness. "Wait right here, Moose, *darling,* and I'll be right down."

Even a blind half-wit would realize he should maybe wait outside at this point. But as huge a moose as Moose was, he was clearly pretty light in the wit department. The idiot cracked open the beer, then, to our collective horror, started to comment on the game, talking at our dad about football, sportsmanship, coaching, no "I" in "team," and whatnot. My father responded in half words and long exhalations of smoke, the whole time his jaw popping in and out as he clenched his teeth. My brothers and I shot looks at each other, eyes big with disbelief. We sneaked a few looks at our father but didn't dare look too long for fear of setting something off. The air was tight with rage. The tension froze and flattened my guts. There were so many times we thought Dad would lose it and there would be a tremendous explosion, walls would be pulverized with fists and furious roaring, but so many times the outrage and gut-ripping frustration would just stalk around us like a monster.

When I couldn't take any more, I took the dogs for a walk. My usual escape. I was gone a good ten minutes. When I got back, Mom, in a tiny blue dress, was snarkily saying goodnight to my father.

"Nicetameetcha, Hen! Yeah, ha-ha," Moose says, sounding like he had genuinely made a new friend. Then they left.

It was clearly time for Mom to move out. Her parents were finally helping out financially, so she could get her own place. If it hit the fan, an ambulance could be called or something.

I know my mom did not want to move out. She certainly didn't want a divorce. She loved my father with an addict's white-knuckled desperation. Not too terribly appealing to my dad, who just hid from her in plain sight. He was cloaked in an invisible Mom deflecting sheath and nobody could penetrate, except maybe Doug Flutie.

My dad didn't want a divorce either. Rather, he didn't want to deal with having to get the ball rolling himself. He wanted Mom to go away, sure, he wanted the whole *thing* to go away, but she had nowhere to go, and my dad wasn't going to send her into the street to become a ward of the state.

Finally, Mom's millionaire parents stepped in to help when her songs of "My Awful Children" and "Everybody's So Mean To Me" went down some spots on the charts and she started pushing her latest single, "I'm An Abused Wife."

The only things my dad ever hit were walls and six-packs of Heineken.

One day, Mom must have been emboldened by some feminist drivel on television or one of her new friends, whom she had convinced my dad was mistreating her. She strode up to my father with her jaw fixed and said, "Henny. I want a divorce."

Now, I know, in every wet twist of my red guts, that she hoped and prayed in a fever that my father, confronted with this finality, would say, "No, Suzi, please. No. We can work this out, let's just talk about this. I don't want you to go." In her mind, she had the whole romantic scenario lined up where he would whip off his invisibility cloak, get up and hold her, rocking her gently until all was forgotten.

"'kay," came the reply.

∽

"Stormy's going to live with me," I heard Mom say to her friend on the phone.

"What? Dad?" I looked at my dad, who just mouthed something, looking irritated. There was no discussion. He was so glad she was leaving, if I had to be sacrificed for his comfort, so be it. I barely was around, anyway. Because of the crazy at home, I lived in a dorm during the school year. And, besides every now and then in school or when I got suspended, Dad and I rarely saw each other or spoke. We were strangers, so he was probably happy to see me go, too. He loved me, I know, but he didn't like me much in those days.

Mom found a tiny two-bedroom about two miles from my dad's house, just a bike ride, for me. She could go ahead and *think* I was living with her, but I planned to squat at my dad's. He wouldn't kick me out, or even say anything if he saw me camped on his couch. I was such a runaway cat that he never knew if I was coming or going, anyway. So the whole living-with-Mom hideousness was easily avoidable, I figured.

My dad was so thrilled Mom was finally moving out, he volunteered John and himself as movers. The morning of moving day I took off, avoiding the house until it was over. I imagined the whole thing would be done by late afternoon, and since I missed moving day (oopsie!), I'd just move later.

When I walked in near dusk, I found the hallway full of boxes and my brother and father standing around looking very uncomfortable in the kitchen. "What's up?" I yelled over Henry Rollins shouting in my ears.

They looked at each other and then at the ceiling. My dad shook his head and went to washing a coffee cup.

Washing dishes was, and still is, very soothing to my father. Many terrible things have been successfully ignored due to a sudsy sink full of plates, pots, and pans.

I pulled off my headphones and looked at John. "Maybe you should go check on Mom," he said.

I was at the top of the stairs when I heard her sobbing. To my left was the guest room where she had been staying. It was empty. To my right was my dad's room, where the sobbing was coming from. I stepped into the bedroom. *Mom?* The sobbing intensified. There were clothes all over the floor with her powder-blue suitcase open and on top of them. I turned towards the sound; my dad's bathroom door was to my left and open enough to see my mom's bare ass.

"Mom?" I pulled open the door.

She was completely naked and incoherent. Her false teeth were in one hand, the other hand holding her up on the sink. Her face twisted around her mouth in a silent grimace, punctuated with snotty sobs for air. She looked like a grotesque imitation of a three-year-old.

"Th-eh-they are being s-so-so mean to me!" she keened into the sink.

"Mom. Get dressed, c'mon, they want to help you." I went towards her and saw a few pills in the sink. She quickly turned on the faucet and started rinsing off her dentures, washing the pills into the drain. "Mom?"

"I'm just everybody's joke around here." She put her teeth in, giving her wet face some shape again. She plopped backwards onto the toilet, clasping her hands together on her jumping knees. "I don't wannagooo." Her tiny wet voice spilled onto the yellow linoleum floor. She was so thin. Only in her forties, but years of cigarettes and metric tons of pharmaceutical mood fixers had aged her flesh to a tissue-thin wrap about her skeleton.

It suddenly occurred to me why she was in my dad's room naked.

She must have asked to stay in the oldest known way women ask for things.

I heard the television go on downstairs and my heart broke for her.

"Fuck, Mom, it'll be okay. C'mon, let's go. I'll help you. Get up." I led her up off the toilet and to her clothing pile. She was listing and swaying a bit from whatever she took, but the crying drifted into sniffles and pouting as she pulled on some cheap elastic pants and a girly, button-down blouse with little flowers on it.

I went to my room and packed a bag to go with her.

From moving into the tiny two-bedroom on the dead-end street, to when I came home to find the door open, a smear of blood on the stairs and a neighbor telling me an ambulance had been called, had only been two months.

CHAPTER TEN:

ANOREXIA FABULOSA, OR, "Does this open sore on my face make me look fat?"

Right after I graduated high school (read: barely squeezed my porky self through the bars), I got punched in the face by a boy I was desperately in love with and it kinda put me off sex for awhile, so I stopped taking the pill. Once I did, lo and behold, I dropped about ten pounds inside of two weeks.

At my heaviest, during my years of running with the moose of crew, I was a bit north of 190 pounds.

Inspired by my new visible wheels of pelvic bone under my remaining chub, I decided to go for it and get as skinny as I possibly could.

It was the summer I turned eighteen. I hadn't been accepted to any college or university, not that I tried terribly hard. I just declared I was taking the year off. For what? Whatever. Mostly to starve myself.

I took a job as a maid in a hotel. Five days a week I would work in my little gray uniform with smock pockets, shaking condoms out of bedding, vacuuming, dusting, hospital cornering, and snooping through people's toiletries. Every afternoon I would borrow a fashion magazine from the sundries shop, then hit the hotel gym. Pumping my legs for hours on the stairmaster while staring at tiny, bird-boned models. At home, over my bed and dresser was a collage of similar images. My walls were a homage to the professionally hungry. I would stare at those pictures, willing my body to shrink around my skeleton, too.

It finally did.

In studying to be an anorexic, I noticed some of the models weren't particularly pretty, but they were nearly void of flesh. Angular and feline, I imagined they were probably invited to parties every night and given cocaine to be kept upright. One of the big lessons I got from my schooling, at that point, was, if you were beautiful, someone would love you. It made perfect sense.

Step one: Stop eating. During that first summer out of St. Mark's, I figured out how to stop eating by taking trucker speed and smoking Camel Lights. I could get away with one piece of dry toast and a half of a honeydew melon every day. So what if my hair was falling out? The Portuguese ladies I worked with at the hotel yelled at me over their lunches. "You too skinny, Tormenta, you gon' get sick!" I loved it. I was so thin people were *worried? Cool!*

Dad was in New Hampshire all summer, again, but when he came home for his weekly check-in, I noticed him acting funny around me. He then came home a little more often. He'd make food and put it in front of me, or bring me greasy beach-vendor food from the water park and stare at me while I barely touched it.

He wants you to stay fat so nobody will want you.

It was challenging to not eat around him under those circumstances as he would get angry when I said, "I'm on a diet, Dad, I can't eat this stuff." Or, "I already ate, Pop, I'll eat it later . . ." Though I hadn't been given any free cocaine or partied with any rock stars yet, one thing was clear: the skinny thing was working.

One morning my dad woke me up. "You going to work today?" I was confused as to why he was home, let alone in my room. I had an alarm clock, after all, and *of course* I was going to work. The condoms and fashion models were waiting for me. Then I realized I was wet. Or my bed was wet . . . warm . . . is the window . . . ?

"Are you okay, sweetie?" he finally asked, waking me up from my delirium.

"Agh can't move, Da." My voice sounded like I had a duck's egg in my throat, and my throat felt like a hot football full of boar bristles.

"Okay, well, I'll tell your work you're staying home again today."

"Agahhhn?" I gurgled.

"He said you didn't show up yesterday, either. I only came down from Boarsie for a minute and thought it was strange that your car was here, and . . ."

I was floating in a thick mist of foam rubber and salted pretzels ripped open and steaming. But I'm face down in the grass . . . so tired . . . just if I could roll over and . . .

". . . and you better goddamn start eating something god dammit you're goddamned emaciated." He left my room. Later I heard his car pull out to head back north.

I had blacked out, sweating, and had not moved for thirty-six hours.

Lying in my damp, fever sheets, I stared at Christy Turlington, Linda Evangelista, and other impossibly beautiful creatures in my collage of anorexploitation over my bed. Thumbtacked among the images was a homemade food chart. What I ate, versus how long I worked out. There were Magic Markered stars next to most days, but there were a few with angry scrawl, "BAD!" "FAT!" and "YOU SUCK!" next to the days where I ate more than five hundred calories.

Swimming in and out of consciousness, I wondered faintly if I had overdone it. It gave me a strange contentment, thinking that maybe I had. I pinched around my tummy at the skin there, bruised from constantly pinching-an-inch . . .

You are still fat and ugly . . . and alone.

Mom was thrilled. She was staying in a halfway house in the next town, and somehow heard that I was sick and not eating. Perfect for her because I wouldn't be able to get away in my weakened state. She would have me all to herself for some horrendous talks of menstruation and tit-grabbing awfulness. Any illness of mine was better than hers because, I guess, she could throw on her Mom cape and save the day.

When I was little, I used to get these things called "tummy attacks." Whenever Mom would be home from the hospital, I would get horrific stomach cramps and tremors. I would sit, crumpled on the toilet and scream into my sleeve from the shocking pain. Mom would always swoop in with medicine and hugs and trips to the doctor. She would fill the house with loud, dramatic phone calls to friends about how worried she was, and "What is a mother to do?"

It was hinted that maybe some chemical or other was getting put in my food to create some drama (intestinally for me, maternally for her). There is no proof of that, but it could very well be that the stress of her comings, goings, staying and staying away, made us all sick.

John had horrible migraines and Henry also suffered terrible stomach ailments around that time.

~

I had mononucleosis, strep throat, and was completely anemic.

"Have you been eating?" asked the doctor, looking at me over his reading glasses, holding the paper with my blood-test results.

"NO. She's gone CRAZY on a diet and NEVER eats." Mom strained her mother muscles at the doctor, flapping her mom cape.

"Mom. You don't live with me. I eat all the time." To the doctor, "I eat all the time."

"I'm your mother and your mother KNOWS."

"Christ."

"Well, Storm, you are severely anemic and fairly underweight. I don't see you getting better anytime soon unless you start eating a little . . . um . . . more." As he looked at me, Mom swiveled in her seat toward me with a dancer's flourish. Now they were both staring at me. He stared like a doctor, she, like someone trying to win an awkwardly-imitate-somebody-weird contest.

"And YOU will DO what the doctor says, young lady. I'll make sure she eats today, I'll take her straight to Friendly's." My stomach scrunched up at that. Friendly's, Mom's favorite public-humiliation theater. Tampons and French fries and alters OH MY!

Christ.

The doctor didn't react to my mom, he kept his eyes fixed on me, so I stared right back at him. "And, Storm, if I hear of you *not* eating, or of you losing any more weight, I will have you hospitalized, you will be hooked up to an IV and force-fed. Do you understand me?"

HOSPITALIZED? I really *am* skinny.

I tried not to smile.

"Yes, absolutely, Doctor." I was already planning what to wear into the city as soon as I could stand up without feeling faint. Cutoff jeans, combat boots, and a baggy Black Flag T-shirt. I wanted to see if anyone noticed how sick I was.

Not only did EVERYONE notice, but I actually got flirted with as if I were a completely new girl! No one had seen me in months, since I was working forty hours a week, and obsessively killing myself slowly with pictures of skeletal teenagers and trucker speed.

To this very day, I have never had more boys hit on me than I did while I was Ribs McGee . . . I looked like a great dane in a leather jacket, but boys strutted around me like black-clad pigeons, making up excuses to talk to me.

The only one who didn't like it was Keith. He hugged me hello then smirked, "Dude. You feel like a xylophone."

I can't say if it was my newfound scrawniness that suddenly made me the prettiest pony in the paddock, or if it had something to do with being so disastrously weakened by caloric deficit, that I was, for once, quiet. I was so tapped I could hardly talk, let alone get up, so I guess it made me really easy to catch or knock over.

My guitar player, Scotty, tells me that skinny, insecure chicks are great because they're easier to nip off from the rest of the herd, they tire quickly, and need to lie down a lot.

I was finally skinny, but had no energy to have sex with anybody. I got some free cocaine from horny guys, but that just led to erection-less make-out sessions.

Then there was that weird hole in my face. It looked like a scrape, but stayed wet, it wouldn't scab over. And I, for the life of me, couldn't figure out what it was.

"Impetigo," the doctor said flatly.

"Whaff's dat?" I said, my mouth full of banana. I wanted him to see me eating so as not to raise suspicion at my unchanged weight PLUS a weeping sore on my cheek. It was a genius idea, I thought, until he prescribed an antibiotic I had to take WITH FOOD, as it blared from its label.

Pretty tricky, that doctor. I basically had strep throat, on my face, weighed around 135 pounds, and was finally getting tired of being sick all the time when the topic of acting school came up.

Suddenly, Grandmother Banks took an interest in my future, and suggested I audition for the American Academy of Dramatic Arts. I don't know how she was connected there, but I sent in an application, interviewed, did two monologues, and sang a song. I moved to New York City and started school in the spring of 1989.

CHAPTER ELEVEN:

St. MARK's School to St. MARK's PLACE.

From St. Mark's School to St. Mark's Place.

The American Academy of Dramatic Arts was a much better situation than St. Mark's. It was a place, I thought, where I could turn my natural tendencies and abilities into viable skills. Where loud and annoying were the raw materials for brilliant and hilarious! I also assumed that I would fit in there, that the school would be full of folks like me: loud, flamboyant, slutty, lonely, and weird . . . hinging on nuts. I was also going to be in New York City! Finally and officially, living away from home and all the headaches that haunted it.

AADA was, and still is, a great acting school. They taught me, in no time at all, that I was a *horrible* actor, one; two, I hated most other actors; and three, though I loved attention, I hated acting in general. Plus, I found, just like at any school before, there was an unwritten, yet obvious, law of beauty favoritism. My first year in New York, the weight came shuffling back to live all over me, save for my boobs and butt, earning me a few barbs of "ugly fat chick," "fat pig," and my favorite, "You have such a pretty face . . . ," then trailing off, suggesting the sad and sorry business going on inside my stretchy black clothes made me a blight on the eyes.

For the first few weeks in New York I slept on a cot in the Banks dining room. They had a sweet one-bedroom apartment on Sutton Place, very posh. But I was not their favorite person, I could tell. I didn't even resemble the kind of person they could even like a teeny little bit. They were only in New York half the week, though, so I tried to stay out of their way, and be as quiet as possible when they were there. I even tried to earn my keep by cooking for them, but my welcome quickly wore out. Grandfather Banks did not care much for my cooking, or me. So I split. I found a place to stay on East 36th Street, close to school. And I found a place where I fit in that was not so close to school; in truth, it was worlds away.

Nobody asked for IDs downtown, so I could go anywhere. There was no shortage of filthy good time hangs in Alphabet City, and The Alcatraz was my favorite. It was a rock 'n' roll bar on the corner of St. Mark's Place and Avenue A. The beautiful bartender there, Raff, became my best friend in New York, and she remains so to this day. Raff was also the raven-haired "Queen Vixen," one of the singers in The Cycle Sluts From Hell, a female-fronted metal band that ruled the Lower East Side. Their hit single was "I Wish You Were a Beer," and they toured with Motorhead. I couldn't believe she was my friend. Raff and I would drink and smoke and fuck and snort whatever came across our faces. There were loud rock shows and sticky strip clubs, drag queens and dealers, bathroom three-ways and bar fights.

I had found my people.

That wasn't the case at school. While enjoying my lowlife, rock 'n' roll dirtbaggery, I started to feel out of place in the sensitive, bookish atmosphere of school. I wasn't any good at acting, nor did I have the slightest clue how to improve. The only acting I was any good at was my haughty who-gives-a-fuckness. My teachers there were some of the best, and I honestly wanted to do better, to be better, but I didn't get it. Despite all my bravado, I envied my classmates, those serious, gazelle-bodied actresses, clip-clopping their dainty golden hooves through the halls. I felt like a big, loud jackass among them.

But I could sing my big, loud jackass off, and that was the only thing going for me at the Academy. Someone at school told me that I was built for Broadway. I assumed that meant fat, but a good singer.

In 1989, though, the biggest shows were *Phantom of the Opera, Cats,* and *Les Miserables,* and boooring! The higher ups at school thought me a *perfect* candidate for that world. I could think of nothing more ridiculous. I wanted to do well at school, and make my dad proud, but, just like with crew, I felt myself being touted for being amazing at something I hated.

Suffice to say, I was not buying the whole Broadway angle. I wanted to be Joey Ramone, not Judy Garland. To my mind, those Broadway musicals were huge, garish pageants of lame. They were way too clean, pretty, and controlled with tidy, wind-up endings. And, from what I could tell, those singers weren't getting to do coke and fuck on pool tables, so it clearly wasn't for me.

Sadly, neither was being in a rock band. It never even occurred to me to try. Even though I was pretending to be all rock 'n' roll, slamming shots and lines, crawling through the rock 'n' roll landscape of Alphabet City, I never considered myself *worthy* of being in a band. You had to be hot to be in a band. I wasn't hot or cool, or at-death's-door skinny, like all the beautifully wasted denizens of The Cat Club and CBGB were.

But in my new, yet familiar, community of misanthropes and freaks downtown, I settled easily into becoming completely fucked up again. I drank until four in the morning, did blow to keep going, and would have to sweat through my scenes and schoolwork. Every Wednesday was Tommy Gunn's night at Cat Club, where Raff's band played along with other punk and glam-rock bands. Some were god-awful, but everybody rules when everybody's wasted, so it was always a good time. Every Sunday was rock 'n' roll church at the Limelight, a rock club housed in a real church. Raff and I would sit in the attic VIP lounge under the spires, and laugh at the models and eyeliner pirates who would be keeling over from drink and AquaNet.

In the late eighties, early nineties, there was a trashy, junkie glam thing going on. The rock 'n' roll clubs were crawling with big, sprayed hair and torn-up tight black rags of denim or leather. Old-school rockers, self-styled like legendary punk rockers Iggy Pop, The Ramones, then Dead Boys, Lords of the New Church, they were giving way to a new school of flashy California glam like Motley Crue, Guns N' Roses, and LA pretty boy waste-oids. Fashionwise, it made for the perfect storm of street-hardened punk and kinda gay and fluffy. We called those boys "eyeliner pirates." And they filled the Limelight every Sunday for our jeering entertainment, and the occasional men's room tonsil romp.

The VIP lounge at Limelight is where I first encountered Jägermeister and chicks.

The first girl I ever slept with was a dangerously young, fox-faced fibber named Dizzy. Her mom called her "Kippy," though her real name was Karen Weitz. She could smoke cigarettes with her vagina at sixteen and could swing her Lilliputian, butter-cream body into any lap, party, or club she wanted, anytime. Dizz was always on the guest list, and was as full of shit as a girl that young and that beautiful could be. I adored her. I also adored Jägermeister, but that love affair ended badly.

"It's herbal," Raff cackled as we slammed cold shots of the German syrup in the dark church attic strewn with cum-soaked couches and wannabes, "It's good for ya!"

That was the battle cry all night as more shots would arrive at our little corner. "You want some more? It's *herbal!*"

Jägermeister. The name means "Master of the Hunt," and they aren't kidding. One can only assume the Germans called it that because the shit sneaks up on you and beats your brains out. The only other thing I know of that still hunts like that (besides date rapists) are Gila monsters.

As soon as you start limping, it's pretty much game over. Before you know it, you're waking up naked in a Denny's bathroom with bruised brains, a phone number on your leg, and a thank-you note on your back, both written in barbecue sauce.

Raff was a beautiful badass. With her Cherokee cheekbones, big dark eyes, and a satin mane of long inky hair, she always looked like an album cover. Her recent ex-boyfriend was a tall, lanky, handsome, dumb-as-a-bag-of-hammers fuckwit. Theirs was an ugly, public breakup. He hurt her, so I hated him, and wished him harm.

A few weeks before Raff and I discovered Jäger, her dumb-fuck ex had thrown her belongings out of her fifth-floor apartment window. I got the tearful phone call and went right away to her place on Avenue B. Some of her stuff had fallen into a neighbor's yard, so I clambered over the fence between the buildings and found her jewelry box.

I was feeling around for her necklaces and rings in the scrubby grass when I heard a metallic *click* very close by.

"What the fock you doin' theya?" came a dry croak of a woman's voice.

"I'm just looking for my friend's stuff." I froze on the ground.

Raff had been shining a flashlight from her yard over the fence. She called down to the voice in the dark. "My crazy ex threw my stuff out my window and some of it's in your yard, I'm sorry we woke you up."

"Ya didn't wake me, I've had a gun on ya for ten minutes," she chuckled. "Youz can look in the mawning, get the fuck outta my yad now."

The fact that DumbFuck nearly got me killed was still fresh in my mind, weeks later, when Raff and I were hanging hard with the Master of the Hunt. We were stumbling out of a cab at her place, when she slurred, "God, every time I see that fuckin' bike . . ." *The fuckin' bike* was a motorcycle given to both Raff and DumbFuck, but he decided to keep it for himself. "I should fill the fucking tank with corn syrup, I swear."

"Huh? This bike here?" I asked, before horse-kicking it against the brick wall of her building. I loved making her laugh, and her cackling echoed through the concrete night world we stood in, as I bounced the motorcycle back and forth between my cowboy boot and the wall. Later, we listed all his known diseases in bold, magic markery block letters across his apartment door. Served him right for breaking her heart and staying in the same building.

For a while, almost getting killed was just a footnote to a fun night. A turning point came when Raff and I stayed up all night at a friend's apartment. The friend was a huge cocaine dealer, and a really nice person. He was also very generous with his stuff, so we ended up doing our weight in coke. On this particular night, we stayed up passing around a grinder, talking that trembling, dry, desperate, coke drivel, and chain-smoking into the morning.

Limping home under God's fierce flashlight of bright sun, navigating through the packs of freshly washed, normal folk, I felt more hideous than I could ever recall. My eyes felt like they had been scooped out with a camping spork, rolled in cat litter, then shoved back into my skull. My skull that crawled with itchy little demons, chirping, *Loser! Loser! Loser!* I stayed home from school. Raff and I wept on the phone to each other. "I am never doing blow again. Ever." She said, her sultry voice truly thrashed and hoarse, "God. Me neither. I am totally fucking up at school. We gotta stop."

She did. I *sort of* did.

Sometime later, I was doing some day-drinking on a Sunday. Raff was working and we were going to hit the Limelight later on. But day-drinking can ruin your night, and this day was going that way fast.

I had made a quickie friend, one of those drug-fueled friendships that happen over bottles and lines, needles and pills. Chemical camaraderie that feels so real and life-affirming while you're getting completely fucked up, but fade as fast as a cherry high.

She was painfully thin, a stick bug in a tank top. She had hair like Chrissie Hynde and a laugh like Danny DeVito, and at one point, I think, I told her I loved her.

She tearfully told me about something bad that had happened to her, and I wept right back at her pretending to understand. She kept buying drinks and I kept drinking them.

The sun was still high in the sky when she clinked her glass against the fourth or fifth shot of Jack she had bought me. I downed it. She had also bought smokes and a slice of pizza. She was my soul mate.

I managed to say, "I gotta stop drinking, I'm going out tonight and I'm already fuckin' wasted!"

"Me, too! I'm going out later, too!" She blew smoke at me. "We should go to my place and take a nap."

"I would totally die for you. Let's go."

Somewhere in our zigzagging, drunken singing, arms slung over each other's shoulders path to her place, I heard her say something about lines.

Fuck, yeah. That'll be great! It'll take the drunk down a peg, and it means she has blow and will all night. My new best friend *rules*! I'll never do coke again *later*.

Though my memory of her apartment is fuzzy at best, it stood out to me right away that the chick must have dough, or she was fucking someone rich. The apartment was pretty decent-sized and had real furniture in it. No milk crates with tapestries draped over them, no futon on the floor or mish-mash, thrown-away dressers. Nicer still was the familiar chop-scrape sound of razor to mirror.

Huzzah!

"Help yourself, I gotta pee." She gestured to a powder-smeared rectangular mirror that sat on a low shelf. There was a decent heap of powder scraped out of a magazine-folded envelope, but only a tiny couple of lines set up for me. I took the razor and scraped the two lines to make one bigger and made a matching line next to it.

I put the straw in my nose and quick snorted the first line up one side and went to do the other when a searing pain torched through my face. "OOOOW!" My hands slapped to my face. I was instantly tearing, drooling, and a sick funky flavor soured the back of my mouth. My friend was out of the bathroom. "Wha' the fuck kinna coke izzat? It fuckin' *hurts!*"

"It's not coke . . . it's dope." Looking down, "Whoa. You did a lot."

Dope??? I was already drunk and now I've horked up a junkie-sized line of smack? I am *fucked*. Maybe she'll have actual coke to keep my heart beating; maybe she can take me to the hospital, or just hold me while I fucking die?!

She floated to the front door and opened it. "You better go," she said flatly.

"Raaafff! I'm dying, Raaafff!"

I barely made it back to the Alcatraz. I had puked twice, somehow getting some in my own boot. My knees had turned into wet, warm cotton, and my body just wanted to soak into the ground. And as soon as I trudged into the bar it did.

"What the fuck happened?" Raff was pissed.

"I thought it was coooke. I did fuggin shmack. I'm gonna die. I'm sorry," I keened from the spitty gum-stuck bar floor.

"Shit." She grabbed the phone and called my apartment. My roommate, a petite feminist NYU student, was home and ready for me downstairs when the cab pulled up. I had a handful of classmates from the academy who lived in my building and all came out to help my pint-sized roommate trying to haul my wasted ass up the stairs.

We all hung out in our place, me fading in and out like a radio station, everyone else taking turns putting ice cubes on my face and neck, slapping or shaking me awake periodically. It was great fun.

What I remember of the vigil was coming to now and then, hearing *The Wizard of Oz* on television, and telling everyone in the room, repeatedly, "I feel soo amazing," then falling back into sweet absence.

Everyone was pissed at me.

The mess I would've left behind, had I expired, was so huge, that even I hated me for being so stupid, among all the other things I hated me for. Not to mention how hard it would be on my dad to know I went out just like mom had always wanted to. And Mom? Well, you can never get over the death of a child, they say. And she *would* say, repeatedly, "You never get over the death of a child," and everyone would stop what they were doing to help her up or down some stairs, make her tea and ooh and aaah over her sadness. My dying would have sucked for everyone.

I apologized to everyone profusely, all those who kept me alive and dealt with my nonsense. I swore that I was done drinking and partying and was going to focus on my schoolwork. Whatever was going to be my final vocation, acting, singing, teaching, or whatever, I was at least going to ace the two-year program I had earned a scholarship for.

I was so determined to clean up my act, I even swore off sex. My desire to be desired had been the cause of so much humiliation and self-degrading behavior that I called a cease-fire on my self-esteem and hung a "closed" sign on my epiglottis. No booze, no drugs, no boning, no problem.

Funnily enough, my grades improved over the course of the semester. I took a job at the New York Roxy, a big, mostly gay, dance club on the West Side, answering phones and signing for packages during the day and going to school in the evening. I missed all the fun that went down in that club at night, but just about every day I would get a personal call from some simpering weirdo, "Can I be your slave?" For a while I humored him, asked him what he wanted, specifically. He just wanted to be bossed around and if he got hurt while the boss was bossing, then booya, basically.

I don't know who he was, if he was kidding or completely deranged, but I heard from him nearly every day. Until of course, I told him to stuff five C notes into an envelope, with his address written on, and stick it through the Roxy's mail slot,

". . . and tell me what time to be there and I'll come kick your pussy ass 'til you pee your pants, you piece of shit," I said jovially. Of course I wouldn't have gone to some dickweed's place by myself, but I would have taken the money.

Never heard from him again.

Despite my fun, yet failed, phone dalliance with the fake slave, the dam of my libido was bulging, cracking, and threatening to destroy the city should it break.

Rumor has it that women hit their sexual peak in their thirties. I was supposed to go crazy in my twenties. I was twenty, and maybe not at my sexual peak, but something was spinning and burning out of control inside me. I hadn't had sex in about eight months and even masturbation started to lose its luster. I needed more stimulation, more intensity. Orgasms were great, but orgasms with a little risk involved, like when one might, I don't know, masturbate in public, were just the ticket to get me over the . . . um . . . hump, as it were. At school, on the subway, at lunch, I could get myself off deftly without a soul catching on, as far as I knew or cared. And I didn't care. Maybe I *was* crazy.

Spring began to warm up the streets and evenings in New York. Sweaters turned to T-shirts, pants and boots to jean shorts, miniskirts and, well, boots. School was out for a week and I was just killing time in the city. I got a cab from work at the Roxy to go see Raff at the Alcatraz. We were going to have dinner, maybe see a movie.

"Avenue A and St. Mark's Place, please."

The cab driver looked like a Jabba the Hutt made out of burnt Naugahyde. His lips were thick, and his heavily lidded eyes drooped over his wide black beard. Middle Eastern music crept out of the radio like incense smoke. He looked like he tasted sour. I was tingling.

Jerk off. Do it.

The cab smelled like sweet woodsy oil and curried body funk. It was hot and sticky in the back seat. Jabba watched me in his rear-view mirror. At first, I didn't think he knew what I was doing, maybe he thought I put one foot on the seat because I was going pull a fast one and jump out of his cab without paying. He'd glance at the road, then back at me. His face betrayed neither titillation nor disgust, maybe he was scared I was nuts. I was a pulsing, prickling glandular exclamation point of need and the heat and the weird and nothing in my head told me to give a fuck, so I didn't. When I realized he was aware of the go-ings on under my miniskirt, I just stared back at him in the mirror. "I know you know. Just drive," I wanted to say. But I was quiet, staying focused on his eyes and my fingers thrumming subtly across the front of my underwear. I realized he hadn't turned on the meter as we pulled up to the Alcatraz. I put my foot down and slid to the curbside door.

"Thank you?" I opened the door, looking at him.

"Havagooday-yuh," he nodded. Free ride.

"Are you out of your fucking mind?" Raff half laughed, half spat. "Jesus *Christ* will you *please* have sex with someone? I'm sick of hearing about this. You could've gotten yourself killed."

"Nah. He was fine. Who's that?" Sitting across the horseshoe-shaped bar from me was a pretty young eyeliner pirate. He stared at me, I stared back, he bought a shot and a beer. I hadn't had a drink in months, but the cab ride set my heart knocking, so when the eyeliner pirate handed me the shot, I pounded it.

"Take his ass home or I'm never speaking to you again," Raff jokingly hissed at me when the boy went for a wiz.

The warm air, the booze, my friend's ribbing, and my throbbing pelvic hunger turned the afternoon into a slick, red yes.

Back at my place he pushed me through the door onto the floor and we rolled into my room. My room was technically a hallway, but wide enough for a futon and a few crates for my stuff. We snogged and bit and rolled around, his hands everywhere in a fury, pinching and grabbing. It was grand. We were tearing each other's clothes off as if there were cameras rolling. I didn't care about his flair for the dramatic, just so long as he would not be disappointed that I had no dick, I was happy as a clam.

As he yanked off my pants, I suddenly remembered, out of my boredom and obsessive masturbating, I had shaved my pubic hair into a trim valentine's heart and dyed it pink.

"Cool!" he roared as he pounced on it with his face.

Cool.

It was lovely, though he kept up the drama with fairly inane dirty talk. It sounded like he was straight-up parroting bargain-bin porn tapes, totally distracting. I took to shoving parts of me in his mouth, which worked great, until he turned me over. In doggy style his mouth was free to let loose all his red hot zingers.

I was biting my own hand trying to "Oh yeah!" and "Ungh!" away the giggles that were threatening to drive away the only erection I had enjoyed in nearly a year. I'm sure he thought I was just overcome with the moment as I shook beneath him.

"Oh . . . oh . . . yeah! Oh, yeah, baby! Here comes the hot sauce!"

His coup de grace came in a plosive burst, a punch of breath as he was getting off. He had clearly said it one thousand times before, but it would be the first time I had ever laughed openly at a man still inside me. The guffaw came so suddenly from my diaphragm, I shot him out of me like a bar of soap out of a wet fist. "Dude, *what?*" I cackled over my shoulder at him.

His face fell from snarling gladiator over a slain foe, to that of a fourteen-year-old with pee on his pants. "What?"

I'm sure I utterly ruined his orgasm, but I was suddenly picturing my ass crack filled with taco meat and shredded iceberg lettuce and I wasn't feeling so sexy either.

"Fuckin' hot sauce. Hot sauce?" I chortled, shaking my head as we dressed. I tried to stifle my giggles, because I didn't want to hurt his feelings any further, but it struck me as so hilarious. When I saw bright pink heart shaped stains on his tummy from my pubic coif, I lost it again.

"Heh-heh. Okay, okay, stop now." He was trying to let himself in on the joke and subtly let me know he was getting a little weary of the bwaaah-haaa-ing.

We trekked down the stairs and into the early evening. The

streets were full of people enjoying the long-awaited warm dark that held promise of a fat hot summer coming. I loved the streams of bodies flowing around me like water through stones, rolling down sidewalks of the city. A never-ending, head-down dance of avoidance and do-si-dos with strangers, New York.

Eyeliner pirate went to buy smokes and said he'd meet me back at the Alcatraz. "Sure you will," I said to myself, turning down St. Mark's from First Avenue. "That guy probably never wants to see me again, not alive at least."

As soon as I got to the bar I beelined to Raff, who laughed in disbelief "Oh, nooo! He was so cute! Oh, well, at least you aren't celery-butt anymore." (Celery-butt was our pet name for celibate.) "You were driving me nuts. Uh-oh." She looked over my shoulder, so I turned around just in time to see the porn parrot enter the bar. Before I could go to him, give him a hug, reassure his manly status, Raff croons across the bar, "Hey! Welcome back! You wanna beer, or maybe some hot sauce?"

At the beginning of my second year at the academy, I moved from midtown to East 12th Street and First Avenue, to be closer to where I felt at home. I loved my colorful new neighborhood. The same gaggle of Hispanic guys was always in rotation on my corner. One day, they asked nicely, "Oye, Blanca, smoke?"

"Sure!" said my stupid white ass, as I tapped out two cigarettes for them. They chuckled and took the smokes and tucked them behind their ears. I thought it was weird and kind of rude, as I got to my door, I heard them ask a bunch of other people for smokes. It took me a couple of days to realize they were selling crack.

After some time of me walking by them and chatting with them in Spanish (something I actually managed to learn in high school), they realized I was not going to buy crack, nor was I going to narc on them. I was "Blanca" (white girl) and they were "Hijos" (young boys). Drug dealers are supposed to be terrible people, I know, and my Hijos were probably guilty of some hairy shit, but my block was always safe.

I always walked home from school. The academy was, and still is, on Madison and East Thirty-second, a healthy walk. I would grab dinner to go, stop somewhere for a beer, get home, and try to learn lines or do whatever homework I had for the next evening. Walking twenty-plus blocks at night in New York City is much like walking during the day in most other places. The streets were bright, the stores open, and you were rarely, if ever, alone on the block. One time, though, I had stayed out at a bar fairly late and was ambling home, whistling Mozart's "Eine Kleine Nachtmusik." I often would whistle or hum to keep myself company during my long walks home. Every so often, others picked up the tune and whistled with me as we flowed down the sidewalk, a clot of strangers, sharing a moment.

This night there was just me and my whistle. "Eine Kleine Nachtmusik" can sound pretty creepy echoing around a wet street with few people around. It's especially creepy when you hear someone whistle with you, and you can't see them. At around Twenty-third Street I picked up the pace, kept whistling because I didn't want to look scared.

A girl spooked is like blood in the water. I kept on and took a jagged route to see if he was, indeed, following me. When I couldn't pretend any more, I turned to see my whistling partner, and saw a man walking behind me to my left, half a block back. He stopped whistling when I spotted him.

I have a vivid imagination, coupled with knowing how fucked some people can be, so, by the time I got to Sixteenth Street, I had already played the scenario, the police telling my dad that they had found a pair of ears in a bag at a construction site. I switched the tune to "Ode to Joy."

I decided he was an actual threat when I ran into a bodega to buy some soup and falafel, and he waited on a far street corner until I came out. I beelined down First Avenue; I was going to go straight to the Alcatraz, someone would be there who knew me and would walk me home or chase the dude off. As I approached my street, I saw my Hijos. "Oye, Blanca! Que tal?"

I told them in Spanish that there was a guy following me and I was scared to go home in case he saw where I lived. One of them, whom I assumed was in charge, told me to go on home and don't worry. He then made a quick sharp whistle and in a minute two other Hijos came out of nowhere "Bueno, go home, Blanca," he said, once he eyeballed the guy.

Mine was only four buildings toward Avenue A from First Avenue, but as I got close to my door, I heard a scuffle behind me. I couldn't make out what they were saying, but the four drug dealers were on that guy like a rash. No punches or any violence broke out, not as I watched, but they roughly ushered him off the block and out of sight.

"Yeah, they don't want any cops comin' 'round here, Goddess, it fucks with their business," my friend R.J. told me over pizza a few days later.

"You think they killed the guy?" I asked.

"Nah, nah . . . just, prob'ly, um, *encouraged* him to never return." He chuckled.

R.J. was a huge black skinhead. He was six foot three and so mountainously muscled that you could almost hear his crisp white undershirts whining at the strain of holding him all in. I know most skinheads espouse some racist leanings, but R.J. didn't care. He liked the clothes. "I like to look clean," he'd say. We never got it on; our brief but colorful friendship was during my sexless, pre-hot-sauce era. Even though we were strictly friends, he called me "the Goddess." I loved it. Plus, he made me feel small.

One evening we were walking arm in arm, laughing at something or other when some skinny guy walking by, spat at our feet, and said, "Fucking nigger lover." And kept walking.

"What? What fucking year is it?" I yelled, and started to turn around. R.J. held my arm tight, and turned me back forward.

"Nah, nah, fuck that guy. I'm walking with the Goddess." He later said he knew the guy and not to worry about it, so it was forgotten, until weeks later.

"It's R.J., Goddess! Can I come up?" his voice crackled through the intercom.

"Sure!" I buzzed him in, and he stumbled through the door panting and laughing.

"Oh, my God . . ." He could barely catch his breath from his laughing. He leaned his long, heavy body against my door and laughed.

"What . . . *what*?" I started to giggle, too. He leaned over, shaking his head. He propped himself up on his knees, his face stretched around his joker mouth. He could barely talk.

"You, you remember that, that dude? Oh my gaw . . ."

"Who, what dude?"

"The dude . . . The . . . guy said 'nigger lover', that skinny dude." He leaned his heft against the door, nearly composing himself, panting.

"Yeah, yeah . . . Come on, R.J.! Whahappened?" I leaned over, too, and put my hand on his shoulder. The laughter, at that point, was just making more of itself. No way was it going to be this funny. "Sorry . . . uh . . . man, so, I seen him down by Tompkins an' he starts talking shit, and, so, I hit him right?" More laughter. "And . . . and . . . oh, my GAW! I guess I did it too hard . . . cause . . . cause . . ."

"Come on, you're killin' me, man!" I laughed.

"His eye came out!" Tears streaming down his face, he pretty much "bwaaa-haw-hawed" at the floor. I felt my face drop in an instant.

"His eye . . . ?"

"C-came out! Oh, my god . . . and . . . and . . ."

I stood up straight, trying to imagine what else will he think is funny, and how the fuck can you punch someone's eye out? "Eyeballs are *big,* man! It was like . . ." He made a squishy noise and gestured his hand to one of his sockets, suggesting something the size of a wet plum burst from the guy's skull. I couldn't swallow. "Can I crash here tonight? It just happened." He was finally calming down but still wore a huge, dopey smile.

"Of course, sweetie."

"I gotta wash my hands. Thanks, Goddess! Oh, my gaw . . ." He shuffled into my bathroom and I heard him lose it again over the running water.

I didn't have the heart to tell him that his story was not funny *at all,* but I let him sleep on the floor next to my bed. In the morning we had pierogi at the little Russian café on my corner, said "See you later" to each other. I don't think I saw him at all after that.

"Emergency phone call for Storm Large. Storm Large, please call the admissions office. Emergency phone call," crackled the intercom in school. I was in the library, in the basement of the academy, brushing up my Shakespeare, and jerking off.

Mom. Shit.

She must be dead again.

I hadn't talked to the Banks since they had encouraged me to not be around them anymore, so I was surprised when the receptionist in the admissions office told me to call my grandmother.

"Your mother's in New York. You should see her," said Mrs. Banks.

"What's she doing here?"

"I had her hospitalized at (insert name of famous mental hospital) and signed her up for electroshock therapy," she said.

What? "Um . . . I'm sorry . . . what did you say, Grandmother?"

"I signed your mother up for electroshock therapy. ECT. They say they're getting great results with it, and your mother says that it's what they recommend since they've finally figured it out; they know what's wrong."

"You are out of your fucking mind. You are going to let your daughter fry . . ."

"Don't you talk to me like that, young lady. The doctor said . . ."

"Fuck the doctor and fuck you."

Click.

My brothers and I always felt that the Banks blamed us for Mom's troubles. But the fact that Grandmother Banks signed Mom up for some draconian, head-frying treatment wiped away any guilt associated with them. I didn't know much about ECT then and I still don't, but in my mind it was like the electrical version of blood-letting.

It killed me, a little, to think of my mother's childlike body being strapped down with wide canvas belts, to have God knows how many volts of juice shot through her, popping and sizzling through her sad little melon. Her five foot two body arching rigid, jumping against the restraints, choking, and making spit bubbles around a rubber mouth guard.

She was in the hospital in New York for a few weeks, but I never went to visit. I had told her, and everyone, long ago, that I would never set foot in *any* hospital for *any* Mom reason *ever* again. I was doing well on my own. I had stumbled, and was still lost, but I was away from her, and the me that had started acting like her. I wasn't about to have her sudden proximity suck me back into her movie.

I stuffed all the guilt and fear into a corner and let New York drown out the rest.

My brother John did go see her. He later told me he was glad I didn't. He described it as though he was sitting with an old fuzzy grape someone had taught how to mumble.

As we went into final exams, it started to hit me that I was going to have to go home, as there were no prospects for me in New York. I was pretty sure I sucked eggs at acting in everyone's opinion, and the only singing people wanted me to do was music that sucked eggs, in *my* opinion.

Final exams at the academy were, naturally, performances. My music final was to sing "Bali Ha'i," from *South Pacific*: A low, sad promise of a faraway land you could escape to. A siren call to leave your shitty life and languish in orchid-scented sunshine. My class had to get up one at a time and sing their bit, get their grade, and sit down to watch the rest. As my fellow singers got up one by one to perform, the combination of their maudlin music and the growing knot in my chest about leaving New York started to get to me.

As my turn was approaching, I had to run into the bathroom

several times to splash water on my face and slap myself, to stop welling up like a girl. Crying completely cuts your vocal range in half, and if I was going to drag my sorry ass back to Southborough a loser again, I was at least going to be a loser with her very first run of straight As.

My turn. I stood at the piano. "Mos' people live on a lonely island . . ." I began. So far so good, I'm not sucking. Close your eyes, breathe, all good, you got this. "Caught in da middle of a foggy sea . . ." My dad just wants me to do well. I want to make him proud one day, and he loves this song. "Mos' people long for another island, one dat they know they would like, to be . . ." The tears started. That winging ache in the back of my throat stretched around to my lips and water shimmered across my lower lids.

Fuck. Keep your eyes closed.

"Bali Haaaiii will call you . . ."

I managed to hold in my tears until the very last Bali Ha'i, and then a single tear traced down my cheek. Perfect, I thought . . . dramatic, yet controlled. I opened my eyes to see half my class weeping and my music teacher rising from his seat at the piano, eyes shining, to bang his hands together at me, heaving, "Yes. YES!" I promptly lost it and fled from the room.

A plus.

My acting final was an interesting piece in which I played the dead sister to a girl conflicted about life, death, and the drama that unfolds between the two. I was the singing narrator, the invisible observer slash commentator. I got a stunning final grade and wild applause.

Mom, who had been released from the famous shock-therapy hospital just in time to make a spectacle of herself at my graduation, was in the front row of the small theater. She shot up out of her seat at the precise moment when the show was *about* to end, yet her sudden lurch upward would snap a few necks in her direction. Just as my lungs were expelling the final moments of sound in the show, the big finish, the closer, all eyes and hearts on me, the dead girl . . . my mom managed to scream *"That's my baby girl!"* before falling onto the lap of another parent, one tit in her hand, "Whooop! Oh, heavens!"

The academy's graduation ceremony was in a nice, cushy theater in the West Forties. Graduates would walk up on stage, people would clap and nod, diplomas handed out, then the newly anointed degree holder would walk the rest of the way across the stage, pageant-waving. That one trip across the boards would be many of our first, and most of our last, footfall on any Broadway stage.

I wore an expensive, sequined minidress my aunt Bitsy had bought me as a graduation present, but my hair was in a wet ponytail and I barely had time to put on makeup in the cab uptown. My name was called; there was respectable applause and nodding from my classmates and those in attendance. I walked across the stage, chubby, pale, and sparkling. In my head, I looked like a homeless person who had stolen a dress from a showgirl to wear to the unemployment office. I took the diploma from the school president, thanked her, and smiled. People clapped. As I walked the rest of the length of stage, I heard my mom howling again from the wings, *"Yaaay, Stormee!* Whooops! Oh . . . ex-*cuse* me! Oh! That's my baby girl!"

She fell again outside the theater.

While she was talking very loudly to my classmate who had helped her up, I hugged my dad. "Dad. Mom is, she's fucking . . ."

"Taking over? Yeah, I know." He smiled his squinty smile, crushing his cigarette with a twist of his foot.

We looked at each other and, in a moment, I completely understood my father. He knew all too well the madness and sadness I was running from. I was too sensitive to fashion myself with an invisibility cloak, or use the locked box of bad feelings trick. That's why he let me run. There were many sleepless nights for my dad, wondering if the phone would ring and it would be *me* in the ER instead of his crazy wife. However, even though I scared the crap out of him, he let me run because it was the only thing I could do. He would have run if his conscience had allowed it. His insides were elsewhere, surely, but his person stayed, numb and tethered, with a vow to protect and love and all the hogwash that comes with the traditionally ingrained, Episcopalian, Baby Boomer mind.

As much purposeful fucking up as I had done, I always swore that, one day, I would make him proud. And in that moment, I realized he always had been; he was just waiting for me to be proud of myself. I had astonishingly lived, schooled, and worked in New York City, on my own, and not only hadn't died, I actually had done all right.

I was twenty-two years old.

CHAPTER TWELVE:

SF, HEROIN, AND THE MOST TERRIBLEST JUNKIE EVER!

Heroin in twenty pages.

Or, confessions of the most terriblest junkie *ever*.

I had no good reason to move to San Francisco, other than my buddy was driving across country to go to school there and wanted help driving and some company. There is no better way to get yourself to hate another person or get them to hate you, than to stick yourselves in a packed Honda Civic to hurtle yourselves a few thousand miles for several days. But it was a free ride, I had a place to crash in this new, uncharted city, and it was the farthest point I could drive to, away from almost every stupid mistake I ever made, without needing a passport.

Two days before we left, I packed two Hefty bags full of clothes and belongings, and went into the living room to sit with my dad.

"I'm not coming back, Pop," I said to the television we were both watching.

"I kinda figured." He sighed, and handed me a small box. Inside was a gold St. Christopher, inscribed on the back, "Bali Ha'i."

Now, my family isn't religious, but we were firm believers in St. Chris.

When traveling, one should *always* have a St. Christopher around one's neck, on their person, or, at least, in the vehicle. He is the patron saint of safe travel because, as my grandmother, Neeny, would tell it, "He spirited the baby Jesus up onto his shoulder, and forged a raging river."

The drive to San Francisco took three days, during which I made a mental list of priorities.

Stop eating again.

Get laid.

Find an agent.

One was easy enough, as I had no money or job prospects. Two was also pretty easy, as a new girl in town is almost as hot as one that's moving away. The third one was tricky, though; in my estimation, the only pretty I was, was pretty chubby. So I'd stop eating, get a job, find someone to screw, *then* find an agent.

Priorities.

I got dropped off on Dolores Street and met my new roommates—a couple of trust-fund fashion brats from New York who would screw all day, hide out in their darkened bedroom, and go, almost daily, to Western Union to pick up scads of cash wired to them from one or both of their parents.

Right around the time I started looking for a new place to live, I had fucked, roughly, twelve guys in a little over a month and took a meeting with the agent in town who had the biggest ad in the yellow pages.

"Well, you're pretty," he said after looking at my headshots and résumé.

On the wall of his small Market Street office were headshots of, supposedly, his clients. One I thought looked like a guy from a Fritos ad. "I mean, you have a very pretty *face*."

Slumping in my chair, trying to look hungry, I sucked in my gut and bit the insides of my cheeks to fake some bone structure. "See, the thing is, you're kind of *big*."

"I lose weight really fast, I just had to gain some weight, recently, because my doctor told me, well, I was, you know, *anorexic*," I said, a little too loud.

"We don't want you unhealthy, Storm." The "we" he was referring to, I assumed, were all the pretty people in the headshots. "And, besides, it's not your weight I'm referring to. You are bigger than most male actors. Do you think Tom Cruise wants to get up on an apple crate to kiss you?" My cheeks popped out from between my molars as I laughed. I imagined Tom Cruise as a pocket-sized Pez dispenser person.

"Is he *really* that little?" I chuckled. The agent didn't even smile.

"No. *You* are that *big*." Ah. He swiveled his chair to face out his window. "Really, all I can see for you is if, I don't know, someone is looking for a warrior woman who rides in on a zebra to kill the men."

"Is there anything like that right now?"

"No," he said in a way that sounded like *goodbye*.

Xena was still a few years away and across the international dateline.

As I left the agent's office I saw a sign in the elevator that read, "$500 a week!!" I followed it up and discovered that I could put my acting degree to good use by selling people subscriptions to the *San Francisco Chronicle* on the phone.

I didn't take any other meetings, or even look into other agencies. But why should I? He said exactly what my head was saying to me. He and his gorgeous, multiheadshot wall said "You're big," but he *meant,* "You're nothing, you won't go anywhere, you are fat and ugly and stupid and . . ." I already *knew* that to be so. Even though I would never be successful, at least I wouldn't be *wrong.*

Then I met Billy the genius.

He looked like Lenny Bruce, smoked unfiltered cigarettes, and was the best guitar player in the world. I knew this because he said so, and he was a genius. He was so amazing that he stayed in his room all day tracking his intricate guitar music, and never played in front of people, because he knew he'd blow their minds.

He was brilliant and haunted, and he wanted to hang out with *me!* An amazing haunted genius wanted my company? I must not be *that* fat, ugly, stupid, or suck that bad after all.

When he admitted to me that he had gotten himself addicted to heroin, *accidentally,* well, I was so honored. I decided to help him. He saw me as sweet, naïve, and lovely, so I figured the best way to get him off smack was to show him how ugly it was.

By doing it myself.

A lot.

I sure showed him, because in no time we were bickering over lumps of black tar heroin in his stinking flat. I was blotchy and swollen and scared to leave. But I wasn't a junkie. I was in love.

Heroin is a sneaky, sneaky bitch.

She's like this mysterious girl you meet at a party, everyone is intrigued by her, but she only wants to talk to you. She lights up when she sees you and pulls you into an intimate exchange. She is achingly beautiful, strange, and, as you get closer to her, you find she has a fascinating dark past. She makes you feel loved and safe and untouchable. Special.

The more you go to her, however, she starts to go a little gray. She doesn't light up anymore when she sees you, and the harder you try to bring back that light, the colder and more distant she gets. Soon you can tell she's sick of you and your whining, she obviously wants to be somewhere else, with someone, *anyone* else, someone more interesting, stronger, and not so fucking needy.

I was a terrible addict. When I say "terrible," I don't mean I was a super hard-core, shooting up in my eyeballs, trick-turning, gold-tooth-selling junkie, I mean to say I was a loser among real addicts. I could still sort of eat, I kept my apartment, and, though I called in "sick" a lot, I never lost my job.

I never shot up. I'd cook the tar (called "chiva") in a spoon with water as if I was, but instead I would just snort the hot, dirty liquid with a straw or a broken pen. The shit was nasty, too. Chiva tasted like a combination of Easter-egg dye, coppery blood, and fresh throw up. I would gag and heave and throw up every single time I used, but I never officially ODed. My heart never stopped and I never went to the ER to get the adrenaline shot. Suffice to say, I was not a real junkie. *Real* junkies are always almost dying, constantly. I was light-years from being a hardcore addict. I only got addicted as a sad side effect of trying to get my real junkie boyfriend to love me.

Loser.

Any addict worth their chips would call me a *chipper, poseur,* or a *tourist.* Looking back I call it *junkie lite.*

I don't know if Billy ever said he loved me, or if he was even remotely kind. We had sex sometimes, but I would really just be waiting for him to care about me, or act like he did. Of course when we had plenty of dope, we had good times. He was ecstatic when I gave him some China White. He kissed me and called me his sweet girl.

One time, we were at the pay phone on the dying lady dealer's corner. We were about to call her, head down into her basement studio, and get our handful of balloons, when a badly disguised undercover cop got in my face, hissing obscenities and trying to come across as a crazy homeless guy. Had I not been so startled, I would've laughed at him.

Billy fixed his bugged icy eyes on the man and stared him down, silently. I stood at the phone booth waiting for this idiot to scram so we could call the dealer. Billy stepped intently between me and the cop, still staring, creepy and hard. My heart did a tiny bump in my chest . . . was he protecting me? Finally the undercover stalked away muttering his pretend nonsensicals but we had to drop it and leave since we had clearly been made.

Later, Billy pushed a man who innocently walked into me and shouted, "Don't touch my girlfriend, motherfucker!" The man staggered backwards with his palms towards us in the universal "Hey, hey, I'm cool, I'm cool" pose, stammering surprised apologies. Billy finally unlocked his eyes from the poor guy and we continued on our way to his place. When it's feeding time, junkies get pretty cranky, and Billy could be downright scary mean at times, but he called me his *girlfriend*.

We had two main dealers. One was a dying woman in a filthy basement apartment on Market Street; the other was a married couple who would deliver. I really liked the married couple; the guy looked like Carlos Santana and the woman looked like a sunken-eyed seventies actress whom you've seen in everything, but whose name you can't recall. They fancied themselves musicians, so they would always bring some home-recorded demo on a hissing cassette tape. The music was terrible, but if we sat through the agonizing twang and inane drivel of junkie lyrics, and made a sufficiently big deal over them, they would, sometimes, bump us a bonus, usually in pill form: "Honey, take this twenty minutes before you boot up and you'll feel like you went through a wall."

"Wow, actually that sounds terrible."

"You won't know what hit you. You'll fucking love it."

And I always did.

When I was high I felt like a rock star. Like I had already accomplished my dreams and everyone adored me. I felt famous, but, most important, I felt loved. That was the drug's greatest trick.

One night Billy recorded me on his four track while we were wasted. It was a Billie Holiday song, "Lady Sings the Blues." She was a *real* junkie and she was amazing. I sang a breathy lilt into the microphone, high as a kite, thinking I, too, must sound amazing. Later Billy took nude pictures of me wrapped in a black lace scarf. I felt beautiful and doomed.

Later when I heard the recording, sober, I could hardly believe what I was thinking. Flat, mush-mouthed, and out of tune, I sounded terrible, like a warped kid's record. And the nude photos? Woof. They looked like pictures of a moon-colored narwhal, hauled out of a sea of sweaty cheese using grandma's funeral veil.

Whoa.

I have no shame in admitting I am incredibly vain. My vanity has saved my ass, many times over, especially with regard to drugs and alcohol. Remember heroin chic? Those numb, bony girls, languishing across fashion spreads with their priceless milky flesh sucked in, drum tight, across long, chiseled bones? Doing heroin was going to make me look like them, right? I was going to look like an expensive, bisexual vampire cat from outer space! Yeah!

Yeah . . . no. I was ugly. My visage was more heroin shit than chic. I mean, you'd think vomiting and lying around all day would make you more attractive, but you'd be wrong.

My flesh was Elmer's Glue-colored pizza dough peeking over sweatpants. My skin was puffy and spotted and my hair was a matted red mess. It's safe to say that, had I been even remotely as hot as one of those smacked-out models, I'd have stayed on drugs and died in gorgeous, skinny squalor.

I figured it was definitely time to stop when I started seeing demons and thinking about killing myself. My spirit was looking down at me, literally and energetically. Pissed, mortified, wondering when I was going to get out of this half-life.

Then there were the demons. Pointy shadowy things, I could only see them out of the corners of my eyes. They would point at me, rocking and shaking in my periphery. I couldn't hear them, at first, but I knew they were laughing at me.

Towards the end of my half-life, I smuggled some China White heroin back to San Francisco with me from a trip to NYC. I put the packets in a condom and tucked them inside me for the plane ride. Billy always got the first taste because he always made the score. But this was mine, so I did a bunch of it by myself, alone in my apartment. He'd get some later.

I sniffed up a healthy line out of the first bindle, and hit play on my stereo. When I was high I loved to get lost in music, become the star, the object of desire, and all my ugly would melt. This particular day, I was David Bowie, living as Ziggy Stardust: beautiful, bones, glamorous, misunderstood, and . . . and . . . lost . . .

I began darting, in and out, through a thick cloud of prickling panic when I found myself slumped in front of the stereo. I had been jet-black gone for half the album. I focused my eyes through my loose, gooey muscles; the CD counter was at track five.

"It ain't easy, it ain't easy, it ain't easy to get to heaven when you're going down. . . ." I did too much. I can't . . . stay . . . hot coffee vomit spurted out and splashed onto a newspaper on the floor. My mouth was stinging.

I came to a few times. The music was loud. I would peek at the little track counter on my CD player.

If I make it to track 11, I'll be okay.

"Time takes a cigarette . . ."

Open your eyes. Stay.

". . . and puts it in your mouth . . ."

Awake. Get a smoke. Open your eyes, Storm.

". . . it lingers . . ."

Open your eyes.

". . . then you forget. You're a rock 'n' roll suicide."

Track 11, "Rock 'n' Roll Suicide," a funny song to live to.

One of the smartest things I did at that time was speedballs. Doing speed mixed with heroin you could stay up and feel the high. The best part was not being able to sleep at all, having panic attacks and hallucinating. It was *smart* because it was such a hideous way to exist that I finally decided it was time to leave Billy and get clean.

Billy and I had started this little game whereby we would buy some dope together, get high, and then he'd start some ugly fight where I would usually end up leaving in tears, leaving him with the rest of the drugs to himself. Great game. He'd always win, though. He was a genius, after all.

There's nothing quite like a rape to put things into perspective.

The rape was technically my fault, thus making it more heinous.

One night, Billy was in a rage. We hadn't slept in days and he was obsessing over a complicated guitar track he was laying down. I was wasted, smoking and listening to the cacophony of his screaming guitar, trying to look supportive. In between takes he would cuss, kick something, rewind the tape, and then go again. Some of his ranting started to creep my way: "You stupid fucking waste of skin. Get the fuck out of my life." He was trying to get me to leave. I pretended not to hear him.

I wanted to tell him he was brilliant. Amazing. What a totally unrealized genius he was, but I was fading. It wouldn't have worked, anyway, my flattery, he would have seen right through it. Much better to go completely blank in general so that his verbal and musical assault would just fade into dream or nightmare background music. Billy might then get bored or tired, and leave me alone.

I spaced out staring at his half-open bedroom door, waiting to disappear, when she walked in.

There were weeping red black chunks torn out of her huge, lumpy gut. Her flesh was a flat gray, like a dry shark, but wobbled with every step and hitch of her gurgling laugh. This corpse of a dead, bloated whore staggered towards me, her arm swung in a loose, accusing point at me. She had red, matted hair like mine and dull bulging eyes, filmed over like those of an old fish. Her livery smear of mouth opened off center . . . opened and closed but the sound that I heard from her was the sound of Billy's repetitive guitar riff, screaming, accusing.

My lungs swelled with ice water, and my skin prickled to a bristling itch as I was hauled upwards by my own shouting, "What the fuck do you want? WHO ARE YOU?"

The whore demon was gone; All that was left was Billy screaming at me how I ruined his take, his life, you cunt. My heart popped woodily against my sternum. I panted and coughed and was suddenly aware of being very cold and damp. Billy's screaming faded in my world even though it went on. I lay back down and tried to get comfortable.

Perched on a lamp over my head was a shadow demon. I looked right at it. It looked right at me. It was sooty and pointy and dust-bunny dry, and in the sweetest voice inside my head cooed, "You know, if you were dead, you would not feel this way."

"Fuck you," I said.

"No. Fuck. You," It giggled.

I shot up and swung my tingling feet to the floor. Billy smoked at me, his huge, bug-lamp blue eyes hateful. He was holding his guitar still but the room was still loud, the guitar amp crackled and buzzed, threatening serious feedback that would rip the air to pieces.

"I . . . uh . . . I gotta . . ." I couldn't say *go*. I didn't want finality. As lame and mean as everything really was in that place, I wanted someone, anyone, to be there. Even if they hated me. And if I made some permanent-sounding declaration, and he listened, took it to heart, and never wanted to see me again, it would be my fault. My heart hung from itchy threads begging pathetically for Billy to say, "Don't," or "I'm sorry," or *anything*. He just stared at me like I was a permanent disappointment. I pulled on some clothes, slowly, in case he might want to stop me from going off into the dark and cold. When he didn't, I skulked out.

On the street, in that biting, spitting cold that is a specialty of San Francisco Februaries, I would find a place to crash. I had done it before. It was around one in the morning and folks would be closing up the bars on Haight Street soon, people would be headed home and one of them would let me tag along.

I ran into an acquaintance on the street. She was cute, older than me in years and miles, but she had an easy laugh and pot at her house and of course I could crash with her.

Thank god.

At her apartment, she couldn't find the pot but she had some crappy wine I started to guzzle. Maybe she had painkillers? No. I was going to go from clammy to a trembling pile of fucked in a few hours, so I just drank. When the sun came up, I would get back to Billy's, back into his stinking graces; maybe there'd be some chiva left.

The little apartment was very warm. She went into the kitchen to get some more wine and came back wearing a filmy slip.

"You know, I really like my body," she said, jutting out one pale hip, handing me the bottle.

Uh oh. "You're totally pretty, yeah," I said. My teeth were starting to hurt. She pat her hands down her sides.

"Yeah, even if I gain weight, I still have this," stroking her hands around her small waist and outwards from the ample curve of her ass, "see?"

Her words stretched out. She had a strange, dry lisp that was creeping into her mouth, as if she were talking through a stiff, permanent, wide-open grin. She was on something. Coke? "Here," she purred, taking my hands to stroke down her sides, "I've always wanted to kiss you."

Just a safe place to crash.

I let her kiss me and I tried to reciprocate.

"I want to taste you," she said. Ugh. I must have been so filthy and smelly. When was the last time I even bathed? And was it before or after Billy and I fucked last? And when the fuck was the last time we fucked?

Even in this unwelcome sexual encounter I concerned myself with whether or not I was going to be yummy? I would have felt sexier had I been flung over a bar toilet in the middle of a plosive intestinal event, reacting to some shit Chinese food. *How the fuck did I get here?*

Whatever drug she was on made everything I did (precious little, if I'm remembering correctly) just fine with her. She scratched and bit and made a big scene about how she was gonna fuckin' come, yeah!!!!

Ugh.

Naked and stinging, I crawled into her bed and faced the wall with my back to her. She slid under the blankets and fiddled around with me from behind while I stayed dead still.

I'm asleep. Get bored and leave me alone.

My skin crawled all over, but I wasn't shaking yet and there was a purple hint of morning in the apartment. In no time she will be unconscious and I will get the fuck out of there . . .

Keys in the door?

I'm staring into the wall, my ears growing hot from aching towards the sound of someone coming into the apartment. Tossing keys onto a table. Jacket coming off, the flumping sound as it gets tossed onto the floor. She is in bed with me but isn't moving. Footsteps into the bedroom then, *"Hmmm."* It's a man's voice making a what-do-we-have-here? hum, a happy surprise. Then, a shirt being pulled off, the slip and leather squeaks of a belt being pulled open, big boots thumping off of big feet, then a zip of a fly and jeans. I could smell the salt and deodorant and cigarette funk of skin in close proximity as he crawled over us pulling the blanket down to reveal a she, whom I am guessing was his girlfriend, and a naked stretch of unsuspecting me, a new girl.

This *must* be his apartment because I am now paying rent to his cock. This is what I had to do. I was sitting somewhere in my skull, arms crossed, with a mix of pity and pissed-offness at my sad-sack existence. Twenty-two years old and I'm blowing another random dude, not for a semblance of affection, not for drugs, not even because he was cute. I never even saw his face. I drew my aching mouth around this stranger so I could stay somewhere warm.

The girl is suddenly awake and screaming: "What the? Don't assume you can . . . you can," she was screeching at him, slapping at his naked torso. He let go of my hair. I flopped back onto the bed and froze.

"Get out!" She slapped him out of the bed.

"Agh! You crazy bitch! A'right, a'right! Fuck! Ow!" He was trying to get his clothes off the floor as she smacked him on top of the head. She threw herself out of the bed to continue verbally assailing the guy into the living room. I braced myself for what might happen after the guy left. She was now awake and in a complete state of meltdown.

I'm asleep.

The door slammed open then shut, the shouting stopped, but her dramatic sobbing rasped in the next room.

I'm asleep.

She screamed something and glass smashed. A bottle? She padded her way back into the bedroom, moaning and crying.

I'm asleep. I'm asleep. I'm asleep.

She sobbed and keened in bed next to me, tried to hold me, but I was a dead heap. I am asleep. After awhile she finally wound down and blacked out. I was crawling and starting to shake a bit, hard to say if I was sick, or just in shock at the utter catastrophe my life had become.

When the sun came up, I got dressed quickly and quietly. Scraped a pile of quarters off her dresser and took the bus down Haight to my apartment.

I had my own room in a flat, catty-corner to Billy's. I never had my keys with me because I was always at Billy's place, but I lived with a nice couple. She was a gorgeous mom-to-be, who worked for an organic juice company, and he was a handyman who sold speed on the side. I knew they'd be home and awake by now, so they could buzz me in.

As I stood on my stoop, waiting for the buzzer to open the gate, I looked up the hill to Billy's door. He was probably high and asleep. No idea where I was and not the slightest inkling of a shit did he give about it. Neither had I, obviously.

Later, alone in my drafty bedroom, the sick came over me, and I remember thinking, *Whoa, this is bad. Not nearly as bad as I thought it was going to be, though.* Like that desperate, quaking skin wave before a bad case of food poisoning, just a little while longer here and it will all be behind me.

My stomach felt suspended in a sick, cold gel and the thunkathunk of my heartbeat sent waves of sick through it and down to my sweating bowels. Just a little while longer though. Home stretch. Atta girl, almost there.

Then it got worse.

Each itchy hair scraped out of every oily follicle, stiff and splintered across every aching stretch and fold of skin. My face was stuck in a dry heave "ugh" around my dried, fat tongue that sat in my mouth like a pantyhose toe stuffed with bark dust. I shook on the bathroom floor, clammy, spooning the toilet. Out of the corner of my tearing eye, I saw the demon staring from lip of the tub. Long, dark fingers folded around its knobby knees, beetle-black eyes flat, emotionless, superior.

Gotcha.

At some point, I no longer had to choose between cleaning up my own balsamic diarrhea, or foamy puke. Both my ends were endlessly leaking and spurting, but were now shooting blanks. I somehow smeared my damp body down the hallway into my bedroom. It all gets foggy from there, save for the pain and the humiliation.

Trying to get into my bed was a nightmare. Anything that touched me sent a crazy acid-splash sensation that shocked my nerves. Satin, worn raw silk, even a baby's breath would have felt like electrified razor wire. My skin felt like it had been burnt crisp and I was smeared with rancid peanut butter and piss. I stank, and everything hurt.

Adding to that agony was the bone-aching ocean cold that my walls and windows did nothing to keep out. Blankets weren't enough of a barrier between me and the cold, so I pulled whatever was around from the floor to cover myself: towels, jackets, and dirty laundry. I must've looked like a sick, milky slug, some hollow-eyed larvae of a huge, meat-eating moth, all slime and twitching under my dank cocoon of rags.

All I wanted was to go to sleep and wake up better.

Junkies pray a lot, I think. They pray for an easy score, they pray for money, and not to get busted. I just wanted to be knocked out. So I prayed. Hard. To God, even.

God, please let me sleep. Knock me out, or kill me, please, God.

I was sure I wouldn't know the difference between sleeping and dying at that point, I just wanted out of my body and brain. Even my tears stank, leaking out of me like cheap salad dressing.

Then someone got into bed with me.

The bed shifted under their weight and a warm, bodily presence pressed into my back. I turned quick and blinked through the dark behind me, gone, like a blown-out birthday candle. There was a soft hum in my ear, like a fan in another room. "Please come back," I said into the dark.

Please come back . . .

The warmth flowed back into my bed, surrounding me. My shaking calmed down and my breathing evened out. I was warm, softening; the edges were blurring and fading.

I soon fell into a sweet, purple sleep. When I woke up again, a few days later, I wasn't better, but I was on my way.

It wasn't long after that the phone rang.

"Stormy?"

"Mom? Hi . . . hello?" I don't know how my mother even had my number, or what she was thinking when she called. But she called at around the exact moment I could form a coherent sentence.

I didn't tell anyone, for a long time, about my run-in with heroin.

It was too embarrassing. I know some people knew what was going on, but once I was clear of Billy and the Demons, nobody brought it up. I especially didn't tell anyone in my family, I hadn't even been in touch with them for months, my mom for even longer.

"I just need to know you're all right," she said after an awkward silence.

"I'm fine, Mom. I'm fine."

CHAPTER THIRTEEN:

LOUDER THAN GOD.

A lot of performers, famous, infamous, and anonymous, get into drugs as part of their job. Truthfully, there are plenty of drunks and drug-addled perverts in every vocation, but for some, it's a prerequisite to be high in order to be creative. Like the drugs will make them a subversive, freewheeling genius, or something. It doesn't help that a lot of people think that all *good* art comes from an altered consciousness. It's a tough argument, because so many artists were and are totally fucked up, yet produce some outstanding stuff. However, you might be able to take the drugs away from the artist and the art would still be cool. To put it another way, you could take a talentless hack, give them the best drugs known to man, and they'd still suck.

⊂≯↖

Bone straight, or chemically twisted, it's a crazy fucking job.

What's it like to do my job? First and foremost you have to love singing or playing, writing, practicing, and performing. You have to love it more than anything and feel like total crap if you aren't doing it. You must also hate money, in the beginning, and enjoy pouring your guts out to strangers in dark bars, who may or may not give a shit. You have a handful of minutes to get them to notice and listen. Bottom line, you have to try to get them to love you. Otherwise you are just so much hot air in the dark. A lot of young singers ask me how they can get where I am. *Where I am* is, in truth, a dismal failure, by music-industry standards. I've sold tens of thousand of records throughout the years, charted exactly once on Billboard, have one video out there, can fill a three-thousand-seat theater in my hometown and two- to five-hundred-seat theaters in some different areas in the United States and abroad. On paper, to most major labels, that's pretty grim, but I am fiercely proud of these accomplishments. I am mostly proud of the fact that I have only been singing a slinging inappropriate banter as my singular income for the last seven years or so. And I have done it all as an independent artist. How I got here was nearly two decades of slogging through bars, clubs, bands, and towns, hiring and firing booking agents, managers, publicists, and hangers-on, following the yes, and trying everything, even if it looked or felt weird. Everything you experience today is part of the story tomorrow.

But a creative life is tailor-made to make drug addicts out of the weakest of us, musicians especially. We're up late at night, sleeping most of the day or traveling, often with shitloads of downtime and ample opportunities, as well as motivation, to get loaded. Oftentimes, musicians start to get all fucked up on drugs to enhance and prolong the sensation of being, basically, a rock star. Most of our awake time is spent in rooms full of booze and intoxicated people who act as though we possess some magic that will keep them young forever. These are the people who buy us drinks or offer us drugs to keep us hanging out with them after gigs.

Sex. Drugs. Rock. And. Roll.

Maybe it's because I'm dyslexic, and see the world all twisted and backwards, but, music got me off drugs. Pat Benatar, specifically.

I got asked to sing Pat Benatar's "Heartbreaker" with a band called Louder Than God. I was still kind of a mess, and looked like a pasty slice of ass, in my opinion, so for my first time on stage in San Francisco, I wore a big, black, zipped-up hoodie, covering up my puffy maggoty limbs. It was their regular Sushi Sunday gig, a free-of-charge rock-and-roll night at a club on upper Haight Street called the Nightbreak. There were usually two or three decent bands, cheap drinks, and sushi, fresh off a cart in the back. It was always a good time.

It was towards the end of LTG's set. The club was packed, it was sweltering inside, and as soon as I stepped out, the lights cooked through me and my breath went sunburn dry. My colon shimmied in my gut and I saw black roses blooming in front of my eyes, swooning in the heat. I held a huge breath, waiting for my cue, and stepped to the microphone. With the black hood pulled over my head, I looked like a bummy punk rock dude, or one of the sand people from *Star Wars*. Nobody knew I was a girl until I started singing.

"Your love is like a tidal wave, spinning over my he-eh-ead!" I gripped the top of the mic stand as if it were my lifeline. My eyes squeezed tight, streaming with stinging sweat tears and black eyeliner.

I threw my head back and the hood popped off. I was burning out of my clothes, everyone was on me, with me, in me, the room, the roar, the floor shot away, I whipped off the sweatshirt to shouts of "Yeeaah!!!" from everywhere.

"You're a heartbreaker, dream maker, love taker, don't you mess around with me. You're a heartbreaker . . ."

I had sung before in public, sure, but this . . . I was out of my body, spinning, soaring, surfing electric, fuck yeah, I jumped around in my head, free of all of my stupid everything, throwing the devil sign back at myself: Yes! Yes! Yes! Yes! There you are! There. You. Are.

The crowd was one thick flesh mass of rags and damp heat. They crushed forward, going completely apeshit at my last screeching note. The lead singer said, "Thanks, Storm!" and started his last song as I hopped off the stage into the crowd. Swept into arms and hugs and shakes and shouts of "Fuck, yeah!" "What's your name again?" and "Ho-lee shit, woman, you rule!"

I felt pure glory, like I had won some sports thing, an undeniable exultant, fist pumping victory. I was flying out of my boots, tingling along every inch of me, completely high. *Really* high, as opposed to the high I had known. No hiding, I was slapped pink and raw, bitten and torn open. The stuff in me that made me feel ugly and alone, sloppy and crazy, I scooped out of my insides and screamed it into the faces of strangers who ate it up, spat it back, and howled for more. These people plugged into the nobody me, this big nothing girl, and got some kind of epic charge out of me, the me who was too busy screaming and burning to hide.

Out of all the cheering and compliments, three different guys asked me if I was in a band and if not, would I like to be in theirs. One in particular was a beautiful heavy-metal guitar player boy with huge tattooed arms, dyed black hair, and pretty blue eyes, and it was rumored he had a dick like a peppermill.

Want.

"I'd love to be in a band with you. Sure."

He was a supersweet guy. He put the rhythm section together before we broke up. It would have never worked. The peppermill rumor was true and . . . ouch.

My music career began rather biblically. The part of the Old Testament where everyone begats everyone? I screwed Johnnie Peppermill. That band was called Mind Power. I stop screwing him, he quit. Then I start screwing the bass player. That band was called Flower. Bass player goes crazy, gets fired, so I start banging the new guitar player. That band was called Dirty Mouth and that one stuck for a while, seven years. In those seven years, I learned how to be in a band.

We wanted to call the first band "Flower" after the skunk in *Bambi*. The best way I can describe our sound was a Zeppelin meets Jane's Addiction. I was a great singer, loud and adventurous, but my lyrics? I'd love to say that everyone's first attempts at songwriting produce cringe-worthy twaddle, but I'd only be trying to make myself feel better. I had filled stacks of journals with embarrassing poetry and long litanies of why doesn't anyone love me and wah-wah-wah-ing. So, my first go-round of lyrics were these precious, maudlin run-on sentences. My early songs were about my mom, heroin, and racism, terrible song material. I'm not exaggerating when I tell you they were really lame. I took myself so seriously, but it still felt incredible. To sing loud into a microphone with my eyes closed, surrounded by my own amplified voice riding on top of booming bass and distorted guitar, ducking around the huge drums like a salmon hopping up a raging river. I was full and empty and present and absent all at once, anonymous but sparkling in the loud, electrified bashing. I knew I wasn't very good, but I knew I would get better. Most important, I was finally sure I was exactly where I was supposed to be.

Once we had ten songs or so, we decided to play our first gig.

The Boomerang was across the street from the Nightbreak and was not considered terribly cool. Anybody could play there, really; it was a perfect venue for our first time. We asked our friends to headline since they could pull some bodies in, so it was The Firemen (featuring members of Mountain Pig and Freak Show Ho Down) and Hate Holiday.

Flower was a mishmash of twentysomethings with no real unifying style. Elroy was a lanky boy of mixed race who had a sweet smile, braids threaded with bright yarn, and looked great with his shirt off. Fu was the drummer, beautiful and black with short, spongy dreads that sproinked in every direction. D was a white thrash-metal enthusiast and totally sober. He was very cute and wore whatever and felt whatever about it.

The whole day leading up to my very first gig with my very first band was about finding something to wear. In San Francisco in the 1990s, there was a new hippy glam resurgence. Bell bottoms, platform shoes, and huge cartoonish sunglasses were considered rock 'n' roll. I got into it as best I could, but I was still so fashion traumatized from being heavier, and having no idea what was cool. I decided to wear white nightgowns and army boots. Perfect. Comfortable, yet grounded, no one would accuse me of trying too hard or thinking too much of myself.

I was absolutely terrified until sound check. Once I had my feet on stage and felt myself facing forward with the guys behind me and at my sides, all I felt was an urgent, "Let me at 'em."

We had a decent-sized crowd for our first time, not packed, but respectable. My dad was even there with his girlfriend Mari. Their relationship was a successful matchmaking effort made by Daphne, Mari's daughter Heather, and me: We had seated the two attractive, yet stubbornly single, people together at Daphne's wedding, a couple of years earlier. They shared a dance at the reception, went on a date the next night. To wrap up their first date, Dad ended up at Mari's house for a beer, and never left.

Besides our family and friends, most of the other people were there to see the other bands. While we played, though, it was clear that for my handful of minutes on stage, those people were mine.

Flower's first gig was unremarkable in the sense of anything amazing happening. But, inside, I felt all my gears shifting and locking together, my machinery in sync with itself. We only played for half hour or so, but I already knew I was going to do this until I couldn't anymore. This was it, lights, noise, screaming and me, hoovering up the attention like I used to suck on drugs or men or anything before. I was throwing myself at people and they threw back. I was going to die on stage or die trying.

There are many theories about making it. You need to get signed is a big one. Signed to a major label was the addendum to that. You need a demo, a great manager, you need to play LA, you need to tour, you need *songs*. Hit fucking *songs*. Then you get on the radio, and . . . and . . . and.

The fairy tale goes like this: An A&R guy would come see a show, listen to your demo, then convince his label you were the next big thing and next thing you know, you and your band are drunk on Cristal in a huge tour bus having a spitball fight with torn-up hundred-dollar bills.

I instinctively knew that the major label thing wasn't going to happen for me. In my laymen's understanding of how the machine worked, a major label would peel off a chunk of cash to spread *around* you, giving you a little bit but making you feel like hot shit. You stand there with the ten bucks they just gave you, because you're awesome, and you feel terribly important. You don't realize right away that you're now on the hook for about one hundred large plus interest, and *maybe* they try to sell your records for you.

Nirvana was the biggest band in the world at the time, and they had started as a college radio phenomenon. The labels caught on long after the kids did. Little has changed since then. In fact, the Internet has made it so much easier for artists to get to their fans and fans to find the next cool thing without all the annoying hard sell of commercialism. Major labels are all but dead these days, and reality television has more star make-or-break power in the short attention span theater of today's pop culture. And radio? The only thing happening on radio is oldies, right-wing ranting, and a shitload of Spanish-speaking church programming. Enduring musical careers are now, as they were then, about the enduring love and loyalty of fans.

And boy, did I start collecting some crazy fans. The Good, the Bad, and the Ugly crazy.

The Good: We played once or twice a month in San Francisco, and my whole life would become about those gigs. I'd have total stage nerves, palpitations, and vomitous sensations before every show, but I would knock myself out like it was the last time I'd ever open my mouth in public. My abject terror was that I would suck, have a shitty show, or lose my voice.

This wasn't just any gig. We were having our CD release party at Bottom of the Hill, a club in Potrero Hill in San Francisco. I was

159

overly excited and chatty, chain smoking and drinking coffee. I stayed at the club after sound check to eat the free greasy-spoon dinner they offered. I had a pint of black bar coffee and a veggie burger with real bacon, plus jalapenos and Tabasco sauce.

Then I took a nap in the dressing room.

When I woke up, my throat was raw and my voice was a little froggy, so I had some Maker's Mark and about five cigarettes while I put on my makeup and my just-for-the-CD-release-party-rubber shirt. We swagger on to the stage to howls of "I love you!" and rowdy cheers, I cough through the first few numbers expecting to warm up and smooth out, enabling me to rock for two hours. Three songs into the show, my voice evaporated. I stood, sweating in my makeup and rubber shirt, in front of four hundred die-hard fans, couldn't make a sound, and went into a full, nightmare panic attack.

The band started the song "Beautiful," a fan favorite. I opened my mouth and prayed, "She was over the top, and out of control, she ran away when she was thirteen years old . . ."

Only air and squeaking bleats of sound creaked out. I told the band to stop, hot tears were mixing with the sweat, I choked out an excuse, "I got something in my throat, I'll be right back . . . the band will . . ."

The packed crowd unanimously roared "No, don't go!

"Do you guys wanna sing it?" I croaked.

Everybody nodded and cheered.

I looked at the band, my guitar player started the opening strains, I held out the microphone to the audience. "She was over the top, and out of control, she ran away when she was thirteen years old . . . but she had her feet on the ground, and nobody pushed her around . . ." The audience sang the whole song. They sang the heck out of it, too. It was beautiful.

LOUDER THAN GOD.

The Bad: O, Canada! She's quite a bit bigger than the United States, with about a tenth of its population. So, when you're driving across country, say, heading west from Toronto to Thunder Bay and beyond, it's a minimum six-hour drive to the next semblance of a town. In between are kilometers and kilometers of woods, farms, hockey stars on billboards, mangy bears, and road signs threatening moose violence. Oh, and a butt load of Tim Horton's. And for you Americans who haven't been up to our neighbors in the north country: Tim Horton's is like a Dunkin' Donuts that just gave up.

We were packing up after a show in Regina, Saskatchewan, headed to a gig in Calgary, about a seven-hundred-and-fifty-kilometer drive. Kilometers might be smarter, but they aren't as big and powerful as our American *miles,* so we were looking at about a four-hundred-mile drag to the next gig. It was the tenth or eleventh gig on a three-week jaunt, and we were all tired, dreading yet another long drive through the bucolic, nonstop, Groundhog Day landscape.

I was in the dark parking lot behind the club, dumping some crap into the van, when I turned and found myself face to face with a human Pez dispenser. She was pretty, or had been once, but she had that faces of meth thing creeping in. A pipsqueak of squirrely sinew, her energy blasted off her with such trembling waves of whacko, it gave me goose bumps. She was also so suddenly close she could have tasted me or started stabbing me with the pen she held in her hand.

"Hi! Oh my *god* you rocked *so hard*! That was *awesome*! I want you to tattoo me!"

"Hi. Um. What?" James was suddenly there and flanked me, so I relaxed a bit. "You want me to . . . ?"

"Tattoo me!" Turns out, she wasn't holding a pen; it was the point of what looked like bouquet of dentist's tools duct taped

161

together. With her other hand she hauls up her tank top, "Right here! I won't even feel it!" She drew an air circle over her skinny torso, indicating a rather large area across her pronounced rib cage.

"Um. No, I think that's, ah, a bad idea. Unsanitary. You know? You want some stickers?" Behind her in the dark was a looming figure, smoking, not coming too close but paying attention to the exchange. He was hanging back, but I knew he was with her.

"She'll totally do it," it said from the shadows.

"I'll totally do it! Totally! It won't hurt. Come on!" she begged. "Just your name, I want your name on me!"

Without fans, a musician is only a bunch of hot air in the dark. Most fans are simply glad to see you live, but some are hell-bent on meeting you, touching you, having a moment with you, and then there exists that special handful, who wants to peel you and dance around in the moonlight wearing your skin. This pasty little wastoid didn't want to hurt me, but she clearly wanted me to hurt her by helping her getting tetanus. I felt pretty powerful and powerless at the same time.

Moreover, I wanted none of it, but I wanted to treat this bony little bag of bad decisions sweetly.

"What if I just write my name on you with a nice, soft Sharpie marker?"

"Oh. OK. Oh! Then I'll just get it tattooed on me! Awesome! Totally do it!" Everyone watched as I pulled out a black marker and she held her shirt up her side. "Do it big, too! Yeah!"

Maybe, because I was tired and punchy, I decided to draw my name so huge on her little body that she would never get it needled in. When I was done, it essentially was a half corset. "Yeah, awesome!"

The S was central on her sunken belly, then the T, then the O was the size of a football from the top of her hip bone to her armpit, then R then M up and down her back.

We all admired my penmanship, as it was very neat and well balanced.

My thinking was that she would never be so fucked up as to get that tattooed on her. Because that would be insane.

"There you go, sweetie. You hungry? You look like you could use a sandwich."

"No way, I'm so fine! I'm totally gonna get this put on me right now! You rock!" She scuttled back to the looming man and they both hopped into a car. "You rock!!!!" she called from the passenger side as they pulled out.

"You know she was serious, right?" James said.

"No way, man. There's no way she'll get that tattooed on her. That's just nuts."

"Uh huh," he said as he went into the van.

The events surrounding the Lilliputian loony tune showing up at our next gig, four hundred American miles and one dozen moose warnings later, are a might too nasty for my beloved editor to allow here. They involve a maxi pad, a boot, and a mix of fake blood and feces that all end up in someone's mouth. However, I can tell you, James was right. She was serious.

The Pipsqueak Pez Dispenser not only showed up, but she pounced on stage and grappled a quick, bony hung onto me. As she went into a stage dive, we saw the loose corset of bandages peeking out from her tiny half shirt.

The Ugly: We toured a bit of the West Coast and were drawing larger and larger crowds in San Francisco. My favorite place to play was the Paradise Lounge on 11th and Folsom Streets; it was my home away from home. I loved the place so much that I swore the day the Paradise Lounge closed down would be the day I moved away from San Francisco for good.

We had a gig at my beloved Paradise this one night when I was sick as a dog with a hideous lung infection. During a vocally dramatic moment on stage, something hacked out of my infected lungs and caught in my windpipe, kicked up into my throat and stuck there, wildly itching and choking me. I dropped to the floor as the crowd and band lost it simultaneously, the band going through its usual smashing sound wall of booming chords and huge cock wagging, the crowd surged forward, caught up in the electric crushing and my crawling across the floor, heaving.

"ROCK 'N' ROLL!!!" A girl screamed from the front. The crowd thought I was having some epic moment onstage where I couldn't even handle gravity, and I must have been convulsing because I was so fucking into it! "Yeah, Stoorm!!!"

I couldn't breathe and I couldn't stop hacking. The thing, whatever it was, was in a perfect spot to gag and choke me at the same time. I'd inhale to get a blast of air behind it and a tickling trail of its slime would thread back down my esophagus making the cough harder and more desperate. I had about nineteen seconds to get whatever it was out of me so I could get to the verse.

I had a roll of toilet paper on stage, in front of the kick drum, for blowing my nose and wiping up my fever tears. I grabbed a heaping wad of it and shoved it against my mouth and with a mighty retching "Haaack!" up came the offending item out of my mouth, ker-plunking into the ball of toilet paper. I looked at it through my bleary eyes and was stunned. It was a grayish, sea-anemone-looking glossy lump of something with protrusions sticking off it, laced with a light bit of blood. It was bigger than a lima bean, had some weight to it, too.

That's when I saw her.

She was a slip of a boy girl, short hair sticking out in spikes from under her baseball cap. She stared hard at me, looking serious, as she extended her hand towards me in a gimme-that gesture.

She wanted my loogie.

I shook my head *no*. She nodded, *oh, yes*. I shook my head again, *No, no, no*. She nodded with matching vigor. Horrified, I slowly held the tissue wad out to her. Her eyes lit up as if I were handing her a ball of folding money that would save her life. She snatched it out of my hand and held it in both of hers with a look of purest adoration and gratitude.

Afterwards, I crumpled in my drummer's car, shaking and sweating with full-on flu, I waited for the rest of the band to come out so I could go home. In my fevered fog and twanging aches, I chuckled at the thought of someone building a shrine to my goo. On the way home, my drummer marveled at the level of crazy some of our fans were getting. I couldn't talk, but I smiled in agreement, knowing that I must be doing something right.

CHAPTER FOURTEEN:

The "GOTCHA"

"**Y**our mom is a good person; she just isn't acting like a good person these days."

That was the gist of the letter that my dad sent to each of my brothers and me, over the winter of 1999. It was right after the night when, during a horrific blizzard, Mom got hold of my brother Henry in one of her, "I don't know how many pills I took, I think I see a tunnel . . ." calls. Henry, with a sick baby at home, had gotten in his car and nearly killed himself skidding through the blinding snow. He reached Mom's apartment just in time to see her being wheeled, high and blathering, into the ambulance that beat him there.

It was a diplomatic way to say ignore your mother, she doesn't care for anyone's comfort or even safety when it comes to her bullshit dramas. We already knew Dad felt that way, but it was striking to see him actively convey anything out loud about her. Mom had been long dead and buried in Dad's head box, he never uttered her name nor made any reference to her since what seemed like forever, but since one of us almost died again at her behest, he had to speak up.

He was preaching to the choir, as far as I was concerned. Mom had been dead to me so many times that it was easy to toss dirt on that grave again. Mom had pulled the "Gotcha" on me not too long before I got that letter, so, let the dead-to-me lay.

The Gotcha was a neat trick Mom would pull whenever I got soft. I'd start feeling a need to reconnect, try to have a relationship with her. This would happen every couple of years. She would be sweet and open, seem healthy, changed, and would sprinkle my heart with tickles of hope for a new beginning. I love you, too, Mom. Then within twenty-four hours there would be a medical meltdown, a tear-soaked snit, some heinous drama that I would find myself in. Like a bait and switch, but instead of a con man showing you a real watch, then switching it for the bogus one, I would be shown a mom to reach for, only to be given a screeching infant who wants to rip your heart out.

Around a year after getting away from Billy and the Demons, and I was on a healthier path, I came back to Southborough for a visit. Mom was in a halfway house. It had been a year or so since I'd been in touch with her, but I figured I was in a much stronger place, so I went to see her.

The word was that Mom was doing much better in her new situation, but I was, as usual, cautious, not wanting to get my hopes up. Slowly, as we chatted, though, I relaxed a bit. She seemed all right. We had tomato soup with grilled cheese sandwiches. I met her new cat, and Mom appeared to be relatively balanced. She seemed to be doing well. We made plans to go to the mall the next day to shop and have lunch. "I'll give you a call and then come pick you up, say noon?"

"Sounds great, darling."

Shopping and lunch, like real mothers and daughters do.

Around noon the next day I call her up. "Hey, Ma! You ready to hit the mall?"

She's sobbing. "I-I . . . I'm sorry Stormy . . . p-please don't yell at meee!"

"What happened? Are you okay, Mom . . . what's going on?" She sounded desperate, like someone had just let her have it, hurt her feelings, thrashed her with a car antenna. "Mom?"

"Pleeease!! I know, I know . . . I'm sooorry! Don't be mad at me, I'm so sorry!"

Then I heard another voice in the background, "Suzi. Hang up. You don't have to listen to that." My blood instantly torched ablaze. *Gotcha.*

She was putting on a fucking show for someone in the room with her. Selling the old "my daughter is so mean to me" ploy. I smashed the phone and raged through the house.

Fool me once, shame on you, fool me forever . . . ? Well? Getting your heart broken and then to have your broken heart bamboozled over and over, over bullshit, made me nuts. She could get me on the phone every once in awhile, pretending to be dying or getting some sucker social worker to call me, sounding like a doctor, telling me she was dying. But I rarely spoke to her. So, when I got my dad's letter, I didn't need to be told again.

Somewhere in the spring of 2000, my band, now called Storm, Inc., was in the studio, tracking some new material. Though I was still stubbornly independent, the band was doing really well; we were more professional, businesslike, and tighter.

The songs had improved as well, so I was excited to record them. This particular time in the studio, however, for some reason, things just kept going wrong. The tape would get fucked up, the guitar couldn't get signal, speakers got blown. It was a friend's studio, far from a slick operation, but we were still paying for the time that was ticking by, getting us nowhere. I was getting pissed.

Finally, when it looked like we were good to lay down some basic tracks, the power went out. The whole studio went black.

"Fuck!" I shouted in the dark, kicking something near me.

"Don't worry, we'll get it!" said the engineer's voice, but I was already headed out to smoke a cigarette and fume in the parking lot. I went to get my smokes out of my bag and saw my pager.

There were three 911 pages from a 617 area code. Massachusetts plus nine one one equals Mom. My pager had voicemail so I checked that first. A stern woman's voice was telling me my mother was in the emergency room and was in dire condition. "This is so-and-so from such and such hospital, call me immediately." According to the time stamp, the voice message had been left only fifteen minutes earlier.

The studio was dead, but the phone in the office was fine. "Such and Such Hospital," chirped the woman who answered.

"I'm looking for So and So, this is Storm Large returning her call."

"Just a moment." Hold. "She's gone for the day."

"She only called me fifteen minutes ago and said it was an emergency."

"I'm sorry. She's gone." I suddenly felt an old tired rage twitch its whiskers in me.

"May I ask, is this person . . . a *doctor?*"

"No ma'am, she's a social worker."

A fucking social worker 911 paging me, sounding like a doctor, again to tell me how my mom is in dire condition, again, and she needs to talk to me . . . why?

My hatred for some of these self-important social workers was hard earned. I imagine it is probably a thankless gig, lots of snooty doctors looking down on you, stinking bodily fluids looking up at you waiting to be sopped up and sanitized. Mom's doctors were starting to give her the "Yeah, right, lady" treatment, so she went to work on the second string for their sympathies. She even got one to pretend she was a therapist when I came to visit her once.

"You're mother's in here," she said holding the door open to a small room near the nurse's station. Once inside she closed the door heaving her porky self onto a table. Then, with her well rehearsed therapy voice, asked, "So, Stormy, tell me why you hate your mother."

"Huh? Mom?"

My mother sat in the corner opposite me in full regression, staring at a spot a foot in front of her jumping knees, squeezing both her two balled up hands between them. She bit her lip like a kid caught in a lie, awaiting punishment.

"Suzi, do you have anything you'd like to say to Stormy?"

Mom shot a miserable glance up at me then back to the floor, "I think Stormy is a-angry w-with me." She pouted and struggled.

"S'cuse me but are you even a doctor?" I said to porky so-not-a-doctor.

Just then mom wailed, "DON'T HATE MEEEE!!" She then threw herself onto the spot she was staring at to bang her head against the floor at the cadence of her chanting, "Stu-pid! Stu-pid! Stu-pid!"

"GO GET SOMEONE YOU FUCKING IDIOT!" I screamed. She ran out. Nurses ran in. I left. Mom stayed.

After that, whenever a social worker would call on my mother's behalf, I would redline into fuck you very much in zero point suck it seconds.

"Is there a Suzi Large in the hospital somewhere?" I ask, trying not to spit the word *fucking* between every *fucking* word.

"Please hold." Holding, smoking, hating, waiting.

"H-heeellooo-ooo?" Mom putting on her weakest voice.

"Mom?"

"Hello, darling." Her award-winning, "I'm so weak but I will sound strong for you, dear," voice.

"What's wrong, Ma?" I ask, knowing exactly what's wrong.

"Are you alone?" *The windup* . . .

"Yup. All by myself. What's up?"

The deep sigh, *aaand the pitch,* "I have bone cancer, darling."
The crowd goes wild!

"And I want us to handle this like a family. I don't want to do what Bitsy did."

My aunt Bitsy, Dad's big sister, had kept her diagnosis a secret from her kids until it was certain she wasn't going to win the fight. I thought it was a classy move by a brave lady. Mom, on the other hand, would have loved nothing more than to see us tearing our hair out every day, beating our chests at her bedside to the rhythm of beeping hospital machines, until the fake cancer took her.

"Wow. That's terrible. Okay. Well. I gotta go, Ma, talk to you soon, okay?"

"Stormy. Are you all right?"

"Fabulous. You just worry 'bout you, okay? Great, talk to you soon. Buh-bye."

Christ.

At home, my voicemail was full, fake doctor so and so with the fake emergency, a call from each brother and my father. I called him back.

"Hey, sweetie."

"Hey, Pop, what's up?"

"I think your Ma is in pretty bad shape."

"No. I talked to her. She just has bone cancer again."

"Actually, sweetie," sighing, "the doctor thinks it's actually something this time. They might need to do surgery to find out what it is. I think John is on his way to the hospital to get some more answers, but stay by the phone tonight, okay?"

My father actually sounded concerned. *Is this real?* I got off the phone and grabbed a beer and paced around my apartment

Is this real? She's dying this time? All my rage and bitterness toward my mom did its old slow turn on myself, stinging me like a scorpion committing hara-kiri.

Great. Now who's the asshole? She's going into surgery and . . . what if she doesn't wake up? What were my last words to her? Some jackass typical "I don't care about you, Mom, die from whatever you want" comment. Christ. Now she'll die alone, under anesthesia without anybody who cares about her in the slightest, to hold her hand or show her there's something worth waking up for.

When my phone rang again, it was my brother John.

"Hey, Sis." The familiar gruff voice of my big brother sounded exasperated.

"Hey John, what the fuck . . . ?"

"I went to go see Ma and she's all propped up in a room like a princess. She's fine, she just has a friggin' tummy ache."

". . . and bone cancer. Don't forget the bone cancer. I hear it stings." We both laughed our old callous laugh. "So she's okay?"

"She's *fine*. She just wants attention." He sounded disgusted. "I'll call you when I hear something, if I hear anything."

Whipsawed again, like a doll being shaken by a frenzied dog. My temper spiked. "You know what, John? I actually don't think I ever want to know anything about her at all. Unless she's dead, okay? I'm serious. I'm calling Dad and Henry and telling them the same thing. She has yanked us around for the last fucking time." I told my dad and left Henry a message. "I don't even want to even know if she's in the hospital, or sick or *anything*, ever again. I only want to hear about that woman if she's dead, and I only want to hear it from you guys, a real fucking doctor, a coroner, or a cop, okay? I love you. Good night."

Angry and smug again I plopped into bed with my sleeping boyfriend, and tried to relax enough to sleep. Somewhere after three-thirty in the morning my phone starts ringing.

I walked through the dark to get the phone.

"Hey, Storm, I'm sorry." It was my brother Henry. ". . . but, how close to death should she be?"

Gotcha.

CHAPTER FIFTEEN:

PENULTIMATE GOTCHA, GOOD-BYE TO THE QUEEN OF PARAPLEGIA.

Mom had an aneurism. She was in surgery for seven out of the ten hours it took me to get from San Francisco to Boston. She barely made it through the operation and was in a very delicate state when she came out. I couldn't see her until the following morning.

Dad told me that the surgeon had to go pretty deep to get to the aneurism that threatened to stop Mom's heart, and they had to cut one or two major cables to get to it. According to Mom's doctor, she was now paralyzed from the waist down. She would never walk again.

I didn't know what to expect as I pulled up to the hospital. The news that morning was that Mom was recovering. She was still very delicate, drifting in and out of consciousness, but they were allowing family to visit.

Mom finally had something wrong with her, for real. Not terribly glamorous or exotic; paralysis brought on by a blood clot. Rather common for someone written up in a medical journal for winning the multiple personality lottery.

But this was real. I wondered if she would be happy about being paralyzed, then quickly cursed the thought from my head

She will never walk again, you asshole. She will never be able to skip down a beach or get up to hug someone and she will now, really, have to deal with something fucking difficult and sad, mostly on her own . . . with and without an audience.

Then I saw her.

The small hospital bed she was in looked like an extra small bed for kids, but it still dwarfed her. She seemed so flat and weightless, like the mummified remains of a twelve-year-old boy. Her toothless mouth hung slightly open, her dry lips drooped in over her gums. Her cheeks and eyes deeply sunken around her baby skull. Her skin looked powdered . . . a talc-dusted mummy doll stuck in a hospital bed to play "Operation."

"Where are your teeth?" I asked the tiny creature that was supposed to be my mom. She didn't answer. She was out cold.

I pulled a chair next to the side of the bed. There was a painful-looking I.V. needle stuck into the tissue-thin meat of her hand. An ugly bruise spread out from under the white tape that held it in place. After years of drugs, smoking, and inactivity, my mom, at fifty-seven, had the flesh of an eighty-year-old, with the stringy veins that come with it. I imagined there had been a ton of poking before the big needle hit pay dirt, so her hand looked beat to shit, lying on the blanket, purple and defeated. I slid my palm under her tiny mangled paw . . . it was cool.

"Mom?" Her lids fluttered but her face stayed stone.

I thought she'd be dead when I got there, so when she wasn't,

I couldn't help but puke up thirty years of random anger and hurt that had shook in my head the whole way to this moment. She was unconscious, but I let her have it.

"I don't hate you, Mom. I never did. All I ever wanted was for you to be okay, so I could have a mom, I needed a mother, but ended up with a sick kid. You, *you* were the child. You made me feel like I could not only never love you enough, but I was *why* you were in so much pain, that it was me making you sick. Do you have any idea how much that hurts? To love someone, to fucking miss you so much, more than you could possibly imagine, and feeling like it's me making you sick? That it's my fault you're gone? Meanwhile you're telling everyone around you how much we all hate you, and hurt you? That is fucked up, Mom. You're not sick. You're sad. I have no idea how to love anybody, least of all myself. And no one can ever love me, either, because they know I'm broken, they can smell it on me, the sick and sad you gave me. But I am not you and I am never going to be. I refuse to end up like this, like you. I won't be the mess you made.

"I realize you're in a coma or something and can't . . . you probably can't even hear me . . . but . . . I don't hate you, I never did. God knows, I tried to, and I'm sure it made being miserable a lot easier believing I did, but the truth is, I love you, Mom. I have always loved you. It just was never enough."

Somewhere along my rant her hand moved. "He-ll-o-oh . . . darling . . ."

Her voice was a painful dry creak. Her eyes opened slightly. Normally, in moments like these, I would roll my eyes at her shtick of grim, hanging-by-a-thread-I'm-so-terribly-ill . . . but I just sobbed.

"Mom, what has happened to you?"

She was so weak it took her awhile to articulate anything. The doctors had pushed a breathing tube into her trachea during the seven-hour surgery. It was out now, but her throat had been scraped raw. "I'm sorry for hurting you and the boys," she said. "I don't know why . . . sorry." She drifted out again as I sat with her a while longer.

Was that real?

She was so heavily medicated that she might have been incoherently babbling. But my heart hoped that it took that much sedation and trauma to strip away all the bullshit and get some real out of her.

"I'm sorry, too, Mom . . . I love you." I kissed her forehead. It was so dry under my lips, like the back of your hand after washing several times with a harsh chemical soap. She was out cold, again, so I whispered goodbye to her, promising to come back.

That evening, having a post-dinner beer with my dad at his house, I told him about the exchange. I asked him if he thought she had meant it. He took a drag off his smoke.

"Sweetie, all that matters is you got to say everything to her. That's all I cared about. I'm sure she heard it . . . it doesn't matter if she *got* it or not."

"I think she did, Pop. She must have. Something is really wrong with her this time." He just smoked and nodded without actually agreeing.

Mom had a heavy round of tests most of the next day and was exhausted, so I didn't get to see her again until late the following afternoon. She was doing much better, though. She had been moved out of the ICU and into a private room.

I ran into one of her doctors as he was coming out and I was headed in. He nodded a hello at me, but looked grim. After introducing myself and thanking him for taking care of her, he looked down and shook his head. "She's never going to walk again. I swear we did everything we could."

"Hey, it's all right, we know you tried . . . wait . . . did you just tell her she's paralyzed . . . for the first time . . . just now?"

"No, but she's been so sedated that I wasn't sure she had really heard it. We offer counseling and rehabilitation here and elsewhere, but I had to wait for your mother to be fully conscious before discussing all of that with her."

"How did she take all that?"

"Your mom took it surprisingly well. I'm more upset than she is, really. She smiled and seemed more concerned with my feelings than her own situation . . . incredible."

I thanked the doctor again, and wished him well as he left. I took a deep breath and steeled myself.

It hadn't even occurred to me that she might not know what happened from the surgery. I was too hell bent on unburdening myself of all my sadness onto my shrunken, near comatose mother. I stood at the door of her room and cursed myself for being so selfish.

Grow up, Storm. If Mom is just hearing that she's paralyzed right now, she might be in shock . . . or desperate. Go in and be strong for her, for a change. She might be freaking out. She might try to kill herself, for real this time, save up her pain meds and . . . then I heard her laughing.

Mom had this musical, girlie laugh, but her throat was still ragged so it was more of a throaty chuckle, but still, somehow, bubbly and light, like lemon soda.

I pushed the door open and peeked in. Mom was propped up in her hospital bed and was chatting on the phone. She saw me and smiled, held up the pointer finger of her free hand in an "I'll just be a minute, darling" gesture. I walked in and sat in a chair facing her while she gabbed.

Her room was sunny and bright. There were a collection of flower bouquets and a few get-well balloons by her bed. Get-well cards stood open like colorful tents on her dresser along with a box of chocolate-covered cherries. The room was sweetened by her lily-of-the-valley perfume. Someone must have brought that to her along with her teeth, because her face wasn't a sunken-eyed voodoo mask anymore. She even had a little more color in her cheeks as she talked excitedly to whoever it was on the phone.

It seemed the doctor was right, she was lucid and alert, even downright chipper. I was trying to decide how to give her my present of Clarins face cream, a fancy brand that I was sure would pull an excited *Oooh!* from her.

I sat in the chair, my hand in my purse, holding onto her gift, and waited. Then I tuned in to what she was gabbing on about.

"It's really remarkable, *I know*. Well, I'm not getting one of those sad old lady wheelchairs, I'm a very strong woman and I will roll that sucker myself. I've done it before . . . yes, with my knee surgery, it's not that bad, really, well, oh, *nooo*, it's easy. We paraplegics have a much more heightened sense of balance. All of the senses, really."

We paraplegics? She was . . . bragging?

"The doctor could tell that I'm incredibly strong, he even said so . . . and he'd never seen a recovery go so well from such an intense surgery . . . I *know* . . . poor thing . . . he's a lovely man."

She was downright ebullient over her situation, her brand-new badge of sadness. *This one people will see! I will cruise around in my shiny new wheelchair, and roll that sucker over all their sore and soggy hearts. Everyone everywhere will feel sooo baaad!* I felt an old animal prick its ears up in me. I heard her say "we paraplegics" at least two more times before I realized I was crushing the box that held her present.

I got up so quickly it startled my mom off the bragging train for a moment. I put the cream next to the phone by her bed. She looked at it, then mouthed "Oooh!" at me, and continued her chat.

"Goodbye, Mom." I kissed her papery forehead. "I love you."

"I'm almost done," she silently mouthed again.

"Me, too." We looked at each other for a moment, I felt tears coming, but also an urge to rip the phone out of her hand and smash it through her sunny, private window.

"You will never see me again," I said quietly.

She air-talked a "Wha . . . ?" to me, midsentence, without skipping a note.

"Goodbye." I left, trying not to run from the room, the hospital, and the planet.

She got me, though, the newly crowned Queen of Paraplegia . . . I had to admit, she got me good.

CHAPTER SIXTEEN:

LOVE, LOSS THE DOT & SEPT. 12

To keep Mom as dead to me as possible, I threw myself into my work. My band had label interest, a big, New York–based management company was courting us, and I had an investor. Kat, a gorgeous, marathon-running mom of four, die-hard philanthropist and supporter of the arts, paid for our album and put us on tour.

It was 2000, and the world hadn't ended, much to the embarrassment of doomsday prophets and those Y2K douche bags. But, just as things seemed to be going well for me, at last, the world blew up. I guess it had to.

We were recording "The Calm Years" and it was going well, the songs and the performances were strong, but my relationship with my band was growing tired. And damn near dead were the feelings between my boyfriend, Michael, and I. Michael had been my guitar player, collaborator, and musical partner for seven years. I still loved him, but we had become like brother and, well, brother. We called each other Dude and felt like band mates who lived together and slept naked in the same bed.

It all imploded when my substitute mom, Rose, died.

Annie Leavitt was number one, Rose was my number two momstitute. She was my rock 'n' roll mom for a few years. She was a painter, a dark and swirly gypsy woman with big soft hips and a dirty laugh. When she got a fat tumor pulled out of her neck, the doctors found it had leeched into and body-snatched an entire vertebra in her upper spine. Thankfully, the surgery was a success and she suffered no nerve damage; she had to wear a neck brace and get about six weeks of aggressive radiation series. But, after her last treatment, she cackled, "Ya-hoo! Gimme a damn cigarette!" It was a new beginning.

Then around Christmas she developed a nasty cough and could only stand up for about five minutes at a time. We talked about taking a road trip somewhere warm. She had relatives in Arizona and I had a big fat van with a bed in the back. We would go after New Year's, when I was done recording "The Calm Years," we decided.

The call came while I was in the studio. Rose was back in the hospital, with pneumonia, they thought. The cancer in her neck had snuck away from the burn of the radiation to make a wet, black nest in her lungs. She didn't even bother with chemo or any other medical option.

I was one of only a few women she wanted with her at the end. I'd record all day in San Rafael, then go back to Sonoma every night, to help out any way I could.

The morphine was a pink liquid Rose dubbed *Marilyn*. "Time for a little more Marilyn, Stormy!" We let her have as much as she wanted, but it wasn't enough to keep her back from locking into spasms in the middle of the night. Her lungs were so packed with cancer, that there was barely a teacup's worth of room in there for her to breathe with. We all took turns sleeping in bed with her, so when a lightning cramp would split her from sleep, we'd be there to rub her back.

About four days before she died, it was my turn to keep the massage vigil. She woke up with a sleepy and miserable sob and I went to work on the knot. She moaned a grateful sound, likely for the company as well as my gentle kneading, and then settled back down.

The room was quiet except for the whir of the oxygen machine and her clotted little breaths. I kept rubbing her back gently, and started to cry. I whispered into her hair "God, Rose . . . I wish there was something I could say. I talk so fucking much but I can't think of even a few words that even begin to describe what your believing in me has done . . . Something you can take with you so you know how magical . . ."

"Aww, fer fuck sake, I'm not dead yet!" she croaked into the stillness.

"You *bitch*! I was totally having a moment."

"Yeah, well, I'm trying to sleep." She mustered a laugh out of the one cancer-free bit of her lung, I chuckled and held her close. "Stormy. You're bigger than what you're doing. Your band, your boyfriend, Michael. They're great, but you're just bigger."

"Yeah, yeah, you're a little biased, lady, go to sleep."

"I'm a dying woman and what I say is gospel." More struggled laughing. "You're bigger."

"I love you, Mom."

"Love you, too, honey."

Right after she died, I drove from Sonoma back to San Francisco, and broke up with Michael. I started couch surfing at friends' houses, my van, and wherever I could between tours. While on a break in Los Angeles, I ran into a friend in a successful band out of Portland, Oregon. He was playing at the Universal Amphitheater and would I want to come to the gig, then party with them at the Mondrian Hotel on the strip afterward?

Sure. I was homeless anyway. Why not be homeless in a swanky Hollywood hotel for a few days, eating room service, playing rock star? My band split back to San Francisco, I stayed. Then it happened.

I had met the man before and there was no connection, but all of a sudden, the air, the temperature, what I had eaten or drunk that day, the pot brownie he ate, the white on white on white linens in the room . . . who knows. All I can say, at some point during the night my heart and all the meat, fat, and gristle around her, went *boom*.

Mr. Whoopass.

I fell hard, harder than ever before. End-of-the-world, teenaged I-would-die-for-you, Prince, "Purple Rain" hard. I wanted to kill him, eat him, set his bones on fire, and fuck his ashes.

We didn't have sex, though. He was married. He told me that he and his wife were unhappy and separating. Yes, it's an old song, not just sung by touring musicians. However, I wanted so badly for his line to be true, I swallowed it whole. And then some.

But, separated or not, I wasn't going to fuck a *married* man. Not at the Mondrian, anyway. Not where everyone who's anyone cheats on their special someone with some wannabe nobody. No. I didn't want to cheapen what I felt to be the kind of life-changing love I was falling into with this man. I was classier than that, so I didn't fuck him until a few months later, at the *much classier* Four Seasons in La Jolla.

If you're going to go ho, go full-on bag, I guess.

We fucked in a mad fever for three days. Afterward, he had to go to Nevada and I had to get back to San Francisco. My band was headed to the East Coast to do a showcase for the big management company in New York.

When we said goodbye in San Diego, we agreed that we shouldn't talk until a clear decision was made about his marriage. Should they decide to split, give me a call, should they manage to work it out, we'll always have La Jolla, and see ya. My body was bitten and bruised, looking like I had passed out naked in bear country covered in potato chips. During the string of shows in Boston, New York, New Jersey, and Philly, the bruises had faded, but I started to feel funny.

My band got back from the East Coast in August, and by that time I was really feeling tired and, just, off, and I was late.

No way.

It happens sometimes when you're on the road, not eating or sleeping properly. I bought a pee stick. The little pink plus sign in the pee stick window said yes.

Fuck.

I made an appointment for an official pregnancy test at the Women's Needs Center, and decided to not tell anyone. But, after a band meeting, I went to Michael's apartment, the same apartment we had shared for years, for a cup of coffee.

"Dude, are you pregnant?" he said, out of nowhere.

"What? Ha-ha. No. God! Why would you even ask me that?" I had tried to avoid people I knew for fear of giving away my condition. Involuntary tears sprang from my face instantly, each one screaming like a cracked-out cartoon character, "Ye-es! She's pregnant! She's preg-naaant!"

"Shit." I slumped in my chair.

"Oh, Dude. Do you know who the father is?" he asked, reaching for his cigarettes.

I nodded.

"Is the father . . . married?"

One nod before the sobbing started.

"Duuude." He sighed a long plume of smoke.

Michael didn't judge me, though I knew he was disappointed. He was a great friend, took care of me, and let me stay there as long as I needed, before and after.

After the doctor gave me the official, "Yes, you're pregnant, and no, you can't stop being pregnant by swearing that much. Come back on the twelfth," I was shown a picture of my ultrasound. I guess they wanted me to think about my choices, or my options, or something. And I did think about it. The little black-and-white picture looked like a dot floating around some cold cuts. The Dot, that's what I called it. Dot.

This wasn't the first time I had seen the Dot; I had been pregnant once before. He was the first man I took up with after I got off heroin. Not only did he not do drugs, he was a drug counselor! Plus all he wanted to do was fuck all day and night. No way! Me too!

He was a stunning male specimen, and that beautiful, demanding cock of his was the perfect kickstand to prop up my sagging self-esteem. I didn't know what a sociopath was and hadn't heard about sex addiction yet. What could possibly go wrong?

About two months in, I started to feel funny. I was exhausted and sore. I could barely keep my eyes open much past sundown. The day I came home from a doctor's appointment, Kickstand was watching porn in my room.

"Hello!" He said with the phoniest happy soundtrack playing behind him, a pile of naked licking girls moaning at him from the screen.

"I'm pregnant." The words fell with a dull thud. "Which one are you watching?"

"Whu . . . ?"

"*No Man's Land Six?*" Awesome." I crawled into my loft bed, five feet off the ground. It had a tiny sitting area below it. Kickstand shot up from under the loft and stared at me, his eyes shark flat.

"You told me you couldn't *get* pregnant."

That's what I had thought, too; years ago, a doctor had told me my cervix had some scarring and my uterus was tilted. If I ever wanted to have children, he advised, I would need some corrective surgery. I took that to mean, "Continue to fuck irresponsibly, young lady!"

"Look, don't worry about it. I got it, okay?"

"Yeah, I was gonna say." He went back to the lesbian orgy on television. Later, he woke me up pushing my legs apart with his knees cooing, "Well, at least now we don't have to worry about you *getting* pregnant."

The day I had that first abortion was one of the most painful, terrifying, and humiliating days I had ever experienced. And, while I lay in my bed, after the whole ordeal, shaking and bleeding into an adult diaper, Kickstand wanted to comfort me. When I say "wanted" I mean to say "demanded" and when I say "comfort" I mean to say "fuck."

When I told him it was a medical impossibility, he said a blowjob would be sufficient and why was I being so selfish?

So, with Kickstand's performance on my mind, I had decided not to tell Mr. Whoopass of my condition. He was doing his thing, being

187

married, and I was doing mine, being a mess, and putting on a happy face while dying on the inside. Mr. Whoopass was a lovely man, and I was pretty sure he loved me, but I was still too terrified to make the call. Michael and the few friends who *did* know were pressuring me to, though. If we were ever going to be friends, they said, I needed to tell him the truth. The truth that I'm an overly fertile idiot? Yeah, I'll get right on that. I knew they were right, though.

During the agonizing lead-up to the twelfth, when the Dot and I were scheduled to part ways, I went on a road trip to see my best friend in Los Angeles. She was a better human being than I had ever pretended to be, and being around her always helped. A stunning, red-haired, former model, who, after growing disenchanted with the shallow fashion world, shaved her head and traveled to Tibet to help a bunch of refugees get to Dharamsala. She went on to the American University and wrote for *Mother Jones*. Later, she taught English in one of the toughest public schools in Los Angeles, but that September, while the ashes of my stupid life were sputtering, she was going to have a small gathering at her apartment in Los Angeles to celebrate her birthday, as well as her rebirth day.

She had been deeply entrenched in studying the Torah, Talmud, the Zohar, and other Jewish tomes, so she could become Orthodox, the ritual of which was to go into a deep pool of rainwater, called a "mikvah," then, blessed by a rabbi, you emerge a brand new human. Wiped clean and pure. God, if only . . .

Why the heck she wanted *me* in her life at that time is still a great mystery to me. I suppose, if you can't be a good example, be a great cautionary tale.

She, too, told me that I should tell Mr. Whoopass about the Dot. I still refused, even though I knew she was right.

My whole six-and-a-half-hour drive from San Francisco to her birthday party in Los Angeles went like this; "Okay, if I can hold my breath until the next speed limit sign, I'll call him. Oooh, bummer, didn't make it. Not going to call him." Then, "If, the next song on the radio is a Rolling Stones song, then I'll call him. Nope. The Who. Not gonna call him."

Finally, pulling off the 101 into West Hollywood, I looked at my little phone and said, "Okay, if he calls me today, I will tell him." We hadn't talked since early August, nearly a month before, and though the conversation was sweet, we had recommitted ourselves to never speak until he really wasn't married anymore.

So, I knew I was safe. There was no way he would call me, until he did two hours later.

"Hi!" he said, bright as morning. After some awkward small talk, he asked, "I was just wondering if you were okay."

My brain churned through the people who knew I was pregnant, and whether there any way or connection to him that he may have heard. "Sure, I'm great!"

"You've just been on my mind a lot and I had a crazy dream about you."

You said if he called today you'd tell him.

"I know we aren't supposed to be doing this, I just, I don't know," he said.

Yes, you do know. I don't know how, but . . . "Well . . . I . . . *do* kind of need to tell you something."

"Okay."

Deep breath. *Do the right thing.* "Okay. Here goes, ahem . . ." *Lie! Lie!* "I used to be a man. There, I said it."

"Wh . . . what?"

He's chuckling! "Yeah, see, a long time ago, I was a hockey goalie up in Montreal. My name was Gunther, and, well, I was amazing.

189

But during the Olympic trials in the eighties, I made this amazing, game-winning save but my cup slipped out of my jock and, you know, wham! Oh, it was awful." *Good, please keep laughing. Please do not hate me . . .*

"Hey, Storm . . ."

"Wow. I feel so much better having told you . . ."

"Okay, okay. What are you talking about?"

Don't tell him don't tell him.

"I'm pregnant."

Shit.

"Hello?" I held my breath.

"I know," he said, sighing.

"You know? How the fuck do you know?"

"The dream I had. You were having our baby. I was holding your hand in the hospital room; you were in labor."

"That's the dream you had??"

"I was awake, actually. It was more like a head rush. I was in the garage working on my car and I stood up from leaning over and, I don't know, I saw it." Great. He's a psychic. He would later have a dream about the man I started sleeping with to get over *him*. "Listen, let me send you some money . . ."

"Absolutely not."

"Come on, I can't be there, so let me pay for it."

"No."

"Storm, please . . ."

"If you can *dream* my address then you can send me money. Look, I'm fine, I fucked up, and I'm paying for it. You go back to trying to fix your marriage and forget we even talked about this."

Bad enough I was knocked up by a married man but to have him secretly mail me his married man's money to "take care of it" just sounded too gross. I wanted him there, I wanted him to come hold me, I wanted a future. Acting tough was my only move.

He turned out to be pretty resourceful and found a way to get me some money after all. He also insisted that, since he couldn't be there, we should lift the no-talking rule. "I need to know you're all right, okay?"

I wasn't all right by the time I got to the mikvah, but I was pretending to be, for the benefit of my best friend and the rabbis who were officiating at her rebirth. Standing in the temple, watching my friend forging a deeper connection to God, I took a shot at praying. I closed my eyes, held my belly, and had a little chat with the Dot. "Hey, I'm really sorry about this, but you can't stay here this time. I can barely take care of myself, let alone another little human, and you deserve better." I then swore to God if the Dot ever returned, under any circumstances, I would bring it into the world and do whatever I could to give it the best life possible. That was the deal.

I closed my eyes and held my belly. The sun was shining and God was blessing my best friend. I hoped God had a little room in his ears to hear me. I opened my eyes and looked down at my big hands on my belly and, for a split second, saw a tiny hand grab my index finger, hold on, then let go.

An hour or so later, there was an earthquake, a small one. Happens all the time in LA, but I took it as God shaking on the deal.

I drove back to San Francisco a day later, feeling even more pregnant and crazy. Crying intermittently, nausea chewing into my guts, then giving way to desperate, animal hunger. My face had plumped and softened and my boobs looked like they were having an allergic reaction to shellfish. I absolutely hated myself. I felt the Dot was good with our deal, and was moving on, but I was still miserable.

I decided I needed one day of silence, of introspection, meditation, and really try to find a little peace with everything. I would take water, some fruit, and a blanket to the beach, sit by myself and stare at the ocean until I forgave myself. The calendar in my head flipped its pages. *What's today? The ninth, okay, driving back to San Francisco today, tomorrow, the tenth, band business, my appointment is the twelfth, so the eleventh. Tuesday.*

When I got home I took out my real calendar and a pink highlighter. I drew a small heart inside of a bigger heart, to mark the day. Tuesday, September 11, 2001.

September 12, I was sitting in the crammed waiting room of the Women's Needs Center, shoulder-to-shoulder with mostly younger girls, the majority of whom were weeping. All of us were staring up at the television listening to the good folks at CNN talk about how those sorry souls were mercifully unconscious or dead before they even got close to the ground. Well, thank God for that.

I looked down and stared at a parenting magazine one girl was thumbing through, "Lose That Baby Fat!!!" chirped the banner across the cover photo of a lithe and tight mommy jogging with her pink-cheeked miracle in an aerodynamic, off-road stroller. I wondered if that mommy was working out today.

"Storm Lang?"

"Large."

"Really? Wow. Okay, come with me, please. "

It wasn't until a few days later that I got my day at the beach.

The news screeched with discovered plots to blow up the Golden Gate Bridge, to sprinkle anthrax out of helicopters, of a Mau Mau style uprising of Muslim extremists. No one was safe. We were at war, and we should run out and get as much fucking duct tape as we could carry.

I walked barefoot through the cold autumn sand. The sky frowned gray and hard like angry old men beating the drums of war. The Pacific Ocean looked pissed off, too, with big, black waves, slapping, judging. I stood, small and bleeding, surrounded by beautiful, terrible, and huge.

I was a scoured and empty wrapper from some cheap candy bar nobody wanted. Not even close to that tall-walking, loud-talking, hard-rocking motherfucker that no one could touch. My fans thought I was a badass, a ninja, and a killer. Was that ever me? Or had I just been in a crazy panic for these last few years, so blinded and deafened by the me on stage I couldn't notice the weak loser I had always been?

It didn't matter. All that I had been was no longer me, anyway. The me I had built out of fear and fuck yous was gone. I sunk to my knees into the sand, cried and was nothing. Prayed, cursed, and apologized and was nothing. Thought about New York, the lives lost, about how the world was exploding, and I was . . . *a girl* crying alone in the sand. Useless. Nothing.

"I am nothing." I said into the wind. Somewhere, another, kinder voice answered from nowhere and everywhere.

"Exactly."

CHAPTER SEVENTEEN:

PORTLAND EFFING OREGON!

I always swore that I would leave San Francisco for good when Paradise closed down. And I was pretty sure that would never happen, the owner, Robin, and his pal and manager, Terry, were institutions in my world. But times were tough for live music.

Times were tough in the city for nightclubs in general. Under Mayor Willie Brown, some fancy, and hastily built, lofts sprang up around and on top of rock clubs and bars. Rumor had it that the zoning in South of Market, where most of these clubs did business, had been changed from light industrial to mixed use.

It's a lot of building code and policy hoo-ha, but the outcome simply was: Rich people bought real estate in and around buildings that housed these establishments, only to be shocked, *shocked* that those establishments, with their neon bar signs and marquees that announced "Live Music," actually *had* live music, served alcohol, and were open late. So, of course, the very upset, fancy new neighbors went about trying to oust the riffraff, the riffraff being musicians, bartenders, waitresses, security, and a ton of other folks who work in the nightclub world, who were there first, and had been there all along. It had always been okay to make a ruckus down there in South of Market. But seemingly out of nowhere, the new, bourgeois dot com kings and queens were having hissy fits and getting clubs shut down. They did this by calling the cops when anyone would take a guitar solo or take out the recycling at three in the morning.

Rose was gone, the management company in New York stopped returning our phone calls after September 11, my band was essentially bust. I hadn't spoken to nor heard from Mr. Whoopass. I was single, homeless, bandless, and didn't have anything keeping me in San Francisco. It was time to look for friendlier territory to park my van.

Funny how the Universe eavesdrops on everything you say, even think, and sometimes delivers it all, in exact detail, to the real world.

My second-to-last gig in SF was in December. I sang a few songs at my friend's birthday at the Café Du Nord. A man named Frank was in the audience. He told me that if I were ever in Portland to come by his club, Dante's; he would give me a job if I moved there. A week later, my sound engineer, El Fay, told me she was going on a month-long tour, and could I watch her house and her dog, Willma, up in Portland for the month of January.

I had toured through Portland a bunch of times in various bands and always loved the wet, wide, green spaces dotted with some city bits. The smell was lush and fertile with tendrils of roasting coffee and smoke. I also loved the crabby pale residents, every one of whom seemed to be in a band.

Mr. Whoopass lived in Portland.

My last show in San Francisco was New Year's, goodbye 2001, hello 2002, at The Fillmore. Not a bad sendoff.

While headed north on the 5, my phone rang twice. One was Terry at the Paradise Lounge. "Come to the club. They're shutting us down and we're drinking the inventory." And the other was Mr. Whoopass to tell me he was getting a divorce and "Oh, you're going to be in town? What are you doing on Friday?"

CHAPTER EIGHTEEN:

THE LAST GOTCHA.

"**D**on't you think you should visit Mom?" my brother John would say, periodically, over the six years I lived in Portland pretending she was dead.

"Nope," was my regular reply, and John never pushed. He was the only one of all of us who kept up with her. He knew how she was, and where she was. Henry was now a father of two and had fired Mom years before. He had tried to let Mom babysit, to let her be a grandmother, but his new wife put a stop to that. There were a few mishaps with bad driving, one involved a lit cigarette ending up in the kid's car seat, and the other was about some chemically induced blackout where she rolled her car after dropping off his three-year-old son.

Nobody blamed Henry for keeping himself and his family a good distance from Mom, after that. Mom would never meet his third child, a beautiful baby girl named Amelia.

John faithfully remained in contact with Mom. I made him promise to never tell her where I was, give her my phone number, or tell her anything about me, and he always kept his word. Every now and then, Mom would give a card to John, to give to me. He would ask me if I wanted it, if I said yes, he would mail it to me himself.

In her loopy girly handwriting, I'd read about how she was, and what she'd been up to. For years, I got updates this way. There was never any begging, just a sincere promise that things were different. "I am so much better, Stormy."

She told me how she had started making beaded jewelry, had successfully lobbied the powers that be at her facility to put in a small putting green for the residents, had begun an annual fundraising picnic with donated BBQ and live music, and how she was really kicking ass from her little wheelchair.

They were brief little updates. They were all chatty and positive. And not a single one of them mentioned how she had to have her leg amputated.

It had happened some years before. Because of the paralysis, she couldn't feel the bone infection from an undetected fracture in her thigh. When the doctors discovered it, it was too late, so off it went.

Her friend wrote to tell me, in an email, how she was doing really well despite her situation, and wondered if I would ever come see her. "She's doing so much better, Stormy."

But I was living in Portland, now, happy, healthy. My new band, The Balls, was becoming a Portland institution in the mere three years it had been in existence. Mr. Whoopass and I were living together. He played bass in The Balls and we had been performing every Wednesday at Dante's, to more and more packed and whacked crowds. We were in demand in Seattle and in San Francisco, and life was good again.

THE LAST GOTCHA.

"You'll be here in August, anyway, you should really think about seeing her. She's doing so much better, Sis," John kept insisting.

I hadn't seen Mom in nearly six years. A long stretch of safe distance, she *could* feasibly be better, but could she really be that different? I am always suspicious when someone talks about how much they've changed; *trust me, you can believe me, would I lie to you* . . . all those words are red flags to me. Red flags with bold, black lettering, spelling the word, *bullshit*.

However, despite the fact that there was a vast, flapping field of red bullshit flags around Mom, she hadn't told me about her amputation. Not once, didn't even tiptoe around it with her one good leg. The Mom *I* knew would have found the closest handicapped accessible rooftop from which to crow, "Stormy hates me because I have only one leg!"

Maybe the rumors were true and she *was* different.

The plan was lunch. Outside on the facility lawn, where I could easily escape if needed. John picked me up at Dad's. We went to Whole Foods to buy some snacks and sandwiches for our picnic, then we went to go see Mom, the one-legged stranger.

She was in the front entrance of the Elms when we pulled up. She sat in her little wheelchair smoking. As we walked up, the woman she was chatting with outside shouted, "Oh! Well, of course, you're Stormy, you look exactly like your mother!"

"Hi, Mom." I leaned over and hugged her in her chair. She smelled exactly the same, lily of the valley and Kool Mild cigarettes.

There were no tears, no where have you beens, no obvious, needy heartbreak, or how could yous . . . no drama. It was nice.

She took us to the common area and the cafeteria, where we met several of Mom's new favorite people in the world. They were all geriatric, brain injured, or doddery in some way, but they were all in love with her. Haggard old faces would light up, shiny gums, or impossibly perfect-looking dentures would gleam wide at her approach.

"These are my children!" she sang to whomever we encountered. There were only friendly hellos, and nicetameetchas. Not one single surly word nor judgmental look our way. It was *nice*.

Then we went up to her room, opting to eat inside. She showed me her jewelry-making table and all her beads. She told me about selling some of her pieces on eBay and how excited she was about her new skill, her new friends, and life in general. She asked me about my life, where was I living, was I married, how old was I now, was I happy.

I nearly laughed at how odd these questions were for a mother to ask a daughter, but after six years, I suppose, things can change a lot. So I shared my stories about music and Portland and what my life was like and she shared hers.

It started to look like John was right, that she really was better. I decided to go back to see Mom, again, the very next day. By myself, even.

Now we'll see what the trap will be. It's been awhile, but I'm hip to this game. What'll the gotcha be?

I was at orange alert. With Mom, there would be a bait and switch almost as certainly as there would be a pack of cigarettes and an ice cube tray of pills. She would be warm, loving, and a mom, then within twenty-four hours, without fail, some terrible drama would bloom and it would either be my fault or my responsibility to fix it. Either way, I was ready for anything.

I bet it'll be some octogenarian friend of hers, ready to corner me like a lion tamer with a walker, clack their dentures at me for being such an ungrateful daughter, breaking Mom's heart like that, staying away all those years, how could you do that to your poor mother?

I went back, tightly wired, middle fingers at the ready.

"Hello, darling!" she sang. We ended up back in her little room, chatting. Friends came by. Tea was made. More chatting about jewelry, what was my favorite color and would I like some earrings? We had lunch in the cafeteria. More people genuflected before my mother, praised her mightily as she smiled over her macaroni salad and said, "This is my daughter, Stormy!" Then the inevitable "You look just like your mother" comments and further praise on Mom's good works on behalf of the residents at The Elms. They did everything but lay fruit at her feet. It was sweet to see her so adored and accepted at last.

Afterward, as I drove back to my father's house, I noted with some shame that seeing her, being with her, was nice. No drama. Not even a whiff of histrionic, make believe, *everyone hates me*'s. It was casual, mature, and uneventful.

Sparkly beaded, mother-made earrings dangled on either side of my head as I shook it slowly. "That was actually nice," I said to the inside of the car a few times. "Crazy."

It was so nice that we stayed in touch. I gave her my number and address and we kept up a correspondence. We didn't talk on the phone much; we mostly wrote cards. Little notes back and forth. Updates and ideas, talk of friends, pets, life, and the weather, only occasionally did we refer to the past, and it was always to emphasize how much better the present was. I sent her a Christmas card that said, "I'm so thankful you are in my life again."

She died the day before it arrived.

There was a yellow sticker on the returned Christmas card that read:

MOVED LEFT NO ADDRESS

UNABLE TO FORWARD

Gotcha.

CHAPTER NINETEEN:

LOVE YOU, BYE....

I hate moving. I'm pretty sure everyone does. They say it is second only to losing a loved one in terms of stress. We've all been suckered or guilted into helping some person move. In my opinion, it is one of the hugest favors to ask of someone. A favor that should be repaid in kind with meals, six-packs, and endless thanks for being such a good friend. Now, I like to think of myself as a good friend (I am also a sucker), so I have often found myself, my car, and my aching back, in the service of someone else's relocation. Some moves were executed under serious duress, too—a rancorous breakup, or a bad roommate situation—but regardless of circumstance, it's always a pain in the ass. However, with many hands and a plan, it gets done eventually, and after all is said and done, you're popping beers, getting thanked and fed while you watch your friend unpack.

Mom had already moved out, but we still had to deal with her stuff. Her apartment was small, more a large hospital room, with very few belongings of her own, but, for some reason, it seemed to take ages. We moved through the process as if we were bugs suspended in sap, struggling as it hardens into amber.

Maybe it took so long because we weren't really moving Mom anywhere. We were only dismantling the place she had lived for five years or so, deconstructing and relocating items. Taking a thing that existed as a whole and spreading its parts out among many others. Mom was setting up someplace else. She didn't need any of this stuff. She was in a duplex, or rather, two side-by-side Ziploc freezer bags.

We had to figure out where her stuff would go, who would take what, where to donate anything else, and how to do it all without completely falling apart.

Henry was late.

John and I stood around the little apartment and tried to make a plan. There wasn't a lot of stuff to move, but it was taking forever. Every time we picked up a box there was something in it that would stop us, and rip open a memory. Some crazy old familiar thing that made images snap in and out of focus in my mind, like remembering scenes from a movie I saw a million years ago. Did I ever *see* that movie or did I only watch the trailer, *hear* about the movie, and make up the rest? There was jewelry, figurines, a wind-up ceramic ballet dancer that twirled around to an unknown yet totally familiar tune. Did I play with it when I was little, spacing out at its little painted features, winding it over and over again? Was Mom there? Adding to the slow-motion effect was the heavy scent of Mom's perfume. It soaked everything in the place. If it were a cartoon you would see the wavy lines rising off everything depicting the stink of Muguet, a cheap, overly sweet lily-of-the-valley perfume that I'm convinced destroyed her olfactory senses. I have vivid memories of choking in the car with her as she doused herself in the stuff before we went anywhere. It could have also been the menthol cigarettes she paved her respiratory system with that kept her from being able to smell how strongly she reeked like a urinal puck.

She had been dead and gone almost a week, but it was as intense as if she were only gone " . . . *half a tick, back in a sec.*"

None of these memories were clear, but they were all rushing into my head in blurry twists of moments and feelings. There were pictures of us everywhere. Us with missing baby teeth, in corny school pictures in front of American flags, us holding dogs and cats now long dead and buried. Pictures of Mom with Dad or with the Banks. Everyone looked happy in the pictures. Were we happy? Where were we all when it was good, and was it good ever?

We dealt with the big stuff first. Her wheelchair and hospital bed were a no-brainer, they went back to the facility. The nurses and other admin personnel in the place came and took those, but they said no to her cool craft station. Her little bead-making table, with drawers and Tupperware cups filled with pounds of glittering beads of every color, her little pliers and spools of beading wire, they didn't want it? To me, this was the essence of my mom's newly found happiness. Well, that and maybe the metric ton of fancy antidepressants and other pharmaceutical fixer-uppers that filled her bedside table and cupboards. But she had really gotten into her creativity at last and found a useful expression of it. She had made so many pairs of earrings, bracelets, and necklaces that adorned the old ladies in her ward, I felt sure someone there would want to carry on the creativity in honor of her memory. I didn't want it, but couldn't imagine throwing it away. So, I snuck it down into the craft room just by the cafeteria.

Okay, it wasn't technically a craft room but it was a room with chairs and a television and no authority types to say, "Um, what are you doing? You can't leave that there!"

"It's a craft room *now*. You're welcome," I said to no one, as I headed back up the elevator to resume the move.

Mom's clothes would go to St. Vincent de Paul, but, for some reason, Mom's bedding could not be donated. I heard a nurse say it was a biohazard, but that sounded like bullshit to me, it was probably just superstition. More than likely considered bad juju to make your bed with sheets of someone recently deceased. I threw them into my rental car with the clothes and kitchen things bound for St. Vincent's.

All of Mom's pills got flushed. It seemed a terrible waste; some, specifically the name-brand antidepressants, were probably expensive and could have been used by someone in the facility. But again the folks in charge there said no. As I dumped and flushed, I imagined there must be some happy-ass junkie rats floating around on hospital turds, without a care in the world.

John and I cleaned, separated, and packed. Henry showed up at last and looked stricken, but in no time hup-twoed into captain mode and started directing the tasks. John and I would normally be irritated at our ex-cop brother assuming authority, especially since he was late, but we hadn't gotten anywhere. So we followed his lead. Henry liked order, and was good at it.

While we were packing, one by one, many of the elderly residents came by. Some hunched over walkers with tennis balls on the feet, wheelchairs, and electric scooters, some walked on their own, with difficulty, but Mom's door was the only place they would get to pay their respects, and they all came. The old-timers, who could talk, would say hello to us, then stare sadly in at where Mom used to be with her girly laugh and easy hug. They would sigh, lean their brittle bones on the door frame, and talk to us about Mom. They all had sweet stories of friendship, how kind and helpful Mom was to them with this or that. All day, a nonstop parade of ancient bodies, determined to impress upon us how important and special she was, and how she was going to be so terribly missed.

We offered each one of them something of hers: jewelry, books, silly little ceramic creatures, and no one took a single thing. "Oh, she already gave me plenty!" I remember one saying. Many just swore their lives were made better just for having known her.

Mom's best friend was also named Suzi. Suzi2 lived across the street from us in the 1980s, and was a tough-as-nails broad who had been through the ringer a time or two. She had been served and had eaten many a turd sandwich life tossed her way. Not the least of which was her husband. A man I named "Twinkie."

Twinkie had a strange habit of raging through their house when he was home alone. He would shout obscenities at the tops of his lungs and throw stuff around. And he would do this completely naked. Being right across the street, these events were in full earshot, and sometimes view, through the windows.

It was all very amusing until the day Suzi2 sat in our living room crying and shaking uncontrollably. Mom kept filling her glass with Harvey's Bristol Cream, trying to comfort her. I later heard that Twinkie had woken Suzi2 up from a dead sleep, but not because of his naked raging. She woke up to the metallic click of an unloaded gun. While she was sleeping, apparently, Twinkie stood over her, pointing a pistol into her hair over her left ear. She woke up when he pulled the trigger, but kept her eyes closed. He stayed standing over her for a minute or so, not saying a word.

That was what I heard anyway.

Suffice to say, when she and my Mom first became friends,

it didn't faze Suzi2 in the slightest when she came over for a girls' outing, and found Mom speaking solemnly into a mirror.

"Who you talking to, Suz'?"

"Oh . . . the judges," Mom said simply. "I'm crazy and the judges live inside me. They tell me to do things sometimes."

"Okay. Are they gonna let you go to Shopper's World with me today?"

Mom looked into the mirror then back at her, "Yup! Let's go, Lovey!"

Suzi2 had seen Mom two days before she died and had thought she didn't look right, but Mom told her that she was just really tired. They made plans for after Christmas.

Suzi2 came to help with the sorting of Mom's things and to have some lunch. She had a big manila envelope with her and, after lunch, gave me a look signaling a need to talk to me alone.

"Your ma would want you to finish this. I think you should." She handed me the envelope. We were in Mom's little kitchen. All the cabinets were open and her cups and glasses, mugs, and Tupperware were in boxes on the counters and on the floor along with a big garbage bag for all the food she'd left behind, mostly condiments. I opened the envelope and read the heading on the handful of papers inside, "The Circle Adoption Services."

"She started about a year ago, I was helping her, but she just didn't finish it. These folks have her adoption records."

"Her birth mother?"

"Yup. You can finish it because you're her daughter and she's gone now." Her eyes were red but she didn't cry. She was on a mission. "You should finish it, Stormy."

She had a thick as chow-dah New England accent, full on pahk the cahhh, so when she said my name it sounded like "Staw-mee."

I took the envelope and promised I would see it through.

LOVE YOU, BYE....

After Suzi2 left, my brothers and I started hauling the boxes and bags down the elevator and to our cars. Everything we didn't take with us was given or thrown away. I said goodbye to John and Henry and watched them pull away through the sooted wet dregs of a half-assed snowfall. I went to my car, got in, and took a deep breath. My nose and mouth were suddenly full of lily of the valley, smoke . . . Mom?

The sheets. Shit.

Throw them away. Only sheets. Act normal.

I often worry about looking crazy, in general, and that concern always becomes more urgent whenever I'm in proximity to any hospital or mental-health-care facility. For good reason. I could easily picture a couple of big guys in white coats, bringing me inside. They gently tell me what's best for me while feeding me pills, then tuck me into bed with straps that go all the way around it, and a sleepy roommate who had eaten her own hands.

Act normal.

Normal. I was in the parking lot, standing in the wet pre-Christmas cold, next to a giant, mean-looking Dumpster, screaming into the balled-up bedding of my dead mother.

People walked by me, I imagine to visit their family members, to celebrate an early Christmas. They had arms full of bright and shiny wrapped packages and little ones fussing in their just-for-Grandma, itchy holiday finery. A few tossed me uncomfortable glances hurrying through the sloshy cold, probably knowing full well what my deal was. They, too, would soon be tossing out some leftover, allegedly biohazard, belongings of their own dead loved ones.

This soft, Mom-scented pile was the last stuff that had given her comfort. She had been warm and safe, in a warm puff that held

209

her sweet until something woke her up, something made her get up and get her half-awake self into her wheelchair. But the last moments of her living, dreaming, nothing wrong, warm, her Christmas plans humming in her blonde little head, cradled on this pillowcase, breathing softly into these sheets, she was fine. There was an open suitcase on the floor, readying for a Christmas trip to her adopted stepmother's. There were Christmas cards ready to be sent. She was fully intending on living awhile longer. She had gone to bed and nestled in, fully expecting to wake up again, as we all do, every night.

Of course you're going to throw away the last thing that gave her comfort.

Shut the fuck up.

Just like you threw her away. Come on. It's cold. They're just fucking sheets. She didn't even die in them, fer chrissake.

No, she was alive in them, and minutes after she pulled herself out of them she was dead.

Stuff them into the Dumpster. Say goodbye. Do it. What's your problem?

"Fuck you," I said out loud, then shoved the stuff in the wet maw of the big metal box. *Only sheets, they're only sheets.*

Mom was happy at the end. Of course, I only knew her for two days out of the six years I ran and hid from her while she had lost her leg and found herself. I told myself she was happy at the end. She sure had looked happy.

The boy who found her said she looked like she was asleep. Peaceful and pink with no evidence of distress leading up to the end. In every room at the facility, there were emergency call buttons, one by the bed and one in the bathroom. Mom hadn't pushed hers, so it was safe to say she wasn't suffering. Mom loved emergencies, especially when she was the headliner, but she rolled into the great unknown without fuss or fanfare. She simply had gotten up, put her one-legged, paraplegic self into her wheelchair, navigated around her open suitcase on the floor, in the dark, got to the bathroom, onto the toilet and . . . was gone. Just like Elvis. The boy came in the morning to collect laundry and do a general check in and said she looked fine. She had only been gone maybe a half hour.

It was a bit insulting, to my brothers and me, that after a life so hell bent on misery and self-destruction, our mother died as soon as she got some peace. Mom wheels into her little halfway house of happiness, and God or whoever, goes and kicks the plug out. Oops.

The last time I remember seeing Mom happy was in Little Boar's Head. So we would have her service there. In her stuff I found a framed picture, of the five of us, in front of "Kittywake," the shingled beach cottage my dad's parents would rent every summer. In the photo, Mom gleamed next to my dad, my brothers were in matching bathing suits, and I was snapped in mid-yell. I was probably crowing "Cheeese!" Mom was holding my shoulders. Though I was about four in the picture, my white sprout of a ponytail on top of my head was higher than her hip. We were all very tan, and looked happy. Mom hadn't tried to kill us yet, though I later learned she had already begun trying to off herself around the time the picture was taken. It looked like the capture of a happy moment, though. So I kept it, and my brothers and I started to plan the service based on it.

We would do it at St. Andrew's By The Sea, a tiny church on a shady hill just off Route 1A. John, being the oldest, would do the eulogy. Henry would do a reading and I would sing a song. It would be a quick and personal service with all Mom's favorite hymns, mostly Christmas carols. Then we would go to Ray's Seafood for fried clams and lobsters that we could eat outside off sticky red-and-white-checked tablecloths. A perfect send-off for a woman we would never forget, but didn't know all that well.

Dad, my brothers, and I decided to scatter her ashes ourselves before the service. Family and friends were coming from all over, and it was shaping up to be a beautiful, hot July day, but at five something in the morning on the beach, the sun just peeking through the gray dawn over the ocean, it was chilly. We met directly across the street from Kittywake. Our little house, full of happy salt-water-taffy memories, was still there. Sort of. Now a monstrosity stood with it or rather, *on* it. An unfinished construction project literally straddled the original cottage. Some madman had tried to build a new, ultramodern thing, yet still incorporate the original house's footprint for some reason. At some point, though, whoever they were ran out of money and abandoned the whole horrible mess. It looked like Kittywake was getting slow-motion raped by a huge, tacky mansion from Florida.

Henry brought flowers. Dad brought big Styrofoam cups of Dunkin' Donuts coffee and Mom . . . half of her, anyway. The other half had gone to Grandmother Banks, who had her small service for Mom, earlier in the year.

We had one large Ziploc baggie full of dust and weird, nubby . . . bits. We mixed her ashes in with flower petals and both brothers and I scooped up a handful each, to pour into the Atlantic.

One at a time, we waded into the water to, I guess, meditate or pray before we released her.

I took my scoop of Mom and some flowers and high-stepped into the ocean. My feet quickly began to ache from the cold, and I couldn't think of anything to say. I stood holding the gritty stuff in both hands, cupped together, wondering what part of her body I had. Her knee? Her head? She was a small lady, so there weren't a lot of ashes to start with. Did they blend the ashes? I guess they had been shaken pretty well in their bags for some time, six months?

"I'm sorry, Mom." I looked for a sign, her face in the clouds, her voice in the seagulls screeching overhead. Nothing. I secretly hoped for a sign. Something magic, something significant that would tell me she was all good where she was, she was complete, happy, and I was forgiven. For some reason, I assumed there would be something, a nudge, a nod from the other side. *Mom always said that she was magic. One of her doctors told her that. I'm pretty sure it was the same doctor who said I should be crazy by now. Maybe I am. I'm freezing and wet, my mom is dead, I might be holding her actual face in my hands and I'm incapable of coming up with a single fucking worthwhile thing to say. I am an utter ruin of a human being.*

"I'm . . ." Then I dropped her. My hands just opened. Ashes swirled like powdered milk and the flowers floated.

Nothing. I rinsed off my hands in the water and trudged out to my dad. We watched my brothers wading out and he patted my back. I tried to look as if I *had* felt a significant shift, that I had made peace, that all was well, but I just felt wet and cold and pissed at myself.

I went to my hotel and dressed for the service as half of our mom floated away.

I think the minister was a bit appalled with our sendoff, but I could care less. He was a nice man, but this was our deal.

The service was a perfect blend of Episcopal tradition and customized extras. John's eulogy was legendary, quoting from the

Book of Matthew, blending in a ripping rendition of the blessing of the Holy Hand Grenade from *Monty Python and the Holy Grail*. Henry read a children's story, I planned to sing one of my songs.

Henry was always the tough one, the straight one. Besides getting angry once in a while, he was usually fairly stoic. While reading the sweet bedtime story that he read to his children but never heard from Mom, tears started to shine in his eyes. The poor guy hung in there as best he could, but started to lose it towards the end. I was crying openly, but trying to be quiet. Everyone was, out of respect and surprise to see my brother, who looked like a Heisman Trophy in a Brooks Brothers suit, regress to a sad little boy.

I was sitting next to my dad in the first pew of the church. While we watched Henry read, I noticed the wood of our seat would squeak with any movement. Of course, I sat in the loud pew, the only one making any noise in the whole church. If I barely shifted my weight, it would give a sharp creak. Still as I sat, though, the squeak kept chirping out of the old dark wood. I looked around to find what could be making the noise.

Dad. His hands were tightly balled together between his knees and he was completely still. Face forward and set, semper fi square jaw fixed, eyes on his son. He had his glasses on, and he looked so still, as if he were holding his breath. The only movement was the endless track of dripping tears down his stony face. And every minute or so, a tiny sad squeak would escape his flexing throat.

I put my hand on his leg and kept my eyes trained forward until it was my turn to get up and sing.

Well, I *tried* to sing . . . did my darndest. But after my two brothers' incredible moments at the pulpit and my sobbing, squeaking statue of a father, I had cried my throat damn near shut. I got off to a good start, but then lost it at the end. I sang one of my own songs, "Here We Are."

Here we are. Floating around outer space.

We're all looking for the final frontier, my dear, it's right in front of your face.

Here we are. Why are we so afraid?

We're so afraid of ourselves, and each other,

And the humongous mess that we've made . . .

Right around the first chorus, my face slammed shut and I could barely breathe. "Please someone . . . guys? Help me . . . I can't."

The back of the church was full of my cousins from my dad's side, they are all a little bit older than us and had their teenage daughters with them, all of whom knew, by heart, every song I ever recorded. They were all big fans of cousin Stormy. The girls leapt up and sang, "Time and again I'm at the end of my rope, and I feel life's a joke that I've been sharing with you. After all we are all what we are about to be . . . and here we are, heeere we aaare!" It was perfect. My brothers and I paid tribute to Mom in our own individual ways. As individually as we had responded to her and the lack of her. John, fiery, Henry, soft but soldiering, and I fell apart.

Later, Henry and his wife were playing with their kids at the beach, near where we had sent Mom's ashes off. He saw three roses wash up softly in the waves.

Love you, 'bye.

CHAPTER TWENTY:

BIRTH FAMILY, RET, HEART-BURST.

My earliest memory is as a baby looking out from a stroller. Staring up at the little navy blue awning thing pulled over me, and the big blue sky beyond it. I remember I was moving, seeing the tops of school buildings, the clock tower, the gymnasium. I remember the wheels under my back getting louder and bumpier as I was being pushed faster. Then I heard my brothers' laughter behind me, growing distant as they had given the stroller a heave-ho and pushed it down a hill.

This memory is as vivid as any, and I have no idea if it's even remotely accurate. Knowing them, it is a stunt my brothers would absolutely have pulled. They say they remember it, too, somewhat, but with the caveat that they would have *never* let anything *really* bad happen to me. They were way too terrified of my dad.

Memory is a moving target. They say that if five people witness a car accident, there were five different car accidents. In the eighties, there was an epidemic of so-called repressed memories bursting to the surface in some people. Oprah, Donahue, and Sally Jesse Raphael all had people on their shows who had blinding visions, out of nowhere, of themselves as children when they had been molested or beaten. Tons of people came forward to talk about their repressed memories, including Roseanne Barr.

I remember Mom *loving* this idea. Out of the clear blue sky, you could remember whoever did whatever terrible, awful thing to you. And, because you remembered, you could then heal and move on. Your shitty life was totally someone else's fault, and thank God you remembered!

Mom's memories would change with whatever topic was on daytime television, so when repressed memories became kitchen-table subjects, Mom was psyched. She could remember being kidnapped by aliens, raped by Satanists, *and* her brother was the Son of Sam.

I *know*! Isn't it just so awful?

It *was* true that Mom was adopted, though. Every now and then she would talk about finding her birth family, and would say aloud that she was going to hire a private detective or start researching herself to find where she really came from. These fanciful plans would come and go, but then she would find it more satisfying to invent her real background, usually starting with a "What if . . . ?" ending in hardboiled facts that she had completely fabricated.

She never got terribly far in her searching, I imagine, because she was terrified to discover that she was the result of a sloppy drunken oops, or some other, completely common scenario. My biggest fear was being crazy; hers was being normal and not a completely unique little snowflake of tragedy.

"My father was a cop and he blackmailed my mother who was

a beautiful dancer," or, "My mother was a movie star, and she got pregnant auditioning for *Gone With the Wind,*" and so on, you get the idea. "My mother was raped" was a big one.

I had always been a bit curious about Mom's birth family. Insofar as getting some actual medical history besides the cobbled-together mess of half-truths and bullshit fed to all of us by endless doctors and so-called experts. I was in my thirties, past the age of prescribed madness by some years, and decidedly fine. Other than hypersexuality, addiction, hallucinations, panic attacks, and general fits of blackout depression, I was totally normal.

I was just curious.

When I got back to Portland, however, the manila envelope Suzi2 had given me, a packetful of potential answers, stayed on my dresser for months. I didn't think about it too much, but every time I saw it something in me said, "Leave it alone, dude." There was no info inside, just a last form to fill out, get notarized, then send off with a check for thirty bucks. The envelope sat, until spring.

"What if you want to have kids?" asked my girlfriend, Stephanie, who wanted kids. "It would be really helpful to . . . you know . . . *know.*" Steph looked at me with her cartoon, baby-deer eyes. Steph is ten years younger than me, a silky sweet beauty with a giant, natural heart. We are very different but I consider her my baby sister.

"I don't want kids, Steph. Besides, all the eggs I have left in me are the bitter last batch, and nobody wants *those* to come to life. They're all shriveled up in there, sitting in rocking chairs on a porch in my ovaries, smoking, and bitching about their frustrated lives." I put on a sourpuss old lady face and mimed smoking a filterless cigarette and croaked "Gaaah! I coulda *been* somebody!" I cracked myself up. She smiled.

"Seriously, Stormy, don't you want to know? They might be amazing people."

"Or, I could call and be patched through to an insane asylum, or a phone on the wall of some common room of a maximum security prison."

"Or she could be some nice lady who had to make a tough choice a long time ago who would love to know that, well, that her granddaughter is a wonderful person and a kickass talent."

"Hippie."

"I'm serious."

Of course, I was being dramatic about the whole prison thing, but part of me didn't want to welcome more moms into my life. I had lost mine without really having had her in the first place and our whole dance around each other for thirty-plus years went from sad to horrible and rarely varied beyond those two points. Why would I want to meet more of . . . *her?*

My curiosity got the better of me, though, and with my sweet lil' sis, Steph, cheering me on, I filled out the form, got it notarized, and sent it off.

I imagined it would get stuck into a ream of impossible requests somewhere in a Connecticut records room. I pictured a fussy, exhausted file clerk cursing at the pile of work he'll never get to, and the lost children out in the world dumping their impossible dreams of finding long-lost loved ones on his narrow shoulders. I figured if I heard anything it would be at least a year or so.

Two weeks later I get a call from a man at the agency.

"Storm Large?"

"Yes?"

"We've received your request and processed it. Have you gotten your packet yet?"

"My . . . uh."

"Oh, you'll get it any day now. Unfortunately, your mother's birth mother is deceased, but she had children and they would like to talk with you."

"They *what?*"

"Would it be all right if I gave this number to one of the daughters so she can contact you directly?"

"I dunno, is it safe?"

"Safe? She's your aunt."

"I know, but . . ."

"They have a right to know who's looking into their family history. It doesn't have to be on the phone, it can be your address or email."

"No, give her my number. This number, sure. Was she nice?"

"She seemed nice, yes, just very surprised to get the information. You'll hear from her, I'm sure, very soon."

"Okay, um, thank you."

I don't know what I was thinking starting this whole process. Of course the family has to be informed that they're being somewhat investigated. I can't just snoop around private medical records and explore the lineage and records of real people, potentially related to me, without their knowledge or permission. I was worried about *my* safety? They weren't looking for *me.*

Now they are.

Shit.

A day or so later, I get the packet of records from the adoption agency and foster-care providers. The photocopied pages contained Mom's birth record, nurse's notes on the birth and recovery of the birth mother, and then the stretch of years that followed, before my mom was finally adopted. There were a pack of handwritten accounts on Mom's progress in her various, temporary homes.

Mom was born on March 14, 1943, to a twenty-three-year-old

woman named Loretta V. Hospital records said she was born healthy and didn't cry or fuss too much, even though Loretta refused to touch or hold her most of the time.

Mom's name, at birth, was Sandra.

Sandra was described as a "good baby," sweet and cuddly. Loretta took her home for about three weeks, then decided to give her up. Sandra's first round of foster care was a lovely situation. She was held and played with and doted on, plus her birth mother was encouraged to visit her. Loretta was allowed to spend an hour with the baby a few times a week (why they did this is unclear, maybe to get the birth mother to bond with, then take the baby home, and out of the overcrowded system), and, for a short while, she did. When she would come to see her baby, though, she refused to hold her and would only stay a fraction of the time allowed. On one or two occasions the foster agent described Loretta as "distracted," often showing up for these visits with one or several friends, and they were often drunk. Loretta and her posse, one time, were so wasted when they showed up to visit my wee baby mom, they were asked to leave.

She eventually stopped coming at all.

There was no mention of mental illness in the medical records, but the record was everything the birth mother offered to the hospital when she went to have the baby. According to Loretta, her own general health was good. The only information on the father was he was a naval officer, around the same age as Loretta and his name was "Whitey." Where the hospital record had a space to write down the general health of the father, Loretta had written, "clean and nice looking."

I had begun to research the family name to see if anything came up crazy, when she called.

It was my mom's half-sister, Grace, my *aunt* Grace, technically.

"Is this Storm?"

"Yes, hi! Wow. How are you?" *Please don't be insane.*

"I'm fine. I think there's been a mistake." She sounded nervous, but nice enough.

"Oh?"

"My mother couldn't have *possibly* given up a child for any reason."

"Oh. Okay. Well, I'm only going on what the agency told me, so . . ."

"Of course, absolutely. It's just, well, I'm sure she would have *told* somebody, that's all. And this is the first any of us have ever heard of this."

"You have brothers and sisters?" I asked.

"Three."

"Wow, big family."

"Mom was the oldest of five, so . . ."

"Jeez. Have you talked to any of your aunts and uncles about this?"

"They're all gone. Passed."

"Your dad?"

"He passed away a year before Mom did."

"I'm sorry. So, nobody ever mentioned . . . ?" *Mom was a dirty little secret?*

"Nobody. Ever." She was being really sweet and sounded genuinely confused. And though she was not convinced we were related, she still had taken the time to call me. "I'm not sure why the agency thinks my mother . . . I mean, it doesn't make any sense. She loved kids and was the best mother and grandmother any child could ever hope for."

"She sounds wonderful."

"She was, truly. But I wanted to call you because your mother died and, well, you're probably just looking for answers, which I *completely* understand. I feel certain that this is an honest mistake, I'm sorry."

"Well I'm really glad you called."

"My family thinks you might want money."

"What?"

"I don't really know, but when they heard about all this they all got in a tizzy thinking, well, I don't know. You seem very nice to me."

It was clear to me that this woman was the kind and level-headed one in her family. And, after talking with me for a few minutes, knew that I was not after anything but answers. She seemed to suddenly need some as well. I told her I was just looking for closure, and maybe a little medical history.

We chatted lightly awhile longer and decided to check in later after she talked with her family again, told them about our conversation, and showed them my website.

Meanwhile, I researched the family name. And drank and drank and drank.

I started a mighty Chardonnay habit after my mom died. Of course out of grief, and grief is a crazy thing in and of itself. But I have a natural aversion to losing it, so I medicated with white wine and work. No matter how much I drank or gigged, however, I couldn't stop the voices reminding me over and over, that I was glad she was gone. Relieved. And that struck me as the reaction of a deeply flawed and terrible human being, somebody who, if they weren't totally crazy, they were, simply, fucked in the head.

I still hated the idea of therapy, but I knew I needed help. I couldn't sleep and, my drinking? Well, despite the dainty glass and the smooth oak finish, I might as well have been funneling Pabst down my open throat hole while doing a keg stand.

I had done therapy before after getting away from Billy and the demons. But she was just this nice hippie mom with a sliding scale and a dream catcher next to her diploma. One hour, once a week. At the end of which I would ask her, "Am I crazy?" She would smile kindly and say no. I would look at her, look at her diploma, then smile and say, "You oughta know!" Then I'd give her my thirty bucks and go about my day.

In my search for another person with a diploma, I saw, in the back of an alternative weekly, an ad for some weird therapy that was meant specifically for posttraumatic stress disorder. The ad didn't look at all hokey, with the usual picture of glowing, open hands or some smiling hippie mom with empty nest syndrome. It looked scientific. It sounded pretty cool, too.

RET, rapid eye therapy. "Combat soldiers, accident victims, victims of violent crime, and other traumatizing events have been cured by this therapy. Ideal for post-traumatic stress, grief and depression."

Perfect! Sign me up. I hadn't been in a war or a crash, but I figured I was enough of a train wreck to justify going to see this lady.

Her little waiting room was nice, not too hippyish other than the vegetarian cooking magazines and an abundance of plants to the point where it seemed it was *their* house. She came out and greeted me in a soft but clipped voice darted with a German or Austrian accent. She was small and serious, very focused and not a lot of flowery welcome spiel, but she still had a warm and calm presence. She struck me as a super-left-brain scientist who'd been well marinated in the woo-woo world of alternative medicine.

We talked for awhile about what was going on with me, and I let her in on a bit of my mother's history. She told me a bit about what we were going to do, the basic ideas behind RET and how it all worked. All I had to do was relax, and let my eyes follow her little penlight and let the healing begin.

She also said that I would be done after twelve sessions.

Done? There exists a *done* in the world of therapy? A therapist who wants you to get better to the point of not coming back? I then knew I had made the right decision.

"Ah you warm enough? He-ah." She put a blanket over me as I reclined in the plush, wide chair in her treatment room.

"I want you to do exactly as I say, all right? Ah you ready?" I was warm and comfy and totally ready to drift into whatever she suggested twelve more times. Booya. Here I come, health!

"Breeeathe deeply, all ze way into you-uh tail bone. Good."

She had a cartoon psychoanalyst Teutonic clink to her speech, with a sprig of Zsa Zsa Gabor. Low, rhythmic, foreign, and it was lulling me into a stupor. My brain usually rebels at being told to shut up and relax by yammering insults at itself for not being able to shut up and relax, but I was sinking, and all was quiet upstairs.

"Good, now send your energy, like a finger of light, down from your tailbone into ze chair, doown through ze floor, through ze rock ze sand ze soil . . . good, all ze way down, down, down, until you are connecting yourself to ze source, ze molten core of ze Earth. Feel ze heat and ze weight, yes. Now bring zat energy up. Up . . . up . . . up . . . Good. Nice and rooted. Now . . . Open you-uh eyes."

I was completely still, my skin felt weighted across my face and body. So comfortable, had she stopped there and said, "Well done, that'll be fifty bucks," I would have felt just ducky about it. My breathing was smooth, my head and neck were relaxed for the first time in weeks. Not a trace of the ache that had parked on the back of my skull from all the drinking and crying and struggling to control both. Projectile sobs had been blasting out of me randomly, with little or no warning, with alarming frequency, and terrible timing. A first birthday, family gathering, in line at the bank, on stage, giving a blowjob. In the mooshy chair with little Dr. Zsa Zsa, I felt, for the first time in weeks, total calm.

Then I opened my eyes. She had her pen light on, shining in my face, interrogation style, then began barking orders at my pupils. "Left, right, left, right, left, right, left, right. Up, left, up, down, down, down. Right, right, all the way to the upper left. Upper left, around, around. Now, blink very fast. Blinkblinkblinkblinkblinkblink. Aaaaaand relax." Slowing down, all soft and cloudy, she said, "You are whole. You are complete. The world welcomes and loves you. You are loved."

She was reading a laundry list of positive affirmations into my open brain.

Despite the calisthenics she ran my eyeballs through, I was enjoying all the lovely things she was saying about me. And I was still so relaxed, maybe it was the affirmations, but I began to think that this was really going to work. My heart tickled with hope.

"Up, down. Up, down. All ze way upupupupupupupup." And so on for nearly an hour.

My eyes were really achy as I left her office, but I felt amazing, almost as though I were medicated, in some mild barbiturate fluffy puff. I drove home and swore at no one, not even the hippies who insisted on riding their bikes side by side so that I couldn't pass them. I mused at the old me who would have quick-style fantasized some terrible end to their lives, involving being forced to eat a baby harp seal and making them swear allegiance to George W. Bush before

I beat them to death with a bat made out of rare, rainforest wood. Nope. I was actually happy. I had found the thing that would fix me. And not just the grief part, maybe *everything*: the voices, the sadness, the addictive behavior, and general lameness that had kept me low down and fairly useless feeling for most of my life. This was session one of twelve and I already felt completely changed.

That night, I only had two glasses of wine with dinner and didn't cry myself to sleep. It was amazing. I looked forward to my next visit where I would be eleven hours away from being better. I was going to be normal. Fixed.

The next three sessions were just as stellar, inspiring, a bit soporific, but really incredible. I was on my way, imbued with hope and trembling excitement for the new me to burst out, phoenixlike, until the fourth session.

"Up. Down. Up. Down. All the way to the upper left . . . Upper left. Upper left. Good. Aaand . . ."

"OW! Fuck! OW!"

Out of nowhere a cramp clenched in my throat, everything constricting around the tight ball of ache. I couldn't get a full breath and I lurched forward, grabbing at my chest and throat. It was like I had been woken from a nap by getting punched in the collarbone. "Ugh . . . ow . . . wait. Wait . . . ow, I can't breathe. I can't . . . Mom?"

My eyes were open. The therapist was leaning toward me. The room was the same. I felt the pain in my throat and chest. I was awake. And my mother sat cowering in the corner, weeping. "I'm so sorry, Stormy. I'm so sorry."

She was in a gray hospital gown, she shook and stared at me, toothlessly mouthing pitiful apologies. I struggled to breathe. "Mom! What! I see my mother."

"Storm! I want you to bring your energy back up through ze

earth, up through ze floor into zis room. You are in zis room and you are in zis chair and I (clap) want (clap) you (clap) here (clap) now!" She stood up in front of me, looking hard into my face. She looked concerned but not at all panicked. "Is she still there?"

My chest loosened up and I felt a wave of heat spread outwards from where the knot had been. My eyes instantly flooded. As the tears poured hotly down my face I searched the room through their blur. She was gone. "No. She's . . . Oh, my God, am I okay?"

The therapist smiled, I imagine, as warmly as someone that superclinical ever could. "Storm. Zis is wonderful. What a breakthrough we've had here today." She sat back down and shook her head. "Such a breakthrough for so few sessions. I know we're only halfway through with today, but I think you are done, yes?"

"Yes, yes, please." I would have run screaming from the building had I not been so completely exhausted. "Is this normal? I mean, does this happen to everyone?"

"No, no. Everybody is different. Be happy, Storm. Zis was a *good* thing that happened here, today. I want you to go home, and *think* about it."

Think about it.

A breakthrough. I hallucinated my dead mother. The diamond-hard completeness of all my pain around her shoved into my throat and throttled my heart to the bursting point. *Zis is wonderful.*

That night, thinking about it, I felt that my heart must have burst. I had held on to all this guilt and pain, as if I was supposed to endlessly experience it. My addiction to suffering and hurting was finally giving up, and getting the heave-ho by the new positive responses my brain was learning. So, instead of the volley between head and heart and hate, hate, hate, my heart hit its sad ball against a wall while the brain just whistled a happy tune, looking at pretty flowers, or something. And the heart, left alone with its old pain swelling up inside it, burst open like a plum in a microwave and it puked up the crap it had held on to for so long.

It was like that one time I nearly came to death. I called him "the Professor." The Professor was great because he was insanely smart, well read, and a dirty, dangerous bastard in the sack. He was built like a linebacker, but with dark blue hair and tattoos. He was one of the few lovers in my life who could physically overpower me, and loved to do just that. He also loved to bite. He told me once that he fantasized now and again about eating human flesh. Just tearing out a tricep or chomping the goo out of someone's thigh muscle.

He was so great.

One day, he had me pinned like a dead frog in biology class. On my back, legs cranked open, my wrists under the small of my back, bound with one of those curly cords you use to charge your cell phone in the car. The cord was in his one hand behind my back, his other hand rubbing, tickling, and tucking in and out of me. His mouth would softly assist the one friendly hand until he felt me start to lose it. Then, he would immediately stop all niceties, twist and tighten the cord in his mean hand, then push my legs open farther and sink his teeth into my groin. Slowly chomping into the flesh deeper and deeper, all the while making a sweet, yummy sound in complete contrast to the murderous pain he was causing. He could sense the exact moment that I might kick or scream, cry uncle, or just fucking black out, and he would instantly let go his pit bull grip, kiss the sore, purple indentations he had left, trace his tongue around where it hurt, eventually finding his way back to where it ached and begged and pouted for more.

The French call orgasm *the little death*. When the Professor finally let me come, I died, but, maybe because I'm American, I died a *big* death, or a *freedom* death . . . whatever. I'm sure I died.

Every gut in my torso grew legs and thundered upward through the sparkling hot-pepper fizz of the big red booming yesyesYES, screaming bloody stars blasting up my spine, punching behind my face to explode. Tremors flapped in my muscles like towels snapping off sand, my eyes strobed, dimmed, and a whoosh roared in my ears, then falling, hot dead heavy, dissolving like a mouthful of raspberry sugar . . . and gone.

It could have been hours or ages later, but I realized only moments had passed when I heard him say, "Why are you crying?"

Shit.

It's near impossible to look cool when you come, anyway, let alone when you start weeping like a jerk. Much better to just stare at the other person, come spattered and panting, and say, "Yeah . . . *and?*"

But some old wound had dislodged from my subconscious and shook me. I was crying, hard, and I felt like an idiot. "I . . . I'm sorry."

"No, no, what's going on?" He was really a great guy despite the rough exterior and cannibalistic tendencies. "Did I . . . ?"

No, you didn't hurt me, you egomaniac. It's bad enough I'm crying here but I'm not going to let you think you hurt or scared me in any way; put the macho bullshit down. "I'm sorry . . . I, no, you're great, I . . ." Fuck. No matter how you sliced it, he was going to leave here a superhero and me the weeping soft damsel. *Fuckfuckfuck.*

"Hey, shhh, it's cool, just breathe. C'mere." He scooped me up and held me as I wound down, still shaking and crying. Finally, smoothing out and calming my breath, I said, "I saw it."

"Saw what?" he purred into my hair.

"A broken heart. I know what it is." He lay me back down and wiped the tears still leaking down my cheeks into my ears. He was sitting up on the couch now; my legs were stretched around his hips. "It doesn't break because it's *broken,* or damaged, it bursts open with everything you've ever wanted, hoped for, hurt over, loved. It bursts open because it's *full*."

"Uh-huh." He was stroking my throat and I felt him growing hard again.

What is it with guys and the weak, injured girl thing? "It bursts," he said to the temperature of my skin.

I wiped my face with both hands and curled my hips up to meet his. Yes.

Yes.

I decided to go back for my fifth session of RET. I was convinced that I had experienced a major heart-burst moment. That, combined with my semiconscious, near dreamlike state, I must have concocted the image out of the feelings, and then panic did the rest. My heart had burst, and drained like an abscess. This time I would fill it with positive affirmations and swell that sucker up with some hope.

The worst was over. The rest will be cake. Seven more.

"Right, left . . . Right, left . . . All ze way around. Around. Around. Up. Up. Up. UP. And relax . . . You are complete, the world welcomes and loves you. You are pure love."

"OW! Fuck! GODDAMMIT!" I lunged forward again, gulping in a panic. "No!"

"Iz it your mother?"

"No . . . ugh . . . no." The fist in my chest throbbed as I stared to my right. "If my mother had multiple personalities in life, would she have them in death, too?" I kept staring, struggling for a full breath.

"No. I think zat can only be for a living person."

"No? Okay . . . ugh . . . then . . . who's that!" She looked

231

wide-eyed where my eyes were fixed. To my right was a scrawny man, dressed in seventies work clothes; he had brown hair and thick mustache. I knew what had happened to him the moment I saw him.

"What's going on?" he asked me. He seemed a little upset, agitated, like he'd been waiting for a long time

"I don't know what's going on," I said to him. "I think you're dead, I'm really sorry. Maybe you, um, should go to the light?"

"I want you he-ah now!" The therapist clapped me back again.

I could not get out of there fast enough. I paid her, thanked her, and ran to my car crying.

Great. Fantastic. Mom dies and the crazy jumps out of her and into me like a fucking ghost. This is it. I've fucking lost it.

"You're fine," Delta said. Delta was a psychic counselor, and the first person I called. "Now, tell me what you were doing when you saw all this."

I went back over the how cool the therapy was, how it was really working, all the great feelings of simultaneous hope and calm, all leading up to the nosedive into seeing dead people. "Jesus, honey," she said.

"Am I going to be haunted forever?"

"Oh, honey, no, no, no." Delta laughed. She was a former model. A stunning, willowy blonde monument and she had the beer-soaked chuckle of a pure blue-collar broad. "You're fine, but, seriously? No more RET. That shit's too intense for you, honey. You're way too sensitive."

She went on to explain in therapist terms about how, kind of like an acid trip, RET was a shortcut through your brain's natural defenses. The tricking your eyes back and forth allows you to go into an "awake" dream state so your rational mind is essentially asleep. No guard at the gate, so to speak, so you are far more open to suggestion. In the case of a combat soldier, who is so traumatized by what he or she has seen and done, RET is an ideal tool to get through that hardcore soldier mind. For a sad, sensitive girl with mommy issues? Well, it's not unlike using a chainsaw to get a little bug out of your eye.

"Storm, honey, your mother died. It's a big deal. The only way to go through it is to just go through it. There aren't any shortcuts. I'm sorry."

No shortcuts is right. I'm not really a joiner, but it seems like the seven stages of grief are a place everyone gets to be a part of at some point. And they sure do take their fucking time ticking by. Shock and denial, check. Pain and guilt, oh yeah. Anger? Anger was the stage I got to where the record started skipping. It took very little for me to go from zero to homicidal in the few months following Mom's funeral. God help anyone who heckled me at one of my gigs at Dante's. I got into a shouting match with a guy in the balcony who threw ice at me. I grabbed a cube, shoved it in my pants, wiped my sweaty rear with it and threw it back at him.

"Suck on that, you fuckin' dweeb!"

A woman at the bar asked the bartender, my friend, Adam, "Um, is she always this crude?"

"Yup."

"Could you ask her to tone it down a little?"

Adam looked at the woman and smiled. "Well, you can go ahead and try to, darlin'." To which she popped open her cell phone to call her client and recommend that he not come to Dante's for his after-show party.

Her client was Prince. Oops.

Some huge, Paul Bunyan–looking dickhead grabbed my ass at a poker game and I sent his beer flying out of his hand when I spun him with an open-handed roundhouse to the head.

Then I was asked to co-emcee an event with Dennis Rodman. It was all fun until I nearly got into a brawl with some guy in his entourage. He was a hanger-on, a nobody, a remora. You know those fish that hang around under a shark to snag the bits of meat the shark misses, or drops, but are too pussy to go get their own? Yeah, that was this guy. And he was harassing this sweet girl who just wanted me to give her a little birthday spanking. Long story short, I threatened to disfigure him and Rodman had to break it up.

Anger hung around for a long time with his stupid drunk friends, depression and loneliness. Not on the list, but somehow at the party was insomnia. I had to take sleep aids most nights to get any rest at all. They helped a little bit, but one morning I woke up with nasty-looking bruises on my leg, a headache from Hell, and an odd pain in my asshole area. I looked at my boyfriend, who was staring at me from his side of the bed, with a funny smile on his face. "I'm not entirely sure you *want* me to tell you what happened last night," he said.

Apparently I had blackout rugby hooligan sex with him, jumped up and ran straight into a wall, fell over backward holding my knee, and laughed maniacally, "Owwwwww! My head!"

I wonder if that would fall under "upward turn" in the list of seven stages. Because things actually did start to improve after that.

CHAPTER TWENTY-ONE:

ROCK STAR, WHAT THE FUCK IS LADYLIKE?

In the early spring, following my mom's funeral, I got a call from somewhere in 310.

"Hi! We saw a video of you performing and would love for you to audition in person for a new TV show called *Rock Star, The Tommy Lee Project*." He went on to describe the show, a contest for rock singers to vie for the lead position in a, as of yet untitled, supergroup. "Can you be in Seattle mid-March?"

My band was still doing all right, but certainly needed a shot in the arm. The call got me excited, but cautiously so. So many of these things had passed in and out of my life. You know how, describing the month of March, *it comes in like a lion and goes out like a lamb?* The same goes for most of those promising-sounding opportunities. Only they come in like the best thing ever! And go out like an oily fart.

235

But I always treated every *yeah, right* like a possible *yes,* and whether it led to a cool gig or a sorry disappointment, it always led me forward. So, forward ho.

The auditions were at the Crocodile Café, a decent-sized rock club in Belltown. There was a line around the block when I got there and I instantly wanted to just drive the three hours back to Portland and blow the whole thing off. It was embarrassing, all these people, up and out on a wet, cold morning, hoping to get discovered. I was one of *them?*

I already had a decent career; I was living off music as my main source of income. I didn't need this.

This is reality TV, the lowest common denominator of exploitation of the stupid and fame-hungry. I should totally take my dignity and go home.

I parked my car but kept it running. I stared at the line and began to feel incredibly lame as it became inevitable that I would be joining the other reality television hopefuls in their cold and soggy line. *Not cool.*

I felt like I was on a collision course with this ridiculous idea. The trick was to get my head around all the pros and cons, then decide if it was worth the risk to my reputation and credibility. Both of which didn't matter, in the grand scheme of things, since I was never cool to begin with.

For some reason, there is something detestable about an artist who wants to do well, to actually *live* on the work that they do. Most artists who become popular are often considered sellouts or poseurs, and not *real* artists. Like we all have to be all van Gogh, cut ourselves to pieces, and suffer in an insane asylum until the voices tell us to shoot ourselves in the head. He was one of the greatest painters ever, in my uncool opinion, but does suffering in squalor validate you as an artist? Kurt Cobain died miserable, making it seem like he felt the songs he wrote, songs that struck a chord with damn near a whole generation, were somehow fraudulent because of their commercial success.

Cool or not, it's kind of important that you are liked by at least *some* people in order to make a living off your art, whatever form it takes. Nobody buys your art, you're punching a clock, schlepping drinks, or digging ditches somewhere. That's reality.

Hard and thankless as it can be, sometimes, I so love what I do, I can't pretend that I'm not having a blast. Again, *not cool*. But I'd rather burn than be cool, any day.

After much deliberation, I probably said "Fuck it" a couple of times, out loud to myself. Let the hipsters hate. That's what they do. They already thought I sucked for being popular in Portland.

I walked into the front room of the club to get my number and sign in. "Oh, Storm Large, you made it! We were hoping you'd make it. *Love* your video," said the beautiful blonde at the sign-in table. She was all golden warm California-riffic and a striking contrast to the soggy pale Northwest rockers milling around.

"Which video did you see?"

"The one where you're singing and you get in a fight with some guy and steal his cell phone . . . awesome!" The other people waiting for their chance started looking at me as another girl came up.

"Storm! *Awesome* . . . thank you for coming. Here, just fill this out and we'll get you set up. Do you have a headshot?"

"No, sorry."

"That's cool. Just head over here, we'll take a Polaroid, and you'll be good to go."

It became quickly apparent to me and the people around me that I was the only one, in my immediate pack of hopefuls, who had been asked by the casting people to come. People started looking at me, whispering. I started to feel a bit resented, and a little feared.

The dreaded line was, suddenly, awesome.

Everyone there wanted it. There was a desperate vibe growing, as the line snaked inside and we got closer to the stage. I felt a prickle of nerves myself. I didn't *need* this. I just wanted to see how far it would go. No way were they going to put me on television . . . this whole day is just future stage banter. But curiosity had me by the glands and I needed to see this goofy day to its absolute end. I was so convinced that I was going to get the "Thank you *so much* for coming, you *rock*. Buh-bye," that I just decided to enjoy the spectacle, sing my songs, shake hands with the nice Hollywood people, then go get a killer breakfast at my favorite spot in the U district. When it was finally my turn, I was more excited about the eggs Florentine I was going to order than this potential TV gig.

"Hi, there. Fuck me, that's bright," I said into the television lights.

"Storm Large! Thank you for coming," said a man's voice behind the glare. "How's it goin'?"

"Fine. 'Cept my burning corneas, all is well." Chuckles from behind the lights. I was hungry and tired, but brightly caffeinated. I felt my giant inner ham rise and begin to stretch its legs.

I got this.

Even though I won't get on television, these fuckers will love me before I'm done.

"What are you going to sing for us?" said a woman's voice.

"A couple of originals, if that's cool."

"Very cool," said the man. "Everyone turn off your cell phones, I don't want Storm to kick my ass."

"That's not what you said last night." Cheap, but more laughter.

I sang "Ladylike" and "I Want You to Die, a Love Song," much to their delight and applause. They started asking me questions about music, my band, my life, drug use, my boyfriend, and family. I smart-assed and smack-talked half of the interview, but as I relaxed a bit more and genuinely talked with them, a strange thing happened. I started to think I was going to get this audition, get on this show, and holy shit, then what?

The woman conducting most of the interview was a beautiful, slender brunette. She was pretty intense and focused when talking to me, friendly, but most likely with clear instructions to find specific personality and musical types for the show.

When my camera/stage time was done, she stepped outside with me and we talked some more, alone.

"So, you don't do drugs anymore, at all?" she asked with some gravity. "There will be a drug test at the next level."

"I drink a bit and, on rare occasions, I smoke a little pot."

"Stop smoking pot right now, and you'll pass the drug test in a couple months. What about pills, antidepressants, antianxiety?"

"No psych drugs . . . my mom . . . I uh . . ." *Shit.*

"Your mom?"

Shit shit shit. Don't lie.

"My mom passed away last year, she was on all kinds of medicine my whole life. I hate that shit. No, I love life, I'm all good upstairs."

"What was she medicated *for* exactly?"

Shit. "Everything and nothing. I think she was just unhappy, but she was diagnosed with every mental illness you've ever heard of and a few that don't even exist. Long story. It was all bullshit to keep her on expensive dope. I don't believe in that stuff. At all. Is that a problem? My mom?"

"I don't think so, but we have to know this stuff for obvious

239

reasons. Listen, it was really great to meet you. You're awesome. We'll be in touch, okay?"

Did I just get a television gig?

Right before I got on *Rock Star,* I was staying in a hotel in Santa Monica with all the wannabe contestants; there were about fifty of us. While in the hotel, we got the promised drug test (passed . . . phew!), gave interviews, and were intermittently brought into a conference room to sing for producers and the supergroup, who consisted of Tommy Lee from Motley Cru, Gilby Clark from Guns N' Roses, and Jason Newstead from Metallica. It was a weird week.

Besides all the auditioning and showboating, we all had to be psychoanalyzed, and, like any job interview, had to give references for them to check. James was my reference number one, and he called me at the hotel to tell me that the TV people had called him and asked all sorts of questions about me. Did I have a drug problem? Was I under any psychiatric care? Was I a stable sort of person?

James is my best friend and one of the kindest and smartest men on the planet. And he is a sneaky bastard. Sometimes when we're on tour, he has a tendency to tell people I used to be a man. Especially if a guy asks him what I'm like and should he talk to me, does he have a shot, and whatnot. My good friend James then beams and says, "Oh yeah, she's great. She's healing up so well you can barely see the scars anymore, and she's on a way better cocktail of hormones, so the crazy outbursts have stopped, for the most part." If the poor pigeon believes him that far, James will usually go farther to explain, that my name was really Jake Large and that I used to be in a punk band called

SHIM, but that I was so much nicer as a woman, and very nearly passable, save for my gigantic manhands.

"Did you tell them I had a dick, James?"

"Of course I did. But I had to lie about some other stuff."

"Ooh. What did you have to lie about?"

"I told them you were a sweet and nonviolent person."

"I am a sweet nonviolent person," I pouted.

"Well, I didn't tell them about the guy you choked offstage."

"What guy I choked offstage? I never, wait a minute, *that* guy? That guy totally had it coming. And I didn't choke him, I threw him off the stage by a belt that happened to be around his neck."

"Ohhh."

"Remember? I was spanking him with a belt and he kept trying to grab my ass, so I finally looped the belt around his neck and threw him off the stage like a dog. "

"Uh-huh."

"Dude, fuck that guy. I'd do it again, too. What's so fucking funny?"

"I meant the other guy you choked off stage." James was openly laughing. My brain sizzled.

"What other guy?" So many nights on the same stage with so many degenerate fans inviting themselves into my physical space, how can I remember everyone?

"You mean the *girl*? That dumb drunk bitch who tried to grab the microphone out of my hand? I didn't choke her either. I just kinda waterboarded her. I mean, she was choking on the water, and didn't she get arrested for embezzling or something later? She was an ass."

Laughing harder, "No, no, no! The guy you straight up grabbed by the throat and choked."

"Bull*shit*, James!"

"Yes, you did. He was the one who wanted you to sing 'Happy Birthday' to him."

Oh, yeah.

It was a tradition at Dante's, that if someone had a birthday, and asked really nicely, I would haul him or her up on stage and spank them with a belt (for boys, girls got the hand) and then everyone would sing. It became so popular that, after Hurricane Katrina, we raised a few thousand dollars and several hundred welts by setting up a spanking booth at our shows and sending the money to Mercy Corps.

It had been a few years of the spanking thing that I had to dig around in my brain for ones that went awry. "Ohhh, the *birthday* guy?" I remembered a smallish man sneaking on stage and hugging me from behind without warning. Totally inappropriate. Anybody who has been to my shows knows that you don't. Fucking. Touch me. Or interrupt me. Or make sudden moves, loud noises, or be weird.

"I remember him. He startled me. It was self-defense."

"Right."

I had to go to a hotel room to meet with the doctor to get my results, when I got the news.

"So, doc, am I crazy?" *Pleasesaynopleasesaynopleasesayno.*

He chuckled and tapped his pen on the clipboard with my personality profile and mental state detailed and illustrated, all laid out on a graph.

"I wouldn't say that, but, you are . . . interesting."

Shit. He can tell I have totally thought about killing people, that I hear voices and my pedigree is purebred bonkers. "Interesting?"

"Well, you're a fairly typical artist. Sensitive, highly sexual, a little narcissistic, but the weird thing is . . . um . . . how do I put this?"

SHIT!

"You're a man."

"I'm a . . . ?"

"Your brain, the way you make decisions, deal with challenges, it is masculine. You have a manly brain."

I tucked my giant man hands under my thighs, so that he wouldn't comment on those as well, "So, wait, am I gay?"

"Oh, I don't know, that's not what this means; it's just an interesting slant to your personality. It has nothing to do with sexual preference."

"So I could be a gay *man?*"

"Sure," he chuckled. "Do you have any other questions?"

I didn't. Even though he had called me a dude, I was actually relieved to have a doctor, even a Hollywood shrink, say I was not crazy. That alone was worth the price of admission. I didn't need to go on the show. I was plenty happy.

My next interview was in the vast penthouse suite with the CBS and television bigwigs.

"We really want you on the show, but we just don't want any . . . um . . . surprises. Do you know what I'm talking about?" asked one of the executives.

"We understand you've done some . . . *modeling,*" said another.

Oh. That. Yeah. "I've done fetish modeling. Some nudes, but I promise, nothing gynecological." The female producer chuckled, the men did not.

"What's a gag ball?" one of the men asked abruptly.

I explained what a gag ball was, what a gag ball did, and that there were no sex tapes out there of me. It was unlikely that anyone

I had ever slept with would have been able to afford any decent equipment for such a thing, or have the brains to set anything like that up.

Biting my lip, I didn't shoot my mouth off about why they were giving me any crap at all about some pictures of my boobs. Wasn't I auditioning to be on a TV show with Tommy Lee, a man as famous for his awesome drumming as he was for his awesome cock, displayed in all its majesty in his home-made porn?

Acting the lady, I told them I had modeled for a dildo company, but my face and tattoos were obscured and again, only boobs, no baby box shots. I did not tell them that, though the dildo company loved me, I was a bit much for them as well. The photographer told me, "Storm, you are so beautiful, your skin, your body, your mouth; the thing is, you kinda make our dicks look small."

It was the story of my life.

CHAPTER TWENTY-TWO:

LOVE YOU ENOUGH.

I did ultimately go on the show, and it was loads of fun. Nobody got stabbed, and me, my man hands, and my man brain, made a big, manly splash on network television.

Even though *Rockstar, Supernova* was, technically, a reality show, it was mostly about music. The producers were top-notch professionals whose main focus was to put on a great rock show every week. They wanted great performances out of us, as opposed to other reality shows.

Every week, we would choose a song to perform for the judges of the show—Tommy, Gilby, and Jason—along with the impossibly beautiful Dave Navarro from Jane's Addiction. We would perform, the judges would give their humorous two cents of praise or criticism, then the live and TV audience could call and text their votes in for their favorite performers. The three *least* favorites, or bottom three, had to perform an extra song on the next show. Then the judges would choose who, out of the three, would stay another week, and who would be sent packing.

Skeptical as I was, being on television was a game changer for me. It was a good showcase for all my skills . . . well . . . all the skills suitable for television. Tommy Lee was a hilarious and unbelievably oversexed man-child. A total sweetheart. He would tease and flirt with me as part of his shtick as a judge, and we would go tit for tat and have fun. One time he asked to see more of my body and I winked and said, "Tommy, six letters, Google."

I heard, later, that after that comment aired that evening, the Weather Channel crashed from all the Storm Large Images requests. The power of television, baby.

I got to sing my original, "Ladylike," the second to last time I appeared on the show. The next week it was on *Billboard's* Hot Singles List at number five, beating Justin Timberlake for one day. That same show, I also got to perform with Dave Navarro, which was one of the highlights of my career, and one of my best moments on the show; afterward, I knew I was done.

There were only five of us left, and two shows to go.

We were allowed to pick and prepare a song for whenever we ended up in the bottom three, as it is meant to showcase your strength as a performer, since you're singing to save yourself from elimination. We all had big, barn-burner rock songs ready to whip out if our names were called. I had rehearsed "Bohemian Rhapsody" by Queen, an epic rock-opera piece, but, as we were heading into the last two weeks, I changed my mind. I just knew that my time was up. I decided to scrap "Bohemian Rhapsody," and do "Wish You Were Here" by Pink Floyd, instead.

Everyone I had ever loved was watching. My brothers, my dad, all my friends and their friends, a few million strangers, and damn near all of Portland, Oregon; they all tuned in. Everybody in the world who had ever meant anything to me was with me that night.

Except for one, and I dedicated it to her.

Being on television can make best friends out of complete strangers. People who thought I was just weird loud Storm Large from back in the day were suddenly like, "Heyyy, Stormdog! Remember that time you spit in my mouth and pushed me out of a plane? Those were the days, right? Am I right?"

One benefit of that phenomenon was that it brought my mom's half-sister, Grace, and me closer together. She and her family had fun watching me for three months and were no longer hesitant to declare a bloodline.

I have to admit that I hadn't been totally convinced of the relationship, either. Poring through the photos Grace had sent me of Loretta, at multiple stages in her life, along with other family members, I looked for a family resemblance. It wasn't immediately obvious, but shortly after getting off the television show, while on tour through Canada, I got the proof I needed.

We had a gig in Windsor, Ontario, which is a stone's throw from Detroit, and a short drive for Grace. We made a plan to meet there, so she and a friend drove up to have dinner, see the show, and hang out with her surprise niece, the rock star.

The gig was about a week and a half into a heinous tour. Four of us, trapped in a mini-SUV for hours a day, every day. We'd play some gig, either in an actual club (which would be nice), or some crappy bar, pool hall, or tent, then I'd jump offstage to sell and sign CDs and

T-shirts while the boys humped gear into the trailer. We'd then pile into the SUV to head to the hotel for a few hours sleep. Wake up way too early, search in vain for decent coffee (no offense, Tim Horton's, but . . . ew), then drive, sometimes up to fourteen hours, through woods and fields, woods and fields, and woods and fucking fields to the next club or bar to put on another show.

Showbiz, baby.

It was a miserable month and we all wanted to kill each other after the first week.

We showed up at the club in Windsor and were told quickly that crime was so bad there that I should not go anywhere by myself or leave anything in the car. Great.

We had scored some Chinese food (vegetables were a rare commodity in the smaller towns), and I was happy to be sitting in the bar, by myself, pre–sound check, about to eat some greasy broccoli. I had spaced my date with Grace. James walked up.

"Your aunt is here."

"Shit. Can you put her on the list?"

"She's here . . . *now*."

I was so tired and just wanted to eat and space out. Not meet anyone, not do anything. What I really wanted to do was to hitchhike home and be a fucking chef. I'm too old for this shit.

"Where? In line outside?"

"Dude. She's behind me."

I put my chopsticks down and tried to muster up a scrap of energy. I had to get a smile for this woman who had been so sweet, so generous of her time with me. I geared up to be *on*. I didn't want to be a disappointment. I wiped my mouth. "Okay, bring . . ." James stepped aside and a small brunette woman stood quietly behind him. She smiled as she walked toward me.

"Hi!" She threw her arms open for a hug, and I burst into tears.

My mom was totally there, in her face, her smile, her expressions. Grace had darker hair and eye color than Mom, but it was unmistakable. "Oh, my God, it's really you." I towered over her. I lay my cheek on top of her head as we hugged.

"You really *are* tall," she laughed into my sleeve.

My tears were leaking onto her head and I couldn't talk right away. It's a crazy feeling to encounter someone physically, who, until recently, had been just a notion. Someone who, in real life, had actually been out there the whole time, living and growing and feeling, eating, worrying, loving, hurting, breathing, all the while sharing your blood. My feelings on family ties are equal parts childish optimism and eye-rolling cynic, but the child won out in this moment. "I love you," I said.

After meeting in person, Grace and I talked more frequently on the phone about her mother's family. With each call she opened up and spoke a little more freely. So every conversation held more and more revelations and insights into who my mother was, before she even was.

Set up in my usual spot in my favorite café on Hawthorne, I had just finished writing about the first time Grace and I met when she called. We chatted about her kids and what my band was up to, I told her where I was in the book, and how that was all going. We marveled at how our mothers had barely known each other, yet shared so many emotional connections. In their case, the fruit didn't fall far from the tree, even though the tree pitched the fruit as far as it could away from itself.

"You know, it kind of makes sense to me if Mom gave up a child before she met my dad, that would explain . . ." Aunt Grace trailed off.

"What?"

"Her sadness. She was such a great mother and so wonderful with kids, everyone's kids; everyone loved her. But she had this terrible sadness that would take over. It's why she was on so much medication."

"Medication?"

"Antidepressants mostly. For as long as I can remember."

"What about your aunts and uncles? Your grandmother?"

"Mom almost never talked about Granny. It was a bad time for her, growing up. Her dad left, well, Granny kicked him out. My mom had to quit school in the eighth grade. She worked three jobs to help raise her four younger brothers and sisters."

"Jesus. She and her siblings never talked about growing up, nothing specific?"

"Well, Granny got arrested for bootlegging, for starters, and . . ."

"Bootlegging? Wow."

"It was the Depression, then wartime. Granny was a single mother of five and no one could blame her."

"For bootlegging? No. Tough times call for . . ."

"She was a prostitute."

"What?"

"She was a prostitute. She made their house into a speakeasy and would entertain men at the house."

"With the kids there?"

"I think so. She was arrested a few times."

"Wow."

It was safe to assume at that point that my mom's conception was neither immaculate nor even very nice. The more we talked, the more it looked as though Grace's mom, my grandmother, got pregnant while supporting her siblings who were living in what was certainly a flophouse, quite possibly worse, run by my great-grandmother, "Granny." And Mom lived her first three weeks there.

So Granny ran the show, Loretta ran away, and little Sandra got run off. These stories of Mom's introduction to the world certainly set the stage for unhealthy emotional development, sadness begetting sadness begetting sadness . . . but crazy? The question of mental illness still hung in the back of my mouth. Loretta, my biological grandmother, had grown up through some thick shit, out of which sprang Mom, a human representation of that tough existence. Who wouldn't want to pretend it never happened? That's not crazy.

When I asked if anyone had been institutionalized or diagnosed with mental illness, Grace said no, no one, as far as she knew, had been institutionalized. There were only some addictions, loads of depression, and some anxiety. Oh, and Granny the hooker.

It was looking like we were definitely related.

We began to piece together the timing of Loretta's pregnancy, Mom's birth, and the early years of mother and daughter after they separated.

Loretta got pregnant, in all likelihood, in June 1942. The timing of the birth was pretty much one year before Loretta married Grace's father, the man she would spend the rest of her life with, a year and a half before the birth of their first child, three before the birth of their second, and roughly four before my mom was adopted out of an orphanage near Yale University.

June 1942 was right after the Battle of Midway in the Pacific. Supposedly, it was the turning point in WWII, so there must have been rowdy celebrations among young sailors throughout the Navy. What better way for a Navy boy to party than with a prostitute?

"Maybe Granny was *entertaining* some sailors and there was an incident. The birth father was a naval officer named Whitey, that's all we know on that end, but who knows if *that's* even true," I said.

"An incident?"

"I don't know. But *something* terrible must have happened where your mom couldn't stand the sight of my mom to the point of not only never touching or holding her, but burying her completely in some secret she took with her to her grave."

"You mean . . . a rape?"

"I don't know. No." I attempted to soften this thinking-out-loud I was doing. I could feel my aunt getting a little upset, understandably so. I thought about changing the subject. *Let's talk about your kids. Do you have a dog? Something light, give the poor woman a break.* "Maybe, or could your mom have been, I don't know, *working* for your grandmother?"

Way to take it down a notch, dumbass.

"Oh, I doubt *that*. Rape does make sense, though, I guess."

So, your mom was either brutalized by a sailor or was a piece of rent-a-tail, put out by her mother. Change the subject, Storm, for chrissake!!

"I guess not. God, I hope not, for your mom's sake, and, let's forget about all this for now. Okay? God."

"No, no, it's fine. It's just all this stuff . . . a lot has begun to make sense to me about my family, my mother especially. I just love and appreciate her even more for knowing what she must have gone through as a young girl. Even if she wasn't . . . my goodness . . . what a life."

"My mom used to always say her real mom was raped. There's no way to know for sure, of course, but it would be too awful and weird if she'd been right."

We didn't talk much more about it, but stayed in touch. Grace is a kind, Christian woman who cared enough to reach out to a stranger and offer comfort even though she didn't have to.

"So, no one went to the hospital for mental stuff?"

"Well . . ." She was quiet again. Then, "Mom did. She attempted suicide a few times. There was a while there, during high school, I was scared to leave the house out of fear of what she might do to herself."

"Wow. Grace. You have basically described my mom. She did the exact same things."

Grace didn't let me finish.

"My mom knew that suicide was the most selfish act in the world, and my mom was *not* selfish. I truly believe the thing that saved her wasn't the pills or the doctors or any of that. It was our love for her. We loved her enough to bring her back. Once it really hit home, and she got how much we loved her, how we would never give up on her, she stopped doing all that."

I bit my lip and listened to her. My aunt, this sweet woman who barely knew me, was willing to share so much about her life, as well as her mother's life, with me. And she did it for no other reason than to help me understand my mother a little better, and to maybe bring me a little peace. It was clearly painful for her to go back to that scary time, but she loved her mother so much, and maybe, in a way, my situation helped her get a little peace as well. I was grateful to Grace's openness and honesty, and did my best to not betray the fact that my heart was crumpling in my chest like a cold ball of tinfoil.

After we said goodbye, I called my brother John.

"Sterm!" He answered in his usual gruff, big-brother voice.

"Hey, Jern," I said in our usual fake Swedish accent that we, somewhere along the way, started using to address each other with.

I made as much small talk with him as I could, while pacing in the January rain outside the coffee shop. It was a cold, mean rain.

"Okay. Hey, Jern, could we have saved her?" I started to cry.

"What?"

"Could we have saved Mom, did we not love her enough?" John was quiet as I cried in the rain.

"When are you gonna be done with this book, Sis?"

CHAPTER TWENTY-THREE:

CALL ME CRAZY.

You must have chaos within you to give birth to a dancing star.

—NIETZSCHE

It's impossible to say whether or not love could have fixed my mom. It's a blade that guts me, still. *Did I not love her enough? Was it my fault?*

On good days I can safely say it wasn't my fault, but most days, I believe I could have done more. Maybe that's what drives me to do more now. Before it was just to get away from her, to be nothing like her and be free of it all. And in the end, everything I did in *reaction* to her, created the same loneliness in me. The thing everyone called crazy, with all of its endless names and diagnoses given to it, I think was just that. Loneliness. Feeling like you don't belong, you are unlovable, and, ultimately, unloved.

My whole life has been about the search for love: *Will you love me?*

No? Okay, what if I change? Please tell me who should I be, who do you want me to be, so you will love me? So in the end, Dr. Lovey was right. I did end up just like my mom. The sad inheritance of her innate loneliness has dragged me through this life like a runaway carnival horse.

But what a ride it's been.

I have known plenty of seriously damaged minds, so I'm not saying that all mental illness can be fixed with a hug or that it is all some evil conspiracy drummed up by pharmaceutical companies in cahoots with the psychiatric industry, but the crazy my mom was and what she gave me were definitely undeserving of the chemical and electrical hell she went through. There are studies and stories about some mental illness being directly correlated to creativity as well. One psychologist, when he was diagnosed with ADHD, exclaimed joyfully, *"That's* why I'm so awesome!"

I'm not a doctor, but even I can make that connection. Some of the most brilliant people I've ever known were twisted in some way. And Mom had a sweet magnetism, like a movie star. She could sing and dance and draw and, boy, did she love an audience. I am just like her in that way. Maybe, because of when or where she was born, she was told that energy was only meant to attract a husband, and, once she was married, she was supposed to put it away, be quiet, stop drawing attention to herself. Maybe, if my mother had been born into a musical family or a circus family, or if she had been encour-aged to sing, dance, or pursue a creative life, her sensitivity would have been an asset instead of a bunch of evil, destructive voices in her head. It's too late to know that for sure, but her big, raw heart had never found its voice, and that, too, could be the crazy she was. If I had listened to all those voices, in my head and elsewhere, tell-ing me to be quiet, small, and normal, I would have needed some medicated lockdown myself.

After I got off the TV show, I toured pretty much nonstop for a year. When that started to ebb, I thought it might be nice to work closer to home. That was the main reason why I considered doing *Cabaret* at Portland Center Stage.

"We want you to play Sally Bowles in *Cabaret*," said the handsome artistic director at Portland Center Stage. He said it in a way people tell you things expecting you to say OH MY GOD NO WAY! YES OF COURSE, THANK YOU! Sally Bowles is a plum role, and here I was, some reality TV, club singer, being handed the thing. He had no idea if I was any good at acting, but he knew that my fame was still viable from the TV show, and having me on his stage would be like having a unicorn at a petting zoo.

"No." I said, repeatedly over the many lunches I made the poor guy feed me.

One of the perks of being an artist is, when people talk business with you, you often get a meal out of it. Most artists are broke for the majority of their careers, hence the term, "starving artist." I have been fortunate in the latter half of my career to stuff my face while some business or industry types pick up the tab. Charities supply good eats as well. I have raised, easily, more than a million dollars performing and volunteering at countless charity events because I'm a fucking sweetheart and they always have food, and look the other way when I show up with a canvas tote full of Tupperware.

Maybe it was the Vietnamese pho at that last lunch, maybe it was because it was time to suck it up, and admit I was not going to be a rockstar for real, but I said yes. It scared me to do something as highbrow as theater, and galled me more than a little bit to prove the folks at the American Academy right, but for four months I hiked up my garters and hoofed it through the Kit Kat club while the Nazis took over, I got decent reviews, the theater was packed every night, and I had a blast.

"We want you to write a one-woman show about your life," said the handsome artistic director, after the success of *Cabaret* and my not so sucky turn as a unicorn.

"Sure! Sex and drugs and rock and roll, baby!" I said, shoveling brown rice into my mouth.

"Sure, a little of that, but it should be about your childhood, and your mom, too . . ." he said.

Mmmmm . . . yeah . . . no fucking way.

"What a stupid idea, me getting up and talking about my mom? It's a sad story, not funny or cool . . . right? Stupid. I told him *NO FUCKING WAY.*" I bragged to James the next day.

"So, you chickened out?" James smirked.

"What? No . . . It's a stupid idea, nobody wants to see that."

"You chickened out. It's okay, I understand, it's scary."

Calling me chicken was a cheap, manipulative trick. Throw in the added swipe of ego tickling . . . "You know, you totally *could* pull it off, though." Plus James always had yummy vegan snacks laid out for meetings or rehearsals. The little bastard had my number. So, once again, faced with the urgings of the handsome artistic director and a few more bowls of Vietnamese pho, I said yes.

A great artist once said that the thing that scares you the most, is the very thing you must do. Now, I have sung on stage naked with extra boobs drawn on my chest, learned ten songs in five different languages in six days, then sung them with the National Symphony Orchestra at the Kennedy Center, and sung for millions of television viewers, just to name a few hair-raising pulse-quickeners in my career. However, the idea of turning some of my sadder, less-than-flattering snapshots from my life into an entertaining evening of musical theater was easily the most terrifying thing I have ever done.

Every single night, before stepping into the pitch-black, I would pace the concrete floor in the dark backstage, convinced I was going to have an intestinal event *onstage*. I would sweep back and forth in the tight hallway lined with glossy programs with my picture on the cover.

"You ready?" the assistant stage manager would ask me, holding the door for my entrance.

"If by *ready* you mean am I gonna shit my pants, then yes . . . I'm ready."

It would go like that every night for the first month or so. And just when I started getting used to it, baring the not too pretty bits of my soul to a packed house night after night, and I stopped feeling flulike symptoms preshow, my boyfriend of seven years starts to *feel different*.

"I feel different," he said one night in bed.

"You fucking someone else?" I said.

"No . . . I just feel different," he said, I imagine hoping I would get it and leave without much fuss.

"Um . . . okay." Then we screwed, hard and passionately, all end-of-the-world style. Then we broke up. I moved out of his house and commenced couch-surfing and house-sitting for a couple months.

It made going to work pretty hard, since I kind of referred to him in the show as the love of my life. The one who came along and changed everything.

"Somebody slap me! PLEASE!" I begged as I got to the theater one night, after stupidly looking on Facebook to see sweet thank-you notes to my ex for SUCH A FUN NIGHT . . . from girls younger than my van.

OMG! Soooooooooo nice to meet you! LOL

I had been popping Xanax and fighting the urge to vomit all day. I couldn't stop crying. You can't sing when you're crying and you shouldn't sing after you puke.

"Please fucking hit me. James? SOMEBODY!" The band was in mid–sound check and people were gathering in the lobby to get in early. The show was sold out. They all were. What I had thought was a terrible idea, had turned into a smash hit in Portland.

James and the band, though I'm sure they had harbored fantasies of letting me have it a time or two, refused. *I can't hit you, dude* was the consensus among the musicians.

"Fuck. Mark?" Mark Tynan, my stage manager in *Cabaret* and *Crazy Enough*, was always good for a hug and soft, spiritual words of wisdom. I was a mess, snotty and red-faced, in a near panic at my inability to pull my shit together. I knew Mark could do something to calm me down, he'd been doing this forever with far crazier broads refusing to go onstage for far stupider reasons. I was sure he wouldn't hit me, though. It was not his style and Equity probably frowned on that sort of thing, but I needed something to get me back from my fevered pitch of shrieking nerves to my normal and manageable level of neurosis. My leaking, red eyes pleading with him to do something. I cried at him again. "Hit me."

He held me at arm's length by my shoulders and gave me a gentle shake. He was tall and very warm. "Sweetheart . . . look at me." He made me look into his bright aqua eyes. "Breeeeeathe," he said, smiling.

"Please . . ."

"Shhhhhh . . . sweetheart." His eyes pulled mine into them. He breathed deeply, I breathed with him, then he said, "Relax your neck."

Hunh?

WHACK! The band jumped at the sound that suddenly cracked the air. Mark had fully roundhouse, open-handed smacked me and made my left cheek his little bitch.

"Yessss. YES! Other side, other side!" I said, pornographically, my eyes tearing from the bright, pinking sting. KA-RACK!!

"God bless you, Mark Tynan." I saw tiny sparkles as I stumbled into my dressing room to clean myself up . . . finally back on the ground.

"I love you, too," he sang merrily.

I got my makeup and outfit on, did my normal pacing backstage, and headed out onstage sure that I was going to get the runs in front of everyone.

Sucky as it was to perform under those circumstances—broken-hearted, sick, burnt, wiped, and scraped empty—I am a staunch proponent of "The Show Must Go On." I am the show, so on I go. Like that Longfellow poem, "Excelsior." The little guy denies himself comfort, shelter, safety, even love to fulfill his quest, whatever that is. For me, it's performing. Lonely as it's been at times, I'd rather die than give up my crazy life.

And the greatest performances I've ever seen or given are not unlike the most incredible sex one can ever have. It's when you are truly torn open and powerless, and you lose it completely. You can call it God, or spirit, or art, or whatever chaotic mystery that sounds right to you, but when you are stripped of all your defenses, that's when miracles happen. Maintaining composure during those experiences is beside the point. It's so much better to feel like you might not survive the encounter, shit the bed, and touch the infinite.

Even though Mark Tynan had done me a solid with the mighty slap across my face, it was a tough gig. My voice was rough from the day's emotional mayhem, and I cried openly at bows. Only my band could see it. My body flopped over, tears streaming into my hair, but the audience roared to its feet and gave me my sixtieth standing ovation in a row.

James, myself, and the band all convened at his house after the show. We sat on his porch, drinking and laughing and toasting each other. Nobody brought up my meltdown. I had muscled through, no need to tear the scab off. Nothing to see here. We told terrible stories from the road and beyond over chilled white wine and fancy homemade gin drinks. A shambling clutch of stage dogs having a postgig hang, smoothing away the rough day in the balm of a summer night and the company of great friends. I was in a rough patch, but these guys had my back, front, and sides. I still didn't want to fall apart on anyone, but if I had to, I couldn't think of better friends to put Humpty Slutty back together again. I knew I'd be all right.

A few days later it was my fortieth birthday.

Standing backstage, once again with my intestines sweating, the stacks of programs staring at me, my heart broken, and the house full, I was there. Hanging by a microthin thread . . . but alive and wide awake.

I took a shaky breath and walked through the dark to the microphone stand at center stage.

CALL ME CRAZY.

I grazed my lips across the metal screen ball of the microphone, looked up into the dark potent nothing, and mouthed silently as I did before every show: *Thank you. Thank you. Thank you.*

It was another tear-soaked bow at curtain. *I'm fucking forty and all alone.* The applause was a whitewash of rush in my ears, punctuated with whistles and woo-hoos. I stayed bent over until I wasn't completely sobbing. The tears all streaked up my forehead while in the deep bow, maybe it'll just look like sweat. I stood up to call my band over for the second bow and as my tear-smudged vision cleared a bit, I saw the entire audience on its feet still slamming their hands together and cheering even louder, gushing at me with an epic-loving roar.

And every one of them was wearing a pointy paper birthday hat.

What the . . . ? I turned around to my guys to see if they were seeing what I was seeing, and they were on their feet, clapping and smiling, also wearing party hats.

Gotcha.

I dropped to my knees and sobbed shamelessly.

I was sung to, given my favorite red velvet cupcakes stuck with candles, got hugged a million times, and later I was gently stewed with filthy vodka martinis.

It was the greatest gift ever. Not so much all the details of the night, but the knock-over-the-head realization that I am actually doing something right with my life. In a way I am a little crazy, but it works for me. It certainly helps to be a little twisted to do what I do. I have fallen flat on my face. I have also completely ruled. I have humiliated myself in front of hundreds, even thousands of people. I have also lifted and shaken the room, like deep belly muscles in a brain-melting orgasm. Performing is the one thing I've found I can do, that comes *from* me, it's mine, and, at its best, it is a force of good in the world, bringing joy to numerous humans gathered in the dark listening. Even if you think I suck, you are a little happier for getting to hate me.

You're welcome.

THANK YOU

My Dad, for not locking me up, forgiving me, and still loving me. My big brothers, John and Henry, for helping me remember and supporting me through this process. Mari Quirk for being a wild and wonderful sorta-Ma. My Godmother, Aunt Elena; Susie Moore; Aunt Jeane Lutz, who has given so much; Aunt Bitsy (the original big girl who broke the mold); G-Bear; and all my beautiful cousins of the Carey and MacMaster clan who can, right this moment, put this book down and stop reading. The same goes for all my nieces and nephews. Here is the child-friendly synopsis: Auntie Stormy was a big loud silly pants who did some highly goofy and not smart things, but is now, mostly, a nice person. The end. And you kids know the rule: NEVER REPEAT WHAT AUNTIE STORMY SAYS EVER.

My loving friends who costar in some of these shenanigans, who dried tears, cheered me on, understood, brought me wine, slapped me around, made me lie down or go for a walk; in a good many ways, you make me better, and I am eternally grateful: James Beaton, Daphne Leavitt, Heather Quirk, Laura Izon Powell, Mary Raffael, Stephanie Greig Templeton, Lars Fox, Quenby Moone, Joelle Flegal, Scott Weddle, Caitlynne Flynn, Frank Faillace, Laura Domela, Kevin Morris, Kohel Haver, Steve Sharp, Jennie Baker, Adam Lundeen, Sandra "Phoenix" Hillebrand, Eric McFadden, Jim Brunberg, Greg Eklund, Mark Tynan, Kavita Jhaveri, Howie Bierbaum, Narwal Kortney Barber, Byron Beck, Michael Cavaseno, Stephanie Smith and Ma and Pa Smith, Michelle DeCoursy, Elan Vital McAllister, Carmel Dean, Camryn Mannheim, Daniel Stern, Morgan Dancer, Emily Fincher, David Loprinzi, Brian Boom-Boom McFeather Parnell, Keith Smith, Hester Snow, Ashley Richardson, Red Kevin the Viking Dowling, Mike Sablone, Aaron Annis, David Conrad, Sam Gold, Randy Marie Rollison, Wade McCullum, Holcombe Waller, Thomas Lauderdale and Pink Martini, and the ever-shining Yael Esther.

The Big Brain Trust, my incredible writers group: Cynthia Whitcomb, Christine McKinley, Courtenay Hammeister, Daniel Wilson, and my beloved gay husband, Marc Acito. Marc, especially, who helped me road map the first incarnation of this book—and for being a damn good kisser.

My agent, Richard Pine, for listening to Larry Colton, and in turn, bugging me to do this thing and believing in me. You're both nuts. My sweet, first editor at Free Press, Amber Quereshi, whom I made cry and smoosh food all over her head. And thank you Leah Miller, my tireless and patient final editor, who held my giant man hands and walked me through the toughest parts. You're a badass.

My friends from when I wasn't really a rock star but played one on TV: Toby Rand, Lucas Rossi, Paul and Michelle Mirkavich. And Mark Burnett, for running a classy gig. Thank you.

Thank you Chris Coleman, Rose Riordan, and PCS for telling me to sing my story.

Thank you, Larry Colton, for telling me to write it down.

Thank you Jammer, for calling me a chickenshit and making me do both.

And thank you, Michael Shapiro, for listening. Also for knowing how to get all the candy out of the piñata. I love you.

ABOUT THE AUTHOR

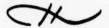

STORM LARGE has been singing and slinging inappropriate banter at audiences around the globe for more than fifteen years, and shows no sign of slowing down or shutting up. She earned an associate's degree from the American Academy of Dramatic Arts in New York City, where her big, dramatic voice impressed her teachers and made musical theater the obvious choice for her. However, Storm resonated more with Alphabet City than Broadway, spending all her free time in gritty rock clubs with the lowlifes, sluts, and geniuses she adored. She pursued rock 'n' roll instead.